Lexical Diversity and Language Development:
Quantification and Assessment

Other publications by these authors:

Ngoni Chipere
UNDERSTANDING COMPLEX SENTENCES: NATIVE SPEAKER VARIATION IN SYNTACTIC COMPETENCE (Palgrave Macmillan, 2003)

Brian Richards
LANGUAGE DEVELOPMENT AND INDIVIDUAL DIFFERENCES
INPUT AND INTERACTION IN LANGUAGE ACQUISITION (with Clare Gallaway)
JAPANESE CHILDREN ABROAD (with Asako Yamada-Yamamoto).

Lexical Diversity and Language Development

Quantification and Assessment

David Malvern, Brian Richards,
Ngoni Chipere and Pilar Durán

© David Malvern, Brian Richards, Ngoni Chipere and Pilar Durán 2004

All rights reserved. No reproduction, copy or transmission of this publication may be made without written permission.

No paragraph of this publication may be reproduced, copied or transmitted save with written permission or in accordance with the provisions of the Copyright, Designs and Patents Act 1988, or under the terms of any licence permitting limited copying issued by the Copyright Licensing Agency, 90 Tottenham Court Road, London W1T 4LP.

Any person who does any unauthorised act in relation to this publication may be liable to criminal prosecution and civil claims for damages.

The authors have asserted their rights to be identified as the authors of this work in accordance with the Copyright, Designs and Patents Act 1988.

First published 2004 by
PALGRAVE MACMILLAN
Houndmills, Basingstoke, Hampshire RG21 6XS and
175 Fifth Avenue, New York, N.Y. 10010
Companies and representatives throughout the world

PALGRAVE MACMILLAN is the global academic imprint of the Palgrave Macmillan division of St. Martin's Press, LLC and of Palgrave Macmillan Ltd. Macmillan® is a registered trademark in the United States, United Kingdom and other countries. Palgrave is a registered trademark in the European Union and other countries.

ISBN-13: 978-1-403-90231-3   hardback
ISBN-10: 1-4039-0231-3   hardback

This book is printed on paper suitable for recycling and made from fully managed and sustained forest sources. Logging, pulping and manufacturing processes are expected to conform to the environmental regulations of the country of origin.

A catalogue record for this book is available from the British Library.

Library of Congress Cataloging-in-Publication Data
Lexical diversity and language development : quantification and assessment / David Malvern ... [et al.].
   p. cm.
Includes bibliographical references and index.
ISBN 1–4039–0231–3
1. Language acquisition. 2. Lexicology. I. Malvern, David.

P118.L438 2004
418′.0071—dc22
                                                               2003070656

Printed and bound in Great Britain by
CPI Antony Rowe, Chippenham and Eastbourne

To our families

Contents

List of Tables   xi

List of Figures   xiii

Acknowledgements   xv

Part I   Measuring Lexical Diversity

1 Introduction   **3**
    Lexical diversity versus vocabulary richness   3
    Overview of the content of this monograph   4
    Lexical diversity   5
    Research using lexical diversity as a variable   6
       Analysis of historical documents   7
       Studies of authors' style and dating works of literature   7
       Forensic linguistics   7
       Demographic influences on vocabulary use   8
       Second language and bilingualism   8
       Language assessment   8
       Linguistic input and interaction   10
       The 'noun bias' issue   11
       Language impairment and delay   11
       Specific language impairment   12
       Intervention studies   13
       Language in dementia   13
       Aphasia   13
       Schizophrenia   14
    Conclusion   14

2 Traditional Approaches to Measuring Lexical Diversity   **16**
    The number of different words (NDW)   16
    The type–token ratio (TTR)   19
    Mean segmental type–token ratio (MSTTR)   25
    Other linguistic measures of range   25
    Transformations of TTR   26
    Conclusion   29

3 A Mathematical Model of Lexical Diversity   **31**
    A seminal paper   31
    The harmonic series hypothesis and further developments   36

	Using population statistics	40
	The most complete formulation	41
	A mathematical model for diversity	47
	Operationalising the model	49
	A mathematical expression for ideal curves	50
	Producing the graphs from real data	51
	Standardising how the measurement is made	54
	Making the measurement, D, and *vocd*	55
	Summary	57

Part II Validation of the Model and its Application to Language Corpora

4 Early Child Language 1: the New England Corpus — 63
Testing *vocd* — 63
Investigating sensitivity to sample size — 64
  Method — 65
  Results — 66
Reliability — 68
  Stability — 68
  Internal consistency — 68
Morphemicisation — 69
Criterion-related validity — 70
Discussion — 71
Conclusion — 73

5 Early Child Language 2: the Bristol Corpus — 76
The Bristol Corpus — 76
Measures from the Bristol project — 78
Method — 80
  The preparation of transcripts — 80
  The calculation of D — 81
Results — 81
  The three versions of D — 81
  D (stem forms) — 84
  Criterion-related validity — 86
Discussion — 89
Conclusion — 93

6 Lexical Diversity and the Investigation of Accommodation in Foreign Language Proficiency Interviews — 95
Background: the oral interview — 95
Method — 98
  The students — 99
  Student variables — 100

Results		102
The students		102
The relationship between teacher D and student measures		104
Conclusion		108

7 A New Measure of Inflectional Diversity and its Application to English and Spanish Data Sets — 110
   Inflectional diversity in the New England Corpus — 111
   Inflectional diversity in the Bristol Corpus — 111
   The Spanish data — 113
   Conclusion — 116

Part III Different Word Categories and their Diversity: Type–Type versus Type–Token

8 Comparing the Diversity of Lexical Categories: the Type–Type Ratio and Related Measures — 121
   Type–type ratios — 121
   Rare words — 123
      Diversity versus sophistication — 123
      Intrinsic versus extrinsic measurement of rarity — 125
      Extrinsic rarity measures in bilingual and second language research — 127
      Laufer and Nation's lexical frequency profile — 128
      Early child language and 'The home-school study of language and literacy development' of Dickinson, Snow and Tabors — 129
      The relationship between rarity measures and sample size — 131
   Vocabulary composition and early lexical style — 134
      The effect of sample size — 136
   The 'noun bias' issue — 138
   Nouns versus verbs: the effect of sample size — 142
      An empirical demonstration — 142
      A proposed solution to the sample size problem — 147
      Programming for limiting relative diversity (LRD) — 148
      LRD for Anne and her mother — 149
   Conclusion — 150

9 Lexical Diversity and Lexical Sophistication in First Language Writing — 152
   Overview of the study — 153
   Method — 154
      The data — 154
      The quantitative text variables — 155
      Coding schemes and analytical procedures — 161

Results		162
Trends in the text level variables		162
Inter-correlations		170
Regression analysis		170
Discussion		171
Differences by Key Stage and Level		172
Predicting National Curriculum Levels		172

Part IV Conclusion

10 Overview and Conclusions — **179**

Flawed measures and confused results	179
A more robust measure	180
Interpreting the values of D	181
Cross-linguistic comparisons of lexical diversity	183
In conclusion	184

Notes		185
Glossary of technical terms and acronyms		187
References		203

Appendices

I	Key to the CHAT Transcripts in Appendices II–IV	221
II	Extract from a Transcript in the Bristol Corpus	222
III	A French Transcript from the Reading Corpus	224
IV	Extract from the Manchester Corpus Illustrating the %mor Tier	226
V	Documentation for *vocd*	228
	Using *vocd*	228
	Sample size	228
	Preparation of files	228
	The minimum command line	229
	The output from *vocd*	229
	Text-handling options	230
	Combining options on the command line	234
VI	Example of standard output from *vocd* using a transcript from the New England Corpus	235
VII	Output from the limiting relative diversity (LRD) option in *vocd* using a file from Anne (anne03a.cha) in the Manchester Corpus	238

Index	244

Tables

2.1	NDW calculated by different standardisation methods for Transcript A and Transcript B	19
2.2	TTRs calculated for Templin's data from 50 utterances	21
3.1	Binomial probability	32
3.2	Theoretical (Sichel's formulation) and mean observed values for TTR, b, c, K and proportions of types for hapax legomena and hapax dislegomena in sub-samples of different sizes from Macaulay's *Essay on Bacon*	45
4.1	Mean TTR for different parts of the transcripts ($N = 38$)	66
4.2	Mean D (sequential sampling) for different parts of the transcripts ($N = 38$)	66
4.3	Mean D (random sampling with replacement) for different parts of the transcripts ($N = 38$)	67
4.4	Mean D (random sampling without replacement) for different parts of the transcripts ($N = 38$)	67
4.5	Descriptive statistics for test–retest of D (random sampling without replacement) and the paired differences between each application of *vocd* ($N = 38$)	68
4.6	Descriptive statistics for D (random sampling without replacement, retracing and exclude file filtered out) for inflected forms and word stems ($N = 38$)	70
4.7	Spearman correlations between non-morphemicised and morphemicised versions of D and age and other language measures for the New England Corpus	71
5.1	Distribution of sample by sex and family background	77
5.2	Descriptive statistics for D (stem forms) at each age	82
5.3	Rank order correlations between D (stem forms) and other language measures at each age	86
5.4	Item–total correlations and alpha coefficients for standardised D scores	88
5.5	Pearson correlations between D (21–42 months) and later language aptitude tests	89
6.1	Student variables ($N = 34$)	100
6.2	Spearman rank order correlations between D and other measures for all students for whom D was calculable ($N = 27$)	102
6.3	Spearman rank order inter-correlations between the subjective ratings provided by 24 teachers of French ($N = 34$)	103

6.4	Spearman rank order correlations between teachers' D and measures of students' language ($N = 34$)	105
6.5	Spearman rank order correlations between measures of students' language and Teacher A ($n = 12$) and Teacher B ($n = 22$)	106
7.1	Correlations between ID stems and other measures of language development	113
9.1	Descriptive statistics for t-unit length	163
9.2	Descriptive statistics for text length	165
9.3	Descriptive statistics for spelling	166
9.4	Descriptive statistics for word length	167
9.5	Descriptive statistics for word rarity	168
9.6	Descriptive statistics for lexical diversity	169
9.7	Inter-correlations between text variables and Level	170
9.8	Regression analysis predicting Level	171
9.9	Contribution of each variable to Level	171
9.10	Inter-correlations among word-level variables	174
9.11a	Regression analysis for Key Stage 1	175
9.11b	Regression analysis for Key Stage 2	175
9.11c	Regression analysis for Key Stage 3	175

Figures

2.1	TTR plotted against tokens for the spoken language of a two-year-old and academic writing for an adult	23
3.1	Distribution of words of increasing probability of occurrence as a proportion of the active vocabulary	43
3.2a	Theoretical TTR curves calculated for b held at 0.01 and for $c = 0.01, c = 0.02$, and $c = 0.03$	46
3.2b	Theoretical TTR curves calculated for c held at 0.01 and for $b = 0.01$, $b = 0.02$, and $b = 0.03$	46
3.3	A mathematical model of lexical diversity	48
3.4	Rising curves passing through the points for mean TTRs calculated from Templin's data	49
3.5	Ideal TTR versus token curves showing increasing diversity with increasing $\mathcal{D}$	52
3.6	Flow chart for *vocd* (default version)	58
5.1	Mean D for inflected forms, stem forms, and root forms plotted against age	82
5.2	TTR plotted against age	83
5.3	Indicative values for D (stem forms)	85
6.1	Scatterplot of D values for each teacher against students' GCSE points	107
6.2	D for each teacher against students in ascending order of GCSE points, showing median D and the interval plus and minus 2 × semi-interquartile range for each teacher	107
7.1	Mean D for inflected forms, stem forms, and root forms against age	112
7.2	The difference between D for inflected forms and D for stems and roots plotted against age	112
7.3	The development of three versions of D for five Spanish-speaking children	115
7.4	The development of three versions of D in English- and Spanish-speaking children	115
7.5	Trends in inflectional diversity (ID) in the Bristol and Spanish children	116
8.1	Cumulative noun and verb types plotted against number of words for Anne at 1;10.7	143
8.2	Averaged type–type measures plotted against number of words for Anne at 1;10.7	144
8.2a	Averaged noun types/verb types plotted against number of words for Anne at 1;10.7	144

8.2b	Averaged noun types/(noun types + verb types) plotted against number of words for Anne at 1;10.7	145
8.2c	Averaged verb types/noun types plotted against number of words for Anne at 1;10.7	145
8.3	Cumulative noun and verb types plotted against number of words for Anne at 2;9.10	146
8.4	Averaged type–type measures plotted against number of words for Anne at 2;9.10	146
8.5	Type–type ratio (verbs to nouns), derived from dividing TTR verbs by TTR nouns, plotted against tokens	147
8.6	Mathematical note on type–type ratios	148
8.7	Verb/noun LRD for Anne and her mother over 11 conversations between 1;11.04 and 2;9.10	150
9.1	T-unit length plotted against Level at three ages	163
9.2	Text length plotted against Level at three ages	164
9.3	Spelling plotted against Level at three ages	165
9.4	Mean word length plotted against Level at three ages	166
9.5	Word rarity plotted against Level at three ages	168
9.6	Lexical diversity plotted against Level at three ages	169
10.1	Means, 10th and 90th percentiles of D for speech of children from 18 to 60 months, French as a foreign language (aged 16) and ESL (adults); and for writing of children aged 7–11 years and adults	182

Acknowledgements

David Malvern and Brian Richards first discussed the measurement of vocabulary diversity in 1988 when, in response to an article by Brian in the *Journal of Child Language*, H. S. Sichel sent a copy of the 1986 paper that was influential in much of the work reported in this volume. Attached was a note saying simply, 'This may help you with your research.' In spite of some early experiments with Sichel's equations and repeated earnest declarations that 'We really must work together on this some time', it was only thanks to a pump-priming grant from the Research Endowment Trust Fund of The University of Reading in 1995 that the research could begin in earnest. Further funding that allowed the work to continue until the autumn of 2002 was obtained in two awards from the Economic and Social Research Council (ESRC): 'A New Research Tool: Mathematical Modelling in the Measurement of Vocabulary Diversity' (R000221995) and 'Mathematically Modelling Vocabulary Diversity and Lexical Style' (R000238260). The latter, plus a postdoctoral research fellowship, again from The University of Reading's Research Endowment Trust Fund, brought Pilar Durán and Ngoni Chipere into the team.

A large number of people have contributed to the research reported in this monograph and to the process of its publication. Many have done so over a considerable period of time, and some may not even realise how significant their contribution has been, such as those, too numerous to acknowledge by name, who have engaged in email discussion with us, reported bugs in our software, sent us copies of their publications, and made us aware of new developments. Among those to whom we would wish to give special thanks for help, advice, support, reading drafts, and sending us information are Shanley Allen, Rolien Bastiaanse, Ruth Berman, Carol Boulter, Gina Conti-Ramsden, Mark Cox, Susan Edwards, Paul Fletcher, Mike Garman, Suzanne Graham, Tom Klee, Larry Leonard, Brian MacWhinney, Liz McCabe, Paul Meara, Amanda Owen, Margaret Perkins, Tracey Pinchbeck, Nan Ratner, Dorit Ravid, Mair Richards, Elvira Samnée-O'Brien, H. S. Sichel, Stacy Silverman, Ursula Stephany, and Stephanie Stokes. We should also like to acknowledge the help provided on a regular basis by staff of the Statistical Advisory Service at The University of Reading, particularly the Head of School, Derek Pike.

Programming for the *vocd* software was carried out by Gerard McKee of the Department of Computer Science at The University of Reading and we are also grateful for Raymond Knott's advice as consultant during the early stages of development. Similarly, thanks are due to Brian MacWhinney and Leonid Spektor for their input and for integrating *vocd* into CLAN.

We should also like to express our thanks to those who helped us with specific chapters in this volume. For Chapter 4, Barbara Pan, Steve Reznick, and Catherine Snow provided us with additional information about the New England Corpus, including publications, precise ages, and CDI scores. For Chapter 5, we should like to thank Gordon Wells for his support and encouragement. We are also grateful for his permission to use the Bristol data for the analyses reported in this chapter and to include part of Jonathan's transcript in Appendix II. Thanks are also due to Sally Barnes who assisted in searching for missing data, to Peter Skehan for making the scores on the language aptitude tests available, and to Paul Croll, who provided the EPVT scores and advised on the development of a single scale for D across recordings. The CHAT files used in Chapter 6 were meticulously prepared by Francine Chambers, Fiona Richards, and Mair Richards. We would also like to express our gratitude to the teenage learners of French in this study and to the school that made the authentic recordings of their GCSE French oral examination available to us, and to the 24 teachers of French who assessed the tapes. In the analysis of children's writing in Chapter 9, the data were obtained from the University of Cambridge Local Examinations Syndicate (UCLES). Paul Meara gave us invaluable assistance in running the P_Lex program. Additional analyses in Chapter 10 that provide values of D from different populations were made possible by Peter Skehan and Benny Teasdale with their data on English as a second language. Elena Lieven kindly gave us permission to reproduce part of Anne's transcript from the Manchester Corpus in Appendix IV.

Some of the material in Chapters 3 and 4 is taken from: McKee, G, Malvern, D. D., and Richards, B. J. 'Measuring vocabulary diversity using dedicated software.' *Literary and Linguistic Computing*, 2000, 15 (3), 323–37. It appears here by kind permission of Cambridge University Press. A large part of Chapter 6 was previously published as: Richards, B. J., and Malvern, D. D. 'Investigating accommodation in language proficiency interviews using a new measure of lexical diversity.' *Language Testing*, 2002, 19 (1), 85–104. We should like to thank Arnold Publishers for allowing us to reproduce it here.

Finally, we should like to thank Jill Lake our commissioning editor at Palgrave Macmillan Publishers for her help and support at all stages in the development of this monograph and Penny Simmons of Password Publishing Services for her eagle eye and enduring patience.

Part I
Measuring Lexical Diversity

1
Introduction

Lexical diversity versus vocabulary richness

A review of the literature on quantifying vocabulary richness gives the sense of a quest for the Holy Grail – the search for a single, all-embracing, but elusive measure of the quality of vocabulary deployment that is independent of the quantity of speech or writing to which it is applied. The next goal is always 'a better and more fruitful measure of lexical richness' (Vermeer, 2000, p. 79). For some, the terms lexical diversity and vocabulary richness appear to be synonymous (e.g. Ménard, 1983; Arnaud, 1984; Wimmer and Altmann, 1999), diversity being indicated by the number of different words in a sample of speech or writing of a set length. Others seek 'better' alternatives that take the difficulty or relative rarity of words into account (Vermeer, 2000; Daller, Van Hout and Treffers-Daller, 2003). By contrast, still others acknowledge that these different measures can complement each other, providing valuable supplementary information about usage and style (e.g. Ménard, 1983).

As an example of the latter in the context of second language learning, John Read's 'Assessing Vocabulary' (Read, 2000, pp. 200–5) conceptualises vocabulary richness as a multidimensional feature of students' writing consisting of four main components: 'lexical variation', 'lexical sophistication', 'lexical density', and 'number of errors'. Lexical variation means the same as lexical diversity – the range of vocabulary and avoidance of repetition – and is measured by comparing the number of different words with the total number of words written, traditionally using the type–token ratio (TTR). Lexical sophistication is the appropriate choice of low frequency vocabulary items that include 'the use of technical terms and ... uncommon words that allow writers to express their meanings in a precise and sophisticated manner' (p. 200). Lexical density, attributed to Ure (1971), is usually calculated as the proportion of word tokens that are content words rather than function words and is a dimension that discriminates between written and spoken language. Read regards it as having a more important role in the assessment of spoken discourse. Finally, the error dimension, which is based on Arnaud (1984), takes into consideration spelling, lexical choice, mistakes in derivational morphology, interference from other languages, and 'false friends' (see Arnaud, 1984, p. 19).

In this volume we wish to avoid giving the impression that we are seeking a single, perfect measure of lexical richness. We are concerned with quantifying the development of vocabulary in both speaking and writing and take a similar view to Read that vocabulary richness is multifaceted and can be measured by interrelated but separate variables. In a series of empirical studies we use three of Read's components as variables, the omission being lexical density. Errors, however, play only a relatively minor role in our investigations, being confined to spelling errors in one study of first language writing.

Overview of the content of this monograph

Initially, our concern is with the considerable difficulties of measurement associated with lexical diversity, or 'lexical variation' to use Read's term. These problems are considered in Chapter 2 and a solution to them is proposed in Chapter 3. In the chapters that follow, the validity of our proposed solution is put under scrutiny and applied to two sets of early first language spoken data (Chapters 4 and 5) and to foreign language oral transcripts (Chapter 6). Chapter 7 uses early language acquisition corpora from two languages to show how a comparison between a lemmatised and non-lemmatised corpus can provide insights into children's development of grammatical morphology. Chapter 8 looks at type–*type* ratios – measures that compare the diversity of different word classes or categories of words, including those that address individual differences and cross-linguistic differences in style of vocabulary development in children, and those that assess the composition of their active vocabulary from samples of spontaneous speech. We provide an empirical demonstration of the sensitivity of one particular type–type ratio to sample size, and propose a solution derived from the work on lexical diversity in earlier chapters. This chapter also reviews approaches to quantifying Read's dimension of lexical sophistication, that is to say, the usage of low frequency or more difficult vocabulary. Chapter 9 contains an analysis of a large corpus of first language writing using six statistical language measures including lexical diversity, lexical sophistication, word length, and spelling errors. We will be particularly concerned with the interrelationships between the first three of these and the extent to which they uniquely predict levels of writing proficiency. The final chapter will provide a critical evaluation of the impact of the choice of vocabulary richness measures and methods of calculating them on recent research. First of all, however, in the rest of this chapter we will consider the notion of lexical diversity and examine the kinds of interpretation that various investigators have assigned to measures that quantify the number of different words in a language sample. We will attempt to give the reader an indication of the scope of such measures by looking at ways in which they have been applied in language research, particularly language development, and taking account of their theoretical justification.

Lexical diversity

We use the label 'lexical diversity' rather than lexical variation in this volume because this is the more common term in the child language literature, which was the starting point for our interest in this area. We note that Laufer (2003) uses lexical diversity to mean a combination of lexical variation and lexical sophistication, but we use it only to denote the former. As noted above, we treat lexical diversity and lexical sophistication as being subsumed under vocabulary richness.

Language researchers and applied linguists working on a wide range of topics frequently need indices that quantify the range or number of different words in a text or conversation. Such measures are variously conceptualised as reflecting:

- 'lexical range and balance' (Crystal, 1982);
- 'verbal creativity' (Fradis, Mihailescu and Jipescu, 1992);
- vocabulary 'flexibility' (McCarthy, 1954; Sherblom and Sherblom, 1987);
- 'semantic abilities', 'semantic proficiency' or 'semantic factors' (Walker, Roberts and Hedrick, 1988; Watkins, Kelly, Harbers and Hollis, 1995; Ukrainetz and Blomquist, 2002);
- overall language quality or 'language maturity' (Stewig, 1994);
- elaborated versus restricted codes (see Hesse and Hesse, 1987);
- total vocabulary size (Thomson and Thompson, 1915; Wagner, Altmann and Köhler, 1987);
- the tendency to use rare versus frequent words (Spreen and Wachal, 1973);
- the readability of a text (Tuldava, 1993);
- the linguistic complexity of a text (Simonton, 1989; Crain-Thoresen, Dahlin and Powell, 2001);
- the extent to which information is condensed and its 'granularity', that is to say, the degree to which narration is fine-grained and detailed (Dewaele and Pavlenko, 2003);
- authorial style (Smith and Kelly, 2002);
- from a more negative perspective, particularly in the investigation of language disorders, measures are often seen as an index of repetitiveness manifested as perseveration in dementia and schizophrenia; speech automatisms in aphasia; echolalia in autism and mental deficiency; and topic bias (a tendency to return continuously to a limited number of topics)

linked with autism, learning disability, and head injuries (see Perkins, 1994, pp. 323–6 for an excellent overview);
- 'the cognitive load imposed by the on-line constraints of spoken [versus written] language' (Strömquist, Johansson, Kriz, Ragnarsdóttir, Aisenman and Ravid, 2002, p. 47, following Chafe, 1982).

Whatever the construct being investigated, however, there is a general underlying assumption among those concerned with educational development, language learning and acquisition, and language impairment that a high lexical diversity is 'a good thing', an indication of a combination of vocabulary size and the ability to use it effectively. Of course, it goes without saying that this is in some respects a naïve oversimplification, and Jarvis (2002) has suggested that in second language writing a high diversity beyond a certain threshold can be associated with poorer quality of language. As Broeder, Extra and Van Hout (1993) have pointed out '... the mark of a good speaker is that he selects words from his word stock in an optimal way in relation to the communicative situation, rather than produce as many different words as possible' (p. 149). One only has to examine the carefully crafted repetition and antithesis in the opening paragraph of Charles Dickens's *A Tale of Two Cities* ('It was the best of times, it was the worst of times, it was the age of wisdom, it was the age of foolishness...') to appreciate the truth of this statement. Besides, as Broeder and colleagues have pointed out, in an ongoing text or conversation 'there is a dependency between successive occurrences of words' (Broeder et al., 1993, p. 149). In other words, as expressed much earlier by Thomson and Thompson (1915, p. 55), 'the first appearance [of a word] assures for that particular word and its associations a livelier connection for some time with the elements in the focus of attention.' Nevertheless, in spite of the mathematical difficulties in finding appropriate methods of measurement that will be discussed in the next chapters, empirical studies have found lexical diversity variables to be valid as developmental indices and as theoretically motivated measures in profiling a range of language disabilities.

Research using lexical diversity as a variable

As noted above, lexical diversity variables have been applied to many areas of linguistic investigation. These include journalism; lexical innovation and loss; literary style; language register; the discourse of job interviews, of group conflict, and of psychoanalysis; the communicative effectiveness of messages; language addressed to elderly people; political speeches and persuasive styles; studies of personality, communicative reticence, schizophrenia, and emotional disorders including stress, anxiety, and repression; the linguistic environment of the home (child-directed speech), and first and second language classrooms; assessment of first and second language ability; senile dementia, autism, language delay, and language impairment. Below are listed in more detail some illustrative publications to exemplify the use of lexical diversity indices and the motivation behind their use. Note that our aim here is to demonstrate the range and extent of usage, the need for such measures and their relation to theory. The inclusion of a study does not, therefore, attest to the validity of its methods, an issue that will be dealt with in the following chapter. Apart from the first example, which we include because of its interesting theoretical underpinnings, we focus for the most part on some of the more recent research topics in the various fields.

Analysis of historical documents

Carpenter and Hersh (1985) treat lexical diversity as an index of military morale during the American Revolution. The personal correspondence of British military personnel was analysed and an increase in lexical diversity over time was interpreted as demonstrating worsening military morale resulting from passivity and reduced aggression. The construct validity of lexical diversity for this purpose is based on the assumption that heightened motivation or drive would favour the selection of 'more familiar, practiced, or expected words' (p. 186).

Studies of authors' style and dating works of literature

Some researchers apply lexical richness measures as indices of authorial style to literary corpora in order to date works whose authorship is known (e.g. Smith and Kelly, 2002). Trends in lexical diversity over an author's creative life are used to build a statistical model from which the chronology of previously undated works can be predicted. Not all authors increase their lexical richness during their working lives – there may even be a decline. Nevertheless, significant trends can be identified.

Forensic linguistics

In forensic linguistics some authors have used a lexical diversity measure as an index of the veracity of witness statements. In an experimental study of interviews with imprisoned offenders who witnessed a staged theft, true and dishonest statements were compared on lexical diversity and a range of other measures such as the use of hedges (Colwell, Hiscock and Memon, 2002). Higher diversity was predicted for the untrue statements because of the careful phrasing of the fabricated elements, but the theoretical foundation for this seems rather weak given contrary views expressed elsewhere that lying leads to more stereotypical responses that reduce TTR values (Osgood, 1960, quoted in Colwell et al., 2002, p. 289). Nevertheless, the prediction was borne out by the analysis. Other applications in the field of forensic linguistics have been the authentication of police statements, wills, and suicide notes.

Demographic influences on vocabulary use

Lexical diversity variables recently numbered among 42 vocabulary measures in a study of the influence of social class, educational background, and gender on vocabulary usage. Language samples took the form of personal interviews of 415 34-year-old Swedish adults as part of a longitudinal study of educational progress (Härnquist, Christianson, Ridings and Tingsell, 2003). Gender and educational background, but not social class, were found to predict TTRs that had been adjusted for variation in sample size.

Second language and bilingualism

In the area of second language (L2) and bilingualism, Daller, Van Hout and Treffers-Daller (2003) have conducted research on two groups of German–Turkish bilinguals into the effectiveness of several measures of lexical diversity and vocabulary richness in the study of language dominance. Two other recent publications have also used a lexical diversity measure as a dependent variable in identifying the mutual influences of bilingual speakers' languages, and especially the effect of the second language on the first. First, Laufer (2003) researched the influence of the second language (Hebrew) and length of residence in Israel on the first language (Russian) of 26 Russian immigrants through an analysis of written compositions. Lexical diversity in the first language was found to diminish with length of residence, but not significantly so.

Second, a study with a similar purpose was conducted by Dewaele and Pavlenko (2003) who elicited oral narratives of films from five groups: monolingual Russian speakers, monolingual English speakers, L2 speakers of English (interviewed in English), L2 speakers of English (interviewed in Russian) and students of English as a foreign language. The choice of lexical diversity as a dependent variable whilst justified by its sensitivity to level of lexical detail, which is itself a function of 'granularity'. This latter term is defined in the work of Colette Noyou and her colleagues who refer to the extent to which the narration 'entails the presentation of a detailed series of micro-events'. That is to say, 'Lexical granularity is reflected in productivity and lexical diversity values, as higher levels of resolution will result in longer and more fine-grained retellings with more specific (and low-frequency) words' (Dewaele and Pavlenko, 2003, p. 124). The analysis showed strong differences between groups on lexical diversity and a weaker effect for gender.

Language assessment

In the fields of both first and second language assessment, lexical diversity measures have frequently served as general-purpose measures of spoken and written language development.

Second language speaking and writing

Vermeer (2000) compared a series of measures applied to the spoken language elicited by interviews of children learning Dutch, both as a first and as a second language, between the ages of four and seven. Jarvis (2002) also compared different lexical diversity measures in a study of second language written narratives completed by 210 Finnish and Swedish adolescent learners of English as a foreign language. Jarvis investigated relationships between the various indices and amount of instruction, quality of writing, first language background, and scores in vocabulary tests. His conclusion was that lexical diversity, when measured by reliable indices, was positively correlated with the quantity of formal instruction and L2 vocabulary knowledge. The extent to which lexical diversity was associated with the quality of writing depended on the writer's L1.

Assessment of first language speaking and writing

One highly ambitious project that has assessed vocabulary diversity in first language speaking and writing is Ruth Berman's Spencer Foundation study 'Developing literacy in different contexts and in diffcrent languages' (Berman, 2000). This research, which was conducted across seven languages (with the subsequent addition of Catalan), compares children at three ages, plus adults, producing language in two genres (narrative and expository), and two modalities (speech and writing) (see Berman and Verhoeven, 2002). Their measure shows main effects for age, genre, and language, but not for modality.

Assessment of early speech

First language assessment of lexical diversity can be compared with norms or a 'reference database' (e.g. Miller, 1996a, 1996b; Miller, Gillon and Johnston, 2002), or can be used for cross-validation in the refinement of developmental indices for different languages, such as mean length of utterance (MLU) for Icelandic (Thordardottir and Ellis Weismer, 1998). Such data have also acted as a criterion derived from the spontaneous speech of children against which the validity of formal vocabulary tests or parental checklists can be judged. For example, Ukrainetz and Blomquist (2002) validated vocabulary tests by correlating scores on four expressive and receptive language tests with the total number of different words in 150 spontaneous utterances spoken by 28 children aged 4;9. Similarly, for vocabulary checklists filled in by parents, Pan, Rowe, Spier and Tamis-LeMonda (2002) tested the validity of the MacArthur Communicative Development Inventory (MCDI) as applied specifically to two-year-old toddlers from low-income families. Expressive vocabulary scores from the MCDI were correlated with the number of different words produced during a ten-minute interaction with their mothers.

Influences on the language sampled in research and clinical assessments

Elsewhere in the field of assessment, researchers have been concerned with the effects of context, setting, or activity, and adult interaction style on the assessment of children's language ability, both for research purposes and in clinical contexts. Hoff, Baker, Isaza, Romanoski and Vasquez (2002) compare the number of child word types produced in three settings: book reading, toy play, and mealtimes at two points in time, at approximately 22 and 24 months of age. The authors warn that playing with toys, which is one of the most frequent activities used to elicit spontaneous speech, does not guarantee the most advanced level of language from the child.

Similarly, Bornstein, Painter and Park (2002) found that a wider range of child word roots was sampled at a time judged by the mother to be 'optimum' than when the child was playing alone or with the mother. One study that considered the effects of interaction style on children's language production, in this case a comparison between 'questioning' and 'commenting' by the interlocutor during clinical assessments, is Yoder, Davies and Bishop (1994). Yoder and colleagues used the 'prorated number of lexically free words' as the dependent variable, that is to say the number of children's different words that were productive, as a percentage of non-imitative utterances. The researchers found in favour of a style that includes topic-continuing wh-questions.

Linguistic input and interaction

In investigations into the comprehensibility and complexity of the language *addressed* to young children acquiring their first language, lexical diversity has been used to compare different contexts and activities such as story reading, toy play, and remembering a family outing (Crain-Thoresen et al., 2001). It has also been a criterion to judge the extent to which adults adjust their language to high and low levels of comprehension in children with expressive language delay (Van Kleeck and Carpenter, 1980). Girolametto, Bonifacio, Visini, Weitzman, Zocconi and Pearce (2002) contrasted the lexical diversity of Italian and English mothers and their language-delayed children. Both Italian mothers and children had higher scores than the Canadian mothers and children.

Hoff and Naigles (2002) used the number of different words addressed to two-year-old children by mothers as an index of the 'data-providing' aspects of input in comparison with social–pragmatic measures, such as topic-continuing replies, as predictors of gains in child vocabulary. Because child vocabulary was also measured by the number of different words in spontaneous child speech, word types are used both as an independent and the dependent variable in this study. Results showed that a combination of lexical diversity and MLU explained 24 per cent of the variance in children's total word types. Further research by Hoff and her colleagues (Hoff, McKay and Noya, 2002) also used the number of word types addressed to children as a predictor of later vocabulary development in a study that aimed to disentangle the effects of maternal socio-economic status (SES) and quantity and quality of input. They conclude that 'it is the lexical richness of maternal speech, not the total amount of maternal speech, that predicts child vocabulary and mediates the relation of SES to child vocabulary' (p. 1).

The 'noun bias' issue

A large number of recent studies that have considerable importance for child language acquisition theory use the relative diversity of nouns and verbs, both in the spontaneous speech of the child as well as in the input to investigate what was originally thought to be a cross-linguistic tendency for nouns to dominate early vocabularies (the 'noun bias' issue). These studies, which follow up Gentner's (1982) natural partitions hypothesis, will be reviewed in Chapter 8 of this volume, together with a detailed consideration of the measures they employ.

Language impairment and delay

The lexical diversity of spontaneous speech as a measure of vocabulary production is frequently employed in studies of language delay and language impairment in children to profile different populations and to evaluate the effectiveness of interventions. Scott and Windsor (2000) tested ten 'general language performance measures' (p. 324), including lexical diversity on the spoken and written discourse of language-disabled school-aged children and age-matched and language-matched controls. In spite of a significant difference between the target group and the age-matched group for narrative writing, there were no differences on speaking. The authors conclude that their measure (number of different words in 100 word tokens) is less useful for older children with language impairments of the kind shown by this group.

In profiling the expressive language of children exposed to cocaine prenatally, Delaney-Black, Covington, Templin and colleagues (2000) conducted a prospective study of 458 Afro-American six-year-olds, 204 of whose mothers had taken cocaine. Other independent variables included tobacco, lead level, social class, gender, maternal verbal ability, and exposure to violence. None of the language variables distinguished between the two groups, but when all children were divided into high and low language groups on the basis of a combination of two lexical diversity measures (number of different words and TTR), they differed significantly on cocaine exposure but not tobacco or lead levels.

Elsewhere, the number of different words has been used to show developmental trajectories of children with developmental dysphasia (Ouellet, Cohen, Le Normand and Braun, 2000), and pre-term children have been compared with age-matched controls on verb frequency and diversity by

Le Normand and Cohen (1999), with control children obtaining significantly higher scores on both. The authors interpret their findings as showing that 'impaired language development is a cognitive consequence of prematurity independently of birthweight' (p. 235). Finally, in the investigation of stuttering Silverman and Ratner (2002) evaluated the validity of two measures of lexical diversity in differentiating a group of normally fluent children with peers who stutter.

Specific language impairment

One area of particular interest is the research on specific language impairment (SLI), a syndrome that affects 3 to 5 per cent of the population. SLI is characterised by persistent language difficulties in children whose development, including hearing and non-verbal intelligence, is otherwise normal. The characteristics of SLI are discussed in Leonard (1998). It is not a homogeneous condition and exhibits a wide range of language difficulties in a diverse population (Miller, 1996b). These may include poor articulation, particular problems with grammatical morphology, and later reading difficulties. Nevertheless, reports of delayed learning of early vocabulary, word-finding problems, naming errors, and mapping difficulties (Leonard, 1998) have led researchers to adopt spontaneous speech measures that reflect the diversity of general vocabulary in developing profiles of SLI through comparisons with age-matched and language-matched control groups.

Fletcher and Peters (1984) found that a count of the number of different words discriminated between children with SLI and age-matched controls. In addition, findings of particular difficulties with verbs (Jones and Conti-Ramsden, 1997) and describing actions (Leonard, 1998) appeared to be reflected in a reduced number of lexical verb types in spontaneous speech samples (Fletcher and Peters, 1984; Watkins, Rice and Moltz, 1993; Conti-Ramsden and Jones, 1997). This appeared to be accompanied by an increase in the usage of general, all-purpose (GAP) verbs rather than verbs expressing more specific meanings (Watkins et al., 1993).

As a result of such findings, researchers have found a need to measure the diversity of different word classes, especially nouns and verbs (for example, Leonard, Miller and Gerber, 1999) as well as the general diversity of all vocabulary. Different studies have produced conflicting findings, however, and recent research that has used a more rigorous methodology for measuring diversity, such as work by Stokes and Fletcher (2000) on Cantonese-speaking children with SLI, found that verb diversity failed to discriminate between these children and the control groups. Such inconsistencies have caused researchers to consider the extent to which some of the findings have been an artefact of the way in which diversity was measured, particularly where the size of language sample has been inadequately controlled.

These issues have recently been addressed in detail by Thordardottir and Ellis Weismer (2001) in a comprehensive overview of the measurement issues. In their own study of a large sample of children, they find no difference between children with SLI and normal control children on verb diversity when sample size is controlled, or on the usage of high frequency GAP verbs. Further discussion of the measurement issues can be found in Owen and Leonard (2002).

Intervention studies

In intervention studies lexical diversity has frequently been used as a dependent variable, for example, with late talkers to compare different treatment methods (Ellis Weismer, Murray-Branch and Miller, 1993) and to identify developmental profiles (Ellis Weismer, Murray Branch and Miller, 1994). Recently, Geers, Spehar and Sedey (2002) used it to monitor the progress of hearing-impaired children following cochlear implants. They related development to the degree of usage of speech or sign language by creating a single transcript that contained all spoken words and signs in a 20-minute speech sample. They concluded that users of speech obtained higher language scores, including lexical diversity, and were more likely to be placed in mainstream educational programmes. Elsewhere, in research into stuttering, Onslow, Ratner and Packman (2001) used lexical diversity as an output measure to judge the effectiveness of laboratory control of stuttering by means of a form of response contingent stimulation called 'Time out ... . from speaking after stuttering' (p. 651).

Language in dementia

Difficulties with lexical retrieval in patients with senile dementia or dementia of Alzheimer type (Pinker, 1999) have led to the adoption of measures of overall range of vocabulary in studies that typically compare these patients with healthy controls of a similar age (e.g. Bucks, Singh, Cuerdon and Wilcock, 2000) or patients with other conditions such as Wernicke's aphasia (e.g. Blanken, Dittman, Haas and Wallesch, 1987). In Bucks and colleagues' (2000) study, lexical richness, comprising measures of diversity and low-frequency words, was effective in discriminating between the groups. Because different word classes may not be equally affected, for example difficulties in naming have been reported as being more severe than producing verbs and function words, production measures for different word classes are often devised, including measures of the diversity of nouns and verbs (e.g. Blanken et al., 1987).

Aphasia

In studies of adult aphasia, vocabulary diversity has been seen as a useful general index of lexical ability that reflects conversational proficiency and discriminates between aphasic patients and normal controls (Holmes and Singh, 1996) or between fluent and non-fluent aphasics (Wright, Silverman and Newhoff, 2003). In addition, the observation that, in contrast with

Alzheimer's patients, aphasic patients have more difficulty with verbs than nouns (Luzzatti, Raggi, Zonca, Pistarini, Contardi and Pinna, 2001) and that the diversity and frequency of lexical verbs is lower for people with aphasia than normal controls has led to the employment of measures of the diversity of individual word classes to allow comparisons with controls, within-subject comparisons across word classes, and comparisons across languages (see for example, Edwards and Bastiaanse, 1998).

Schizophrenia

Marked differences in language behaviour in schizophrenic patients have given rise to a large literature in this area (Meara, 1978). As noted above, perseveration, the repetition of words or phrases, often out of context, is a recognised symptom that has resulted in a long tradition of applying lexical diversity indices to the speech (e.g. Fairbanks, 1944) and writing (Mann, 1944) of schizophrenic patients. Research published in the 1980s suggested that the TTR discriminated reliably between 'thought-disordered' and 'non-thought-disordered schizophrenics' and was strongly related to motor disturbances (Manschreck, Maher and Ader, 1981) but that, while it might be a predictor of response to treatment and remission, its clinical usefulness as a diagnostic of schizophrenia or of thought disorder was limited (Manschreck, Maher, Hoover and Ames, 1984). Nevertheless, TTR has continued to be employed as a measure of repetition in schizophrenia research, but it does not necessarily differentiate reliably between schizophrenic subjects and normal controls (Sanders, Adams, Tager-Flusberg, Shenton and Coleman, 1995).

Conclusion

It can be seen from the research described in this opening chapter that measures of vocabulary richness, and particularly lexical diversity, have been applied in a wide range of contexts and for many different purposes. In some cases, such as Alzheimer's disease, their use results from a move towards assessments based on more conversation-like interviews, reflecting a dissatisfaction with standard batteries of decontextualised tests or even picture descriptions in favour of data that have relevance to the real-world needs of patients (Bucks et al., 2000). Both within and between the various research topics there are vastly differing conceptualisations of exactly what is being measured and why. This is reflected in wide variation in the extent to which the measures have any clearly articulated construct validity or theoretical underpinning in relation to their field of application. In many cases the measure is a highly general index, little more than a rule-of-thumb indicator of development, in some ways analagous to the use of mean length of utterance (MLU) in the study of early language development. In other cases, there is little more than a common sense but poorly supported justification, for example that lying gives rise to higher diversity of vocabulary usage because fabrication entails more careful phrasing. In many other cases, however, the theoretical underpinnings are much clearer, and this is particularly the case where the diversity of individual word classes is assessed in order to advance theoretical understandings in areas such as SLI, aphasia, Alzheimer's disease, and the 'noun bias' issue. The meaning of a general lexical diversity value for pooled vocabulary will be more difficult to interpret because of complex interrelationships between different patterns for different word classes. Nevertheless, we find Dewaele and Pavlenko's (2003) exposition of the concept of 'granularity' as a rationale for their measure to be a particularly useful example of justifying, explaining, and interpreting its use in relation to their own particular purpose. And this is a crucial point because the validity of any measure cannot be judged in the abstract, but has to be related to the purpose for which it is to be used.

In this chapter we have made a case for the need for valid and reliable measures of lexical diversity, whatever their theoretical justification. In the next chapter we will examine the considerable difficulties of calculating measures that live up to these requirements and the confusion that has prevailed in their interpretation.

2
Traditional Approaches to Measuring Lexical Diversity

As we have indicated in the previous chapter, measuring lexical diversity is not as straightforward as it may seem, and to demonstrate the issues involved in its quantification we first need to consider in some detail an apparently simple approach and then discuss the most influential metric, which we shall show is fatally flawed.

The number of different words (NDW)

A number of researchers, notably Miller (1991) and Klee (1992) have used the number of different words (NDW) contained in a language sample. This is the simplest measure available and clearly addresses an important aspect of diversity, namely the range of vocabulary deployed. In Klee's study, which looked at children between the ages of 24 and 50 months, two results demonstrated its potential as an indicator of development. First, NDW correlated strongly with age. Second, it appeared to differentiate between normally developing children and those with specific language impairment (SLI), as these two subgroups in the sample produced significantly different NDW from each other. In spite of this success, however, on closer examination NDW is not as simple a measure as it first seems, and it is worth looking at the various ways in which NDW can be calculated in order to illustrate many of the matters that need to be addressed before arriving at a more robust measurement of diversity. To do so, we shall consider two language samples; the first (Transcript A) contains 60 different words, and the second (Transcript B) 50.

First and foremost, NDW is a measure of *range*. Undoubtedly, the range of vocabulary displayed by a subject contributes to how diverse the lexis employed by that person happens to be. Transcript A has the greater range, and in that sense appears to show greater diversity than Transcript B. Doubts arise, however, when we learn that Transcript A has in total 200 word tokens, while Transcript B consists of only 100, and therefore like is clearly not being compared with like. How many different words appear in a language sample will in all probability depend on how many words there are in total and this is the heart of many problems in the measurement of lexical diversity.

In order to compare like with like, some sort of standardisation is desirable and two kinds have been used. Both Miller and Klee, for instance, standardised the length of transcripts as measured by utterances. Klee (1992) in the study of normally developing children and children with SLI calculated the number of different words in 50 utterances, and Miller (1991) in '100 complete and intelligible utterances' (p. 215). As noted above, Klee found the NDWs standardised in this way discriminated between the two groups of children and correlated strongly with age. Nevertheless, although in terms of utterances like is being compared with like, there is no guarantee that language samples of the various individuals will all be of the same length. That will depend on the number of words in each utterance, or the mean length of utterance (MLU). Miller's (1991) own work demonstrates the problem this raises. In his study of 192 children aged three to 13 years, he found that NDW (100 utterances) correlated strongly with age ($r = 0.75$ and 0.80 for conversations and narratives respectively), but it was even more strongly correlated with MLU ($r = 0.94$ and 0.89). MLU is well established as a measure of language development (see Brown, 1973) and increases with age and language ability (Wells, 1985, Table 3.3, p. 123).

Basing NDW calculations on a fixed number of utterances confounds diversity with MLU. In other words, the older the children, the longer the utterances they produce and the more total words there will be in their language samples. Comparisons of NDW of older and younger children, or between children developing normally and children with a language impairment will tend to favour those with the highest MLU.

A popular alternative, intended to standardise at the point of data collection, has been simply to count the number of different words produced in a set number of minutes. This procedure has been advocated by Catherine Snow and colleagues (Rollins, 1994; Snow, 1996) and has recently been used by Geers and colleagues (2002) in a study of children's speech development following cochlear implants. The method has a similar flaw, however, as it confounds lexical diversity with increasing volubility as children develop. Wells (1985, p. 112, Figure 3.1) demonstrates graphically how the amount of speech sampled in a set time period increases with age and language ability, so again there is no guarantee that every transcript will contain the same total number of words and there is every likelihood that children who talk more in the set time will receive higher NDW scores. In spite of this, it is worth noting that Geers and colleagues (2002) regard the fact that their measure combines lexical diversity and volubility as a strength.

It is possible to ensure that NDW is calculated over the same number of words by delaying the standardisation until the start of the analysis, when, having collected the data, every transcript can be reduced to a set length.

Thordardottir and Ellis Weismer (2001) achieved this by truncating all the transcripts in their study to 315 words. Truncation is the simplest method of standardisation, and has a kind of fairness in as much as the comparison is between the first standard number of words produced by each subject. The number of words for the set length can be chosen in advance, or determined by the length of the shortest transcript collected, but in either case it can be argued that not every transcript is treated the same. Transcripts that are already of the standard length will not be cut at all, while longer ones may be reduced to a fraction of their original length. The fact that some language samples will be cut more extensively than others creates the risk that the truncated sub-samples do not represent whole transcripts in the same way for every subject. In both cases there is a waste of data, as no account is taken of the material cut by the truncation.

Truncating the two language samples in our illustrative comparison to the size of the smaller (100 words) results in NDW (first 100 words) for Transcript A of 40 and of 50 for Transcript B – thereby reversing the relative order of their diversity as measured by the raw NDW. A smaller standard length could be chosen on the grounds that it is fairer to apply a truncation to both. If a standard length of 50 words is chosen, the values for NDW (first 50 words) for Transcripts A and B are both 18, implying equal diversity.

There are better ways of reducing transcripts to a standard length. In order for the sub-sample to represent the whole transcript, random sampling would be an improvement. First, a standard number of words, fewer than the smallest transcript available, must be chosen (for our illustrative example, say, of 25 words), and then a random process chosen to select the given number of words for the sub-sample to be analysed. There are two possible random processes. The words can be selected entirely at random, but a decision needs to be made as to whether or not to replace a chosen word into the transcript before the next word is selected (in which case the same word can be selected again and again). Random selection without replacement is the more obvious choice. If it is thought to be important to preserve the structure of the language in the transcript, on the other hand, a sub-sample of 25 (in our case) words could be taken in sequence from the transcript, with the starting point chosen at random. These two processes would produce NDW (random 25) and NDW (random sequence 25).

Although in either case the random selection provides the opportunity for every word in the transcript to appear in the chosen sub-sample, and in that sense ensures a kind of representativeness which makes use of all the data, different trials will select different samples and could lead to differing results. Better still would be to take a number of randomly chosen sub-samples (by either method) and average the NDWs found for each. This average would approximate to the expected value for NDW, and in our example yielded an NDW (expected 25) for Transcripts A and B of 5.8 and 9.2 averaged over four

Table 2.1 NDW calculated by different standardisation methods for Transcript A and Transcript B

	Transcript A (200 words)	Transcript B (100 words)	Apparent Result
NDW (total)	60	50	$NDW_A > NDW_B$
NDW (first 100 words)	40	50	$NDW_A < NDW_B$
NDW (first 50 words)	18	18	$NDW_A = NDW_B$
NDW (expected random 25)	5.8	9.2	$NDW_A < NDW_B$
NDW (expected sequence 25)	5.2	8.5	$NDW_A < NDW_B$

trials of entirely random selection, and 5.2 and 8.5 for an average of four sequences chosen at random.

NDW is not as straightforward a measure as may be thought, therefore. Raw NDW has its use as a measure of the range of vocabulary in a language sample, but is limited when comparing the lexical diversity of different samples by being dependent on their size. Some standardisation of transcript length is required, but as shown above there are different ways to do this. Table 2.1 summarises the results of the various standardisation procedures applied to the two example transcripts, and illustrates that not only do they lead to a variety of numbers, which makes it difficult to compare the results from studies which use different standardisation procedures, but also that the method of standardisation can change the overall result as to which transcript has the bigger NDW, and this undermines it as a reliable measure of diversity.

The type–token ratio (TTR)

All the words in a language sample are tokens, but each individual word is a type. When a word is repeated, then, there will be two (or more) tokens of one type. The *token* count for a transcript is the total number of words it contains, while the *type* count is the number of different words in it. This nomenclature is behind the naming of another widely used, and in child language studies perhaps the most influential, measure of lexical diversity – the type–token ratio or TTR.

TTR is calculated by dividing the number of different words or types in the language sample by the number of tokens, or the total number of words it contains. Being a proportion of a total, TTR can take values between 0 and 1, with higher values representing greater diversity. The assumption appears to be that because the number of different words is expressed as a proportion of the total number of words, the size of the language sample is therefore taken into account, and TTR will provide a more robust indication of lexical diversity than NDW. As will be demonstrated below, this assumption is false, but the prima-facie case for it can be illustrated by comparing the TTRs for two language samples taken from Shakespeare's *Julius Caesar*. The first is Anthony's soliloquy over the body of Caesar which begins, 'O! pardon me thou bleeding piece of earth'. This consists of 22 lines containing 173 tokens with 117 types. As might be expected of Shakespeare, who is noted for his linguistic creativity, it is a good example of highly diverse text. Only 24 words are repeated and 17 of them appear no more than twice. Its TTR is 117/173 or 0.68. The second sample is an extract from Anthony's funeral oration for Caesar, beginning at the line 'So let it be with Caesar. The noble Brutus ...', and extending for a further 23 lines. It is of similar length, 172 tokens, written by the same author for the same character. But it is a public speech to the crowd, and consciously employs rhetorical repetition to rouse the mob, particularly the statements: 'But Brutus says he was ambitious'; 'And Brutus is an honourable man', which appear with minor variations four times within the extract. It is to be expected, then, that there will be less diversity in this second extract, and a lower TTR can be predicted. This time 29 words are repeated, with only ten appearing no more than twice. There are 86 types in all, which gives a TTR of 86/172 or 0.50, smaller than that for the first, as predicted.

TTR and some related measures were given prominence by a programme of research in the 1940s with the purpose of developing quantitative linguistic indices which could be applied to the speech and writing of a variety of populations (Johnson, 1944). TTRs were used to assess the lexical diversity of total vocabulary and in some cases separate word classes.

Many researchers working in the area of child language and language impairment (for example, Fletcher, 1985; MacWhinney, 1994; Pan, 1994; Stickler, 1987) attribute TTR to Mildred Templin. In her seminal work, Templin (1957) conducted a cross-sectional study of the phonology, utterance length and complexity, and vocabulary of 480 children at eight age points between three and eight years. As far as we are aware, however, Templin neither used the term, nor reported values for type–token ratios, other than to comment that there was roughly one different word for every two words spoken:

> By comparing Tables 60 [types] and 61 [tokens], the proportion of different words used to all words uttered in 50 remarks is apparent. This ratio is approximately one different word for slightly over two words uttered. This ratio shows little variation over the range tested and among subsamples, sex and SES groups.
>
> (Templin, 1957, p. 115)

It appears to have been Miller (1981, p. 42) who first calculated mean TTRs on Templin's data, by pooling the data for each of Templin's eight age groups of children. Table 2.2 summarises this finding, from which he concluded:

The consistency of this measure makes it enormously valuable as a clinical tool. For example, if a normal hearing child's TTR is significantly below 0.5 we can be reasonably certain that the sparseness of vocabulary is *not* [author's emphasis] an artefact of SES but is probably indicative of a language specific deficiency.

(Miller, 1981, p. 41)

TTR's apparent constancy over age, as illustrated in Table 2.2 lent it credibility and led to its being used extensively in child language research along with the acceptance of the significance of the value of 0.5. For example, an introduction to the analysis of child language transcripts by Stickler (1987) treats Miller's calculations for Templin's age groups as norms, and uses the 0.5 threshold level as an overall criterion of normality. Similarly, McEvoy and Dodd (1992) in a study of 19 sets of multiple-birth children aged two to four years concluded on the basis of the 0.5 threshold that five children with a TTR of less than 0.33 did not have age-appropriate TTRs.

None the less, if taken at its face value, the result that TTR remains constant at about 0.5 for normally developing children is highly problematic, or at least surprising, if TTR is a genuine representation of lexical diversity. The evidence clearly shows that normally developing children as they get older acquire larger and larger productive vocabularies, and this in itself ought to lead to greater and greater diversity of usage. Not only do they use a wider range of words, but the range includes synonyms and words with greater specificity which contribute to a reduction in repetition. It would require some exceptional mechanism to account for the more advanced children becoming incapable of exploiting these advantages.

In fact, many empirical studies do not confirm the constancy at 0.5, but far from clarifying the theoretical problem they confuse the matter still further by producing negative correlations with age and developmental measures. Examples include Lieven's (1978) case study of two children and

Table 2.2 TTRs calculated for Templin's data from 50 utterances

Age of Sample	Mean Tokens	Mean Types	TTR of Means
3.0	204.9	92.5	0.451
3.5	232.9	104.8	0.450
4.0	268.8	120.4	0.448
4.5	270.7	127.0	0.469
5.0	286.2	132.4	0.463
6.0	328.0	147.0	0.448
7.0	363.1	157.7	0.434
8.0	378.8	166.5	0.440

Adapted from Templin (1957): Tables 60 and 61, p. 116.

Fletcher's (1985) study of Sophie, where in both cases TTRs fell as children got older and their MLU increased. Bates, Bretherton and Snyder (1988) found that for children at 28 months, TTRs were significantly negatively correlated with both MLU and another vocabulary measure. In a case study of a child with Down's syndrome, Layton and Savino (1990) comment on the child's high TTR (0.60) at 7;8 in comparison with Templin's subjects. Other examples can be found in the second language field – the European Science Foundation project on adult language acquisition (Broeder et al., 1993) also found that TTRs fell over time for free conversations and retelling the story of a film.

Similar inconsistencies appear in other language fields and the contradictory and counter-intuitive results which are found throughout the literature indicate that, in spite of its widespread and continuing use, TTR is deeply flawed. TTR is a ratio of NDW to the size of the language sample. It was seen essentially as a way of compensating for the dependence of NDW on sample size, in much the same way as density is a better comparator of substances than mass, as unlike mass, density is independent of how much of the substance is used to measure it. At first, TTR seems to be an improvement on NDW. For the two transcripts in our illustrative example when discussing NDW, TTR = 60/200 for Transcript A (0.30) and for Transcript B, TTR = 50/100 (0.50), which seems to establish their comparison on a fairer basis that takes their differing size into account.

It is true that a ratio provides better comparability than the simple raw value of one quantity when the quantities in the ratio come in fixed proportion regardless of their size. For example, in the case of the density of a substance, the ratio (mass/volume) remains the same regardless of the volume from which it is calculated. Adding half as much again to the volume will add half as much to the mass; doubling the volume will double the mass; reducing the volume to a quarter will similarly reduce the mass to a quarter; and so on. Language production is not like that, however. Adding an extra word to a language sample always increases the token count (N) but will only increase the type count (V) if the word has not been used before. As more and more words are used, it becomes harder and harder to avoid repetition and the chance of the extra word being a new type decreases. Consequently, the type count (V) in the numerator increases at a slower rate than the token count (N) in the denominator and the TTR (V/N) inevitably falls. A graph of TTR against N would show decreasing values, and as an example, Figure 2.1 shows such a result empirically, plotting TTR against token count for both a transcript of the speech of a two-year-old (see Richards, 1987, for details of the subject) and a chapter from an academic book by Richards himself, to illustrate this is not a property of the producer's age but quite general for all language samples.

TTR is a function of token count and, like NDW, dependent on the size of the language sample over which it is calculated. Higher values will be

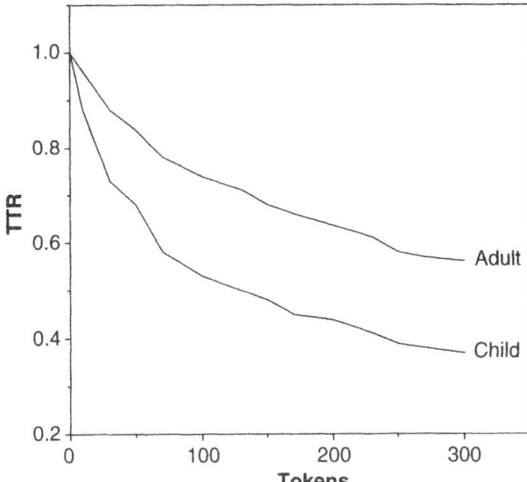

Figure 2.1 TTR plotted against tokens for the spoken language of a two-year-old and academic writing for an adult

obtained from shorter samples and lower ones from larger samples. Analysing the Prince of Wales's speech about the state of the English language at the presentation of the Thomas Cranmer Schools Prize in December 1989, for example, yields a TTR for the first 365 words of his speech of 0.60, but for the whole speech a TTR of only 0.36 (834 types from 2350 tokens). It is clear that the 0.5 threshold is entirely spurious, as it is obvious that any speaker or writer, even Shakespeare, will produce a TTR of less than 0.5 provided that the language sample they provide is large enough. The TTRs of Shakespeare's plays are well under the threshold. They vary from 0.142 (*Much Ado About Nothing*: 2954 types from 20,768 tokens) to 0.201 (*Macbeth*: 3306 types from 16,436 tokens) (reported in Chen and Leimkuhler, 1989, Table 1, p. 46).

These conclusions indicate that for any meaningful use of TTR, some kind of standardisation is necessary, and all the issues to do with how to standardise NDW arise for TTR with equal force. All the methods which have been used for NDW have also been employed for TTR, with as little success. Just the same confounding of diversity with MLU and volubility can be found for TTR as for NDW. Broen's (1972) study of mothers' language use with children aged 18–26 months attempted to standardise by time, calculating TTR on samples obtained in ten five-minute segments of recording – thereby confounding diversity with volubility. In the primer, *Guide to Analysis of Language Transcripts*, Stickler (1987) recommends basing TTR calculations on the middle 50 consecutive utterances from each transcript. The figure of 50 goes back to Templin's use of 50 'remarks' as a baseline for counting the number of words and different words, and Miller's subsequent transformation of these data into TTRs. Others have used different standard numbers of utterances, however; Fletcher's (1985) study of Sophie, for instance, used 100 utterances.

Whatever base is chosen for the standardisation, the increase of MLU with age and/or language ability means that the calculation of TTR is over differently sized language samples for each age and language stage. In Templin's case, the token counts vary on average from about 205 tokens at three years to about 379 at eight (as Table 2.2 above shows). A more recent method is Yoder and colleagues' (1994) 'prorated number of lexically free words' that uses utterances as the standard and divides the number of 'lexically free' types directly by the number of utterances. This or any other type–utterance ratio (TUR) does nothing other than demonstrate explicitly that such measures compound diversity with the number of words in the utterances as is easily shown – let U be the number of utterances, then:

$$TUR = \frac{V}{U}$$

$$MLU = \frac{N}{U} \Leftrightarrow U = \frac{N}{MLU}$$

Then

$$TUR = \frac{V}{\frac{N}{MLU}} = MLU \frac{V}{N}$$

i.e. $TUR = MLU \times TTR$ \hfill (2.1)

Note that in the case of Yoder and colleagues (1994), who confine their analysis to 'lexically free' word types, N and V are the numbers of 'lexically free' tokens and types in the sample and MLU is the number of 'lexical free' tokens per utterance.

As with NDW, the only standardisation for TTR which avoids most of the pitfalls is to fix the number of tokens. As Chotlos noted 60 years ago: 'Usually type–token ratios are not directly comparable unless they are based on the same number of tokens for each individual' (Chotlos, 1944, pp. 85–6). Mark Anthony's soliloquy and speech, cited above, demonstrate a prima-facie case for TTR only because they were chosen to be of much the same length; the TTR for the whole 19,110 words of *Julius Caesar* is 0.15 (compared with 0.68 and 0.50 for lengths of 173 and 172 words respectively). The most successful method of standardising TTR takes all the advice which emerges from the discussion of NDW above; namely to base the calculation on an average of a number of sub-samples of fixed token size. This avoids making comparisons based on differing sample sizes and has the advantage that obtaining a number of sub-samples makes full use of the quantity of data available by taking the mean of the maximum number of segments present in the transcript or text. One such measure is known as the mean segmental type–token ratio, or MSTTR.

Mean segmental type–token ratio (MSTTR)

MSTTR is calculated by choosing a given standard number of tokens, sufficiently small for a number of different sub-samples of that size to be taken from the smallest language sample in the data set. Each transcript is then divided up into segments of the given length and the TTR calculated for each. MSTTR is the average over all sub-samples. It is the equivalent for TTR of NDW (expected). MSTTR was first recommended by Johnson (1944) in a special issue of *Psychological Monographs* on quantifying language behaviour, which contained contributions on MSTTR by Fairbanks, Mann and Chotlos. It was used to compare university students with schizophrenics on their spoken language (Fairbanks, 1944) and on samples of writing (Mann, 1944). Chotlos (1944) analysed the written scripts of 108 school students aged eight to 18 years. The scripts were 3000 words in length, which allowed comparisons between MSTTRs calculated from 100, 500, and 1000 word segments (MSTTR100, MSTTR500, MSTTR1000) and TTR calculated from all 3000 words. Not surprisingly, as each drew on sampling from throughout the whole manuscripts, the four measures were found to be strongly intercorrelated and were interpreted as measuring essentially the same thing.

Following the work of Fairbanks (1944) and Mann (1944), MSTTR100 was used extensively to compare schizophrenics with non-schizophrenics, and patients with various sub-types (for example, chronic versus acute) of schizophrenia (see Manschreck et al., 1981, for a summary). Research has consistently found schizophrenics to have lower MSTTRs than non-schizophrenics. Aphasiology is another area where MSTTR has been found to be a reliable discriminator. Wachal and Spreen (1973) compared the language of 20 hospitalised normal speakers and 20 aphasic patients and found MSTTR to be a powerful and reliable indicator of differences between the groups. In Chapter 6 of this volume we discuss the use of MSTTR30 for students and MSTTR100 for teacher-examiners as a measure of diversity in an analysis of French foreign language oral interviews reported in Richards and Malvern (2000). Although MSTTR is a clear improvement on NDW and raw TTR, it is not without its shortcomings, and these will be addressed in Chapter 6.

Other linguistic measures of range

Neither NDW nor TTR are independent of sample size, and are fatally flawed as a measure of diversity if the number of words is not controlled. Before going on to consider various attempts to transform TTR, it is worth noting that the objection of their dependency on the length of the language sample also applies to similar measures based on ranges and ratios of other kinds of linguistic or related units. Some of the best known are those used by Gordon Wells and his colleagues in the Bristol Study of Language Development

(Wells, 1985). As an example, 'Pragmatic Range' is described in Barnes, Gutfreund, Satterly and Wells (1983, p. 72) as 'The number of different "speech act" functions used by the child by that point' (that is to say, the total for all previous transcripts). Other such developmental indices include 'Semantic Range' (the number of different semantic clause types), 'Semantic Complexity' (the number of different optional semantic modifications of the whole clause), 'Syntactic Complexity' (the range of types of structure), and 'Auxiliary Meanings' (the range of semantic distinctions realised by the child's usage of auxiliary verbs) (see Wells, 1978, for a full description of these). An additional measure, 'Number of Different Auxiliary Forms' (Wells, 1979) or 'Cumulative Range of Auxiliary Forms' (Richards, 1990) counts the different verb forms which occur for the modals and primary auxiliaries.

Turning the range measures listed above into *ratios* offers no advantage. Therefore Richards's attempt to compensate for variations in sample size by calculating the 'range of auxiliary forms/100 structured utterances' for each transcript (Richards, 1990, p. 37) is just as flawed as using TTR. As too would be Yoder and colleagues' (1994) measure and other 'TTRs' such as those calculated for gestures (Iverson, Capirci and Caselli, 1994), signs (Layton and Savino, 1990) and, for infant vocalisations, the number of different sounds divided by the total number of sounds produced (studies by Irwin, reported in McCarthy, 1954).

Transformations of TTR

Various attempts have been made to find a mathematical transformation of TTR which compensates for the sample size effect. Essentially, they are all attempting to find a relatively simple way of representing mathematically how TTR falls with increasing token count, and then to use this as a multiplier or other modifier to turn TTR into a constant over the whole sample. Both Guiraud (1960) with the 'Root TTR' (RTTR) and Carroll (1964) with the 'Corrected TTR' (CTTR) assumed that the fall is proportional to the square root of the token count and arrive at essentially the same measure which is TTR multiplied by $\sqrt{N}$ (Guiraud) or $\sqrt{(N/2)}$ (Carroll):

Guiraud's Root TTR

$$RTTR = \frac{V}{\sqrt{N}}$$
$$= \frac{\sqrt{N}}{N} V$$
$$= \sqrt{N} \frac{V}{N} = \sqrt{N} \times TTR \quad (2.2)$$

Carroll's Corrected TTR

$$CTTR = \frac{V}{\sqrt{2N}}$$
$$= \frac{\sqrt{N}}{N\sqrt{2}} V$$
$$= \sqrt{\frac{N}{2}} \frac{V}{N} = \sqrt{\frac{N}{2}} \times TTR \quad (2.3)$$

Some authors have reported some success in applications of these measures. For example, compared with several other vocabulary indices, Vermeer (2000) obtained relatively high correlations between RTTR and a receptive vocabulary test and found that it was effective in discriminating between children with Dutch as a first and a second language, and Broeder and colleagues (1993) expressed a preference for it as a measure for lexical diversity. Both are affected by sample size, however, as demonstrated in studies of the speech of pre-school children (Hess, Sefton and Landry, 1986; Richards, 1987), or school-aged children (Hess, Haug and Landry, 1989), the writing of L2 English students (Arnaud, 1984), or literary texts (Ménard, 1983). The effect of this rescaling is that the values for these two indices rise over the first few hundred tokens to a maximum and then fall with increasing N. Over the range of values of N about the maximum, the reducing rise followed by what is at first a shallow fall may give an illusion of constancy, but this is only apparent, and eventually both these indices, like raw TTR, will fall towards zero.

With the Bilogarithmic TTR, also known as LogTTR[1], Herdan (1960) adopted another assumption about how the rate of introduction of new types varies with the increasing size of the language sample. This can be summarised as: the rate of increase of types with increasing token count (dV/dN) will be proportional to the TTR for any given value of N. Mathematically, with H being a constant (Herdan's index):

$$\frac{dV}{dN} = H\frac{V}{N}$$

Solving

$$\frac{dV}{V} = H\frac{dN}{N}$$

Integrating

$$Log V = H \log N$$

$$H = \frac{Log V}{Log N} = LogTTR \qquad (2.4)$$

LogTTR would be constant if the initial assumption, which is the equivalent of V being related to N by a simple power law $V = N^H$, stood up to what happened empirically. But that turns out not to be so (see Weitzman, 1971; and Ménard, 1983, for example). Consequently, other logarithmic solutions to the problem have arisen, some from using logarithms to change the curved relationship between TTR and N into one that is sufficiently linear to use regression methods. Härnquist and colleagues (2003), for example, plotted the best straight line fit for TTR against LogN, to form a baseline from which to 'correct' TTR. Similarly, Tuldava

(1993) 'linearizes' the type token curve by 'double logarithm-taking' to arrive at:

$$T = \frac{LogLogN}{LogLog\frac{N}{V} + A} \tag{2.5}$$

where T is the index of relative vocabulary diversity and A is a constant whose value depends on the degree of repetition attributed to the genre or language under investigation. T is an extension of Somers's (1966) S:

$$S = \frac{LogLogV}{LogLogN} \tag{2.6}$$

Three similar, related measures have also been proposed, one by Rubet (cited by Dugast, 1979), the second by Maas (1972) and the other by Dugast (1978, 1979), which are respectively:

$$k = \frac{LogV}{LogLogN}$$

$$a^2 = \frac{LogN - LogV}{Log^2 N} = \frac{Log\frac{N}{V}}{Log^2 N}$$

and its inverse

$$U = \frac{Log^2 N}{LogN - LogV} = \frac{Log^2 N}{Log\frac{N}{V}} \tag{2.7}$$

The last of these, U, is known as Uber. Like Tuldava's T and Maas's a^2, it includes N/V which is the reciprocal of TTR and sometimes called the mean word frequency (MWF) as it gives the average number of tokens used for each type in the text. Obviously, MWF increases with higher and higher token counts.

All of these indices have been subject to extensive testing by various authors over the years and only a few examples can be cited here. Ménard (1983) observed that the constancy of Herdan's LogTTR was doubtful, although it may be applicable over certain, as yet unknown, limits. In a review article, Wimmer and Altmann (1999) raised theoretical objections to RTTR, LogTTR, and Uber (among others), and commented that 'Perhaps we are searching for a stable index in a phenomenon that is itself not stable' (p. 5). The most direct testing is that of Tweedie and Baayen (1998) who plotted the values found for various indices, including RTTR, LogTTR, and Uber over segments of increasing length for 16 texts – the smallest at 24,246 tokens being *The Acts of the Apostles*, the largest Brontë's *Wuthering Heights* at 116,534 words. They concluded that '... the assumption that measures of lexical richness are independent, or roughly independent of text length is invalid' (p. 350). Thorough as the Tweedie and Baayen testing is, it is over large language samples – in fact very large samples. They chose to plot 20 points to cover the whole text, which means even the smallest segment used for determining the values of the indices is over 1200 words in length and the largest sample approaches 120,000. This raises two issues. First, in child language studies, it is usually only possible to obtain much shorter language samples with 1200 words much nearer an upper rather than a lower limit. Interesting though it is, then, the Tweedie and Baayen study is of limited relevance when what is at stake is how stable the measures are at values below the lowest of their 20 points.

Second, in principle at least, a given person at a particular time may have a fixed 'active vocabulary', that is to say, a given number of types known and used, V_a (say). If everything that person said or wrote was transcribed into a language sample, once the active vocabulary had been exhausted in use, for any further language production V would remain equal to V_a and the TTR curve would follow V_a/N come what may. Children, particularly young children, do have an active vocabulary which may be growing over time, but at the point of sampling will be finite and relatively small. All indices would lose accuracy if the language sample were large enough to exhaust the active vocabulary, and most of Tweedie and Baayen's language segments are sufficiently large for that to happen had the authors been very young children. They were not, of course, so whilst this may not undermine their results for adult writing, it does question their applicability to child language research.

In work on children's spoken language, Hess and colleagues (1986) compared segments of increasing length of 83 language samples from children ranging in age from 3;0 to 5;11 and demonstrated that none of TTR, RTTR, CTTR, and LogTTR is independent of sample size over transcripts that ranged from 201 to 361 tokens. Vermeer, in a study of 70 Dutch native-speaking children (mean length of language sample = 887 tokens) and 76 children from ethnic minorities (mean length of language sample = 684 tokens) in Dutch kindergarten, found both TTR and LogTTR correlated negatively with vocabulary tasks for all children, and concluded that 'Initially ... the Guiraud [RTTR] or Uber Indices seem to be adequate measures. However, in later stages of vocabulary acquisition (from [an active vocabulary of] 3000 words on), neither of these measures shows concurrent validity ...' (Vermeer, 2000, p. 77).

Conclusion

In summary, then, NDW is clearly dependent on the size of the sample and, although there are various ways samples could be standardised, there is no universally agreed way of doing so. Taking a ratio, the TTR, seemed to offer a way forward but that too is flawed. It has been established, theoretically and empirically beyond doubt, that TTR falls with increasing token count, and that curves of TTR against N whose points are calculated by averaging a number of sub-samples from the transcript fall continuously with decreasing slope (see Figure 2.1). Simple transformations such as RTTR, CTTR, and LogTTR do not solve the problem at all, but merely change the shape of the curve or alter the scale. Continuing to take logarithms to 'linearise' the curve has not resulted in a constant index, either. There is, too, a potential problem of finding a stable index for very large texts. Once all the types that appear in a text, V_{max}, are used, proceeding further through a text will inevitably be along a curve V_{max}/N. If an author has used all the words he or she is going to by the end of Chapter 8, say, but needs Chapters 9 and 10 to conclude the plot (without introducing any new types) then the TTR against token curve plotted in sequence will fall along the curve V_{max}/N for the token range of the final chapters regardless of how it fell before. In a large enough sample, then, a sequential TTR versus token curve may consist of two sections, the first where V is changing and a second where it is not.

Although none of the indices considered so far have overcome the sample-size effect, the body of work that went into them has much to tell us. Looking for a mathematical way to represent the curve is useful, but applying it to derive a measure is more complicated than simply transforming TTR. Even though Tuldava's method of linearisation, which used regression to fit a straight line after having taken multiple logarithms, did not prove satisfactory, curve fitting to arrive at the index looks a promising method. Some sort of standardisation procedure is needed, preferably based on token size, rather than number of utterances or units of time, and of a size commensurate with the relative small language samples used in child language research. The requirement, then, is to find a valid index sufficiently reliable and stable over the standardisation range for child language samples of a few hundred or so tokens. The next chapter will build on these ideas to do just that.

3
A Mathematical Model of Lexical Diversity

As well as being a function of text length, there is another limitation to using raw TTR for the whole of a language sample – it does not take into account the frequency with which types are repeated. As a simple illustration of the point, we can consider three imaginary texts of 40 tokens containing 20 types. In Text A, each of the 20 types is repeated twice; in Text B ten of the 20 types appear three times and the remaining ten once; Text C is more natural, with ten types occurring once, four twice, three occuring three times, two four times, and one type occurring five times. Neither raw TTR nor any of its simple transformations, such as RootTTR or LogTTR, will distinguish among these three transcripts as they all have the same overall numbers of types and of tokens producing a TTR of 0.5, but they are manifestly different in how they deploy the same vocabulary – they have different frequency distributions.

Throughout the twentieth century theorists have explored approaches to lexical diversity based on the frequency distribution of types within languages. In a paper which set out to investigate whether or not it was possible to predict an author's total active vocabulary (V_a) from a sample text, Thomson and Thompson (1915) laid out the basic theory for such approaches. We will first consider this paper in some detail as, like NDW in the previous chapter, it illustrates many of the issues involved. We will then summarise the main developments of this approach over the intervening 90 years, before outlining the most complete solution to the problem and describing how it can be used to measure lexical diversity robustly.

A seminal paper

In its simplest form, the argument of the Thomson and Thompson paper can be described as an analogy between an author selecting words from his or her active vocabulary and pulling tokens at random from a large urn. In the urn there are as many tokens as there are words in the active vocabulary (V_a), and on each is written a separate type. The author's picking a word for use is modelled by removing a token at random and, having written down its type,

32 *Lexical Diversity and Language Development*

returning it to the urn. For every pick, the probability of pulling out any particular type is exactly the same as for all other types ($1/V_a$), and we have a well-known probability problem solved by the binomial theorem.

Binomial probability is so called because there are two possible outcomes for any type when selecting a token – either the type is picked (probability p) or it is not picked (probability q), and as one or the other must happen $(p + q) = 1$. Furthermore, there is an isomorphism between what happens with two, three, four ... r picks and the binomial expansion of $(p + q)^r$, which is illustrated for one, two, three, and four picks in Table 3.1.

The last term of the expansion always represents the probability of a type not being picked at all. Thomson and Thompson noted that if in a text of length N tokens, V types are selected (the number of types in the text) from a total possible of V_a (the author's active vocabulary), then the number of available types unused by the author must be $(V_a - V)$. By elementary probability theory, it follows that the probability of any one type not being chosen at all is the number of types not chosen divided by the total number

Table 3.1 Binomial probability

Number of Picks	Outcomes (Selected: Y; Not Selected: N)					Binomial Expansion
1	Y 1	or	N 1			$(p+q)^1 =$ $1p + 1q$
2	Y/Y 1	or	Y/N N/Y 2	or	N/N 1	$(p+q)^2 =$ $1p^2 + 2pq + 1q^2$
3	Y/Y/Y 1	or	Y/Y/N Y/N/Y N/Y/Y 3	or	Y/N/N N/Y/N N/N/Y 3	or N/N/N 1	$(p+q)^3 =$ $1p^3 + 3p^2q + 3pq^2 + 1q^3$
4	Y/Y/Y/Y 1	Y/Y/Y/N Y/Y/N/Y or Y/N/Y/Y N/Y/Y/Y 4	or	Y/Y/N/N Y/N/Y/N Y/N/N/Y N/Y/Y/N N/Y/N/Y N/N/Y/Y 6	Y/N/N/N N/Y/N/N or N/N/Y/N N/N/N/Y 4	or N/N/N/N 1	$(p+q)^4 =$ $1p^4 + 4p^3q + 6p^2q^2 + 4pq^3 + 1q^4$
...			...			...

of available types, that is to say $(V_a - V)/V_a$. As we have just noted, however, this is also given by the last term of the appropriate binomial expansion. In this case, the probability of selecting a given type is $p = 1/V_a$, and of its not being selected $q = (1 - 1/V_a)$. As there are N tokens all together, the binomial is raised to the power N, and the final term of the expansion, the one which also gives the probability of a type not being chosen, is $(1 - 1/V_a)^N$. Equating the two expressions for this probability gives:

$$\frac{(V_a - V)}{V_a} = \left(1 - \frac{1}{V_a}\right)^N$$

Solving for V

$$V = V_a \left\{ 1 - \left(1 - \frac{1}{V_a}\right)^N \right\} \qquad (3.1)$$

Thomson and Thompson made use of an exponential form of the binomial, named after Poisson, who formulated it in 1837. It comes from the following limit:

$$\text{Limit} \left(1 - \frac{x}{N}\right)^N = e^{-x} \text{ for large N}$$

Setting $x = \dfrac{N}{V_a}$

$$\left(1 - \frac{\frac{N}{V_a}}{N}\right)^N = \left(1 - \frac{1}{V_a}\right)^N = e^{\frac{-N}{V_a}}$$

Substituting in Equation 3.1

$$V = V_a \left(1 - e^{\frac{-N}{V_a}}\right) \text{ for large } N$$

Thomson and Thompson presented this as a first approximation to expressing the number of types as a function of tokens. Simply dividing both sides by N would give an expression for the TTR versus N curve – the first we have found in the literature. Although based on very simple assumptions, this expression produces curves of the same general sort as those observed empirically – that is as N increases, TTR decreases with reducing slope. Thomson and Thompson acknowledged this was an over-simplification in order to make a start on the problem, but in their discussion they raised a number of issues still being discussed today, nearly 90 years later, and introduced a method which has influenced subsequent studies over those years.

First, they pointed out that the probability of choosing a type for any one pick will not remain constant – if the word *the* has just been chosen, for example, it becomes very unlikely indeed that it will be chosen as the next word. Second, they point out that the context or topic may well produce local clustering of the same type, with such clusters often being widely separated – an example is the name of a character in a book, which may appear often in Chapters 1 and 3, say, of a novel, but not at all in Chapter 2 when the character is absent. Third, they note the obvious, that is to say that some words, particularly function words, appear more often in natural language than others, and go on to use this idea in developing their approach.

Having recognised that some types are more likely to appear than others, they propose that words can be 'weighted' to represent the likelihood of selection. Words of much the same weight can be grouped together, so that the active vocabulary consists of 'a number of groups of varying size each possessing a common weight' (p. 58). In the urn analogy, this could be achieved by having multiple copies of tokens of the same type in the urn. Within a group, there is the same number of copies of each type – the bigger the weight of a group, the more copies of the types. The number of *types* in each group represents the active vocabulary for the group, v_2 for the second group for example. The weight of a group represents the number of copies there are of each type, that is to say the number of *tokens* of each type in the group; for the second group say w_2. In the second group, then, there are $v_2 w_2$ tokens all together. The sum of the tokens in all the groups, $v_1 w_1 + v_2 w_2 + v_3 w_3 + \cdots v_r w_r$, gives the overall number of tokens in the urn. The most probable number of times in a text of length N that *tokens* will be selected from the rth group, n_r, will be N times the proportion of tokens of the rth group to the total number of tokens there are all together:

$$n_r = N \frac{v_r w_r}{v_1 w_1 + v_2 w_2 + v_3 w_3 + \cdots + v_r w_r}$$

Writing $\sum vw$ for $v_1 w_1 + v_2 w_2 + v_3 w_3 + \cdots + v_r w_r$

$$n_r = N \frac{v_r w_r}{\sum vw} \qquad (3.3)$$

In order to proceed to finding out how many *types* from the rth group there are most likely to be, we use this expression (Equation 3.3) for the number of tokens to calculate the probability of picking any one type in the group in n_r picks. Within a group, by definition, all the types have the same weight, so the equal likelihood assumption of the simple relationship will apply. We can, therefore, use Equation 3.2 to give us the expected number of types from the rth group in the text, V_r, by writing n_r instead of N and v_r instead of V_a:

$$V_r = v_r \left(1 - e^{-\frac{n_r}{v_r}}\right)$$

Substituting for n_r from Equation 3.3

$$V_r = v_r \left(1 - e^{\frac{-Nv_r w_r}{v_r \sum vw}}\right)$$

Cancelling

$$V_r = v_r \left(1 - e^{\frac{-w_r N}{\sum vw}}\right) \tag{3.4}$$

The total number of types in the text can be found by adding all the contributions from the different groups together. Dividing this total by N provides a more advanced relationship for the TTR versus token curve, as

$$TTR = \frac{v_1}{N}\left(1 - e^{\frac{-w_1 N}{\sum vw}}\right) + \frac{v_2}{N}\left(1 - e^{\frac{-w_2 N}{\sum vw}}\right) + \frac{v_3}{N}\left(1 - e^{\frac{-w_3 N}{\sum vw}}\right)$$

$$+ \cdots + \frac{v_r}{N}\left(1 - e^{\frac{-w_r N}{\sum vw}}\right) \tag{3.5}$$

which shows that a better solution depends on summing a *mixture* of binomial probabilities, here expressed in the exponential form due to Poisson. This improved solution is still incomplete, however. Problems of how to determine the groups, how many there should be and how to calculate the weights still remain. Thomson and Thompson stated that the more groups there are, the better. Although they went on to demonstrate this by working out weights for solutions based on one group, two groups, and three groups to fit data from a novel, the weights they used were essentially arbitrary and they offered no general method for calculating weights. None the less, in this prescient paper, Thomson and Thompson had introduced most of the features required to find a solution to how the TTR versus tokens curve can be represented.

The most essential insight is that in addition to the *range* of vocabulary used, the *way it is deployed*, or the pattern of repetitions, is significant. As well as the number of types all together, the frequencies with which they appear must be included, and a number of important consequences follow. To do

36 *Lexical Diversity and Language Development*

this theoretically requires probability theory. Binomial probability provides a good starting point, but the simple equal-probabilities-for-all-types urn model is not sufficient and a full solution needs to look at a number of probabilities:

- the probability of a particular type being in a high or low frequency group before selection,
- the probability that the type selected comes from a high or low frequency group, and
- the probability of which specific type from within the group will be selected, which will need a mixture of binomials.

The harmonic series hypothesis and further developments

If we take the notion that better solutions will be found from more and more groups to its logical limit, there will be as many groups as there are words – each group will consist of one word ordered in sequence by the frequency of occurrence for each word. Condon (1928) and Zipf (1935) explored what is known as the 'harmonic series hypothesis' which does just that and provides a rule for determining the frequency (or weights in the terms of Thomson and Thompson) of each. In a harmonic series, each term is a reciprocal of a number which increases arithmetically, that is by adding the same amount each time. A simple example is:

$$\frac{1}{10} + \frac{1}{20} + \frac{1}{30} + \cdots + \frac{1}{10r} + \cdots \tag{3.6}$$

The harmonic series hypothesis states first that if all the types in a text are ranked by frequency, beginning with the most frequent ranked as one, the second most frequent ranked two and so on, then the actual number of occurrences will form a harmonic sequence and their sum a harmonic series which will add to the total number of tokens in the language sample. Because the first ranked has the highest frequency, the frequency decreases as the ranks increase, and the second statement of the hypothesis is that if f is the frequency and r is the rank, $fr^x = K$, where x and K are empirical constants for the sample. Zipf set $x = 1$ which gives one of the so-called 'Zipf's Laws': that frequency times rank is a constant. He further proposed that the evidence suggests that the most frequently occurring word will make up 1/10th of the total token count in a sample, the second most frequent 1/20th, the third 1/30th, and so on. For a text of N tokens, this gives $K = N/10$.

Skinner (1937) tested the $fr^x = K$ rule on the lists of words produced by 1000 normal subjects in a word association test of 100 stimulus words. Each stimulus word produced 1000 response words (one for each person), and by averaging the 100 samples (one for each stimulus word) of these 1000 tokens, he found the rule did not apply well to the first few ranks (high frequency types), nor to the types with very low frequency, but there seemed to be a good fit in between with x = 1.29 and K = 300 (or as N = 1000, K = 3N/10).

Zipf's 1/10th, 1/20th, ... sequence would lead on average to the first ranked word appearing once every 10 tokens in a sample, the second once in every 20 tokens and so on, and once in every 10r tokens for the rth ranked type. In a later paper, Zipf (1937) generalised this to the rth ranked type occurring on average once every kr tokens where k is an empirical constant for a language sample, whose value is 'normally 10' but may vary depending on the repetitiveness in the sample. Carroll (1938) retained Zipf's original suggestion that x = 1 but adopted this greater generalisation to adapt the frequency rule to fr = k/N, suggesting that k is a constant representing diversity. He then used this, and a standard expression for the sum of a harmonic series, as the starting point to derive a relationship between the growth of types and increasing token count, which converted into our notation and after division by N gives for the TTR versus N curve:

$$TTR = \frac{1}{k}(0.423 + k - \log N + \log k) \tag{3.7}$$

Testing this relationship by curve fitting to empirical data, first from 8000 words pooled from a number of respondents to a word production task and then from various literary texts, Carroll reported some success although he too notes that Zipf's law did not apply to the first 30 or so ranked types.

Chotlos (1944) questioned the use of pooled data in both the Skinner and Carroll studies, and investigated both x and k for 18 language samples drawn at random from 108 transcripts of children's writing. Rightly, he identified that for the Carroll equation to apply x must equal one. For the whole samples, he found x varied from 0.796 to 0.938 with a mean of 0.845. If the first 20 most frequent types were eliminated, however, the mean rose closer to one at 0.974, but still exhibited a large range: from 0.808 to 1.255. By computing k for successively longer and longer sequential sub-samples, he found that it was not constant for each individual but subject to the size of the sample from which it was calculated. He concluded that:

> Attempts to represent the relationship between [types] and [tokens] reveals [sic] that the function is of no simple nature.
> (Chotlos, 1944, pp. 109–10)

Nevertheless, many scholars continued the attempt. Much of this work tests itself against different examples of texts drawn from literature, for example Joyce's novels or Shakespeare's plays. Consequently, it is often characterised as stylometrics or what Crystal calls stylostatistics (Crystal, 1987, p. 67). Perhaps the best known is Yule, who studied such considerations as the chance that two noun tokens randomly picked from a text will be of the same type. He derived a constant for a text known as Yule's characteristic K (Yule, 1944). It is a measure of repetition for which lower values represent higher diversities.

Ménard (1983) cites the work of Muller and Evrard from the mid-1960s on a simple method of overcoming the sample-size problem by reducing every text to a theoretical sample of the same length. The method calculates the 'Theoretical Vocabulary' of a sample of fixed length (say 400 tokens) by applying binomial probability in much the same way as Thomson and Thompson did, but it starts from the actual numbers of the types that occur once, twice, three times, and so on in the full text and predicts how many of each frequency of occurrence will be in a sample of the standard length. It is possible to add up all the expected values of occurrence, but computationally easier to sum those of non-occurrence and subtract that from the total types to arrive at how many remain in the sample. As an example, if we take a text of 500 tokens, with V_{500} types, and theoretically reduce it to one of 400 (with V_{400} types), the probability of any given word appearing in the shorter sample is $p = 400/500 = 0.8$ and of not appearing it is $(1-p) = 0.2$. Concentrating on non-appearance, if there are $v_1, v_2, v_3 \ldots$ types which occur once, twice, three times ... in the full text, the numbers expected *not* to occur in the sample are qv_1, q^2v_2, q^3v_3, and so on, that is to say the final term of the binomial expansions for one pick, two picks, three picks, and so on. Summing these gives the total number of types not occurring, and by subtraction we have:

$$V_{400} = V_{500} - (0.2v_1 + 0.2^2v_2 + 0.2^3v_3 + \cdots + 0.2^r v_r)$$

Generalising

$$V_{theoretical} = V - \sum_{i=1}^{r} q^i v_i \qquad (3.8)$$

This 'Theoretical Vocabulary' was suggested as a direct measure of lexical diversity, as obviously the greater the number of types expected in a theoretical sample of standard length, the greater the diversity shown. Ménard gave it cautious approval: 'Solutions satisfaisantes dans les limites de la loi binomiale' (Ménard, 1983, p. 17), but it suffers from being an over-simple application of binomial theory, in that it assumes a constant and equal-for-all probability – a similar over-simplification to that Thomson and Thompson acknowledged in their earlier application of binomial probability.

Others have concentrated on words which appear with a specific frequency, in particular words which appear only once in a text, *hapax legomena*, or only twice – *hapax dislegomena*. Michéa (1969, 1971) and later Sichel (1975), for example, observed an apparent constancy, at a value of about 6, in the ratio of total types to *hapax dislegomena* regardless of token count.

Honoré (1979) suggested that for longer and longer texts, the ratio of *hapax legomena* to the type count increased in proportion to LogN. In 1983 Orlov generated a greater generalisation of Zipf's ideas and introduced a parameter, Z, which 'specifies the text length at which Zipf's law ... holds' (Tweedie and Baayen, 1998, p. 331). All these, and others, lead to expressions from which a relationship for the TTR against token curve can be derived, and to parameters that are in theory constant and could be used as indices of lexical diversity. For the specific studies mentioned, there are:

Yule's K

$$K = 10^4 \frac{\left\{\sum_{r=1}^{N} \nu_r r^2\right\} - N}{N^2} \quad (3.9)$$

where ν_r is the number of types which occur r times in a text of length N;

Michéa's M (and Sichel's S)

$$M = \frac{V}{\nu_2} \text{ or } S = \frac{\nu_2}{V} \quad (3.10)$$

where ν_2 is the number of types appearing twice (*hapax dislegomena*);

Honoré's R

$$\frac{\nu_1}{V} = 1 + \frac{100}{R} \log N \quad (3.11)$$

where ν_1 is the number of types which appear only once (*hapax legomena*);

and *Orlov's Z*

$$V = \frac{ZN}{(N-Z)\log\left(\frac{f_{max}}{N} Z\right)} \log \frac{N}{Z} \quad (3.12)$$

where f_{max} is the frequency of the most common word in the text (the first ranked in Zipf's sequence).

These and a number of other indices were tested over large samples by Tweedie and Baayen (1998), who found none of them provided a constant value over increasing sequential token counts for real data from their 16 test texts. It is of interest to note from their graphs (p. 333), however, that Yule's K was constant for their test using random permutation of the order of the tokens in *Alice's Adventures in Wonderland*, as too was Z for subsamples greater than about 6000 tokens. Also of interest is their graph for Sichel's S which shows it rising to a maximum at about 5000 tokens and thereafter falling very gently. Again it should be stressed that the samples and sub-samples in the tests of Tweedie and Baayen are very large, which in the context of the applications to author stylistics may be reasonable, but which puts into question their relevance to child language studies.

Using population statistics

Brainerd (1982a, 1982b) argued that there is a parallel between the above body of work and similar studies in population statistics. He likened the original aim of the Thomson and Thompson paper, making an estimate of an author's total active vocabulary, to the species–area problem in ecology. One area of work studies the number of animals of various species observed in a geographically defined area, the other the number of tokens and types in a language sample. In the analogy, animals are equivalent to tokens and species to types. In both articles Brainerd refers to a solution to the species– area problem attributed to Arrhenius (1921) which taken analogously and expressed in our type token notation is $V = AN^B$ where A and B are constants and $0 < B < 1$.

Brainerd pointed out that with $A = 1$, taking logarithms will give LogTTR = B, identifying B with Herdan's index, but this is known not to be constant (see Chapter 2). He therefore suggested replacing it with a function of N which would fit with the assumption, on the one hand, that however many animals are observed they come from a fixed number of species or, on the other, that a person has a finite active vocabulary (V_a). This led to the equivalent of:

$$TTR = N^{\frac{LogV_a}{LogN+k}} - 1 \qquad (3.13)$$

Brainerd tested both the original Arrhenius proposal and his extension of it by calculating A, B (Arrhenius) and V_a, k (Brainerd) for works by Kierkegaard of various token size (from 32,238 tokens for the shortest to 213,383 for the longest). His results showed that A increased and B decreased for longer works, and that estimates of V_a varied considerably between the various works, but as the comparisons were between different texts, albeit by the same author, the test was arguably not particularly rigorous.

A similar parallel from biology has been drawn by Marcus, Pinker, Ullman, Hollander, Rosen and Xu (1992) in the context of child language studies. They likened their problem, estimating the size of regular and irregular verb vocabulary, to the 'mark–recapture' technique for estimating the size of a population. Their example was of squirrels in a forest. Fifty squirrels are trapped, marked by painting their tails orange and released. After a pause, 50 squirrels are captured again and the number recaptured, that is to say marked from the previous capture, counted (say ten). On the assumption that all squirrels are equally likely to be captured each time, the proportion of recaptured squirrels to the 50 caught in the second trapping (10/50) will be the same as the proportion of marked squirrels in the whole population (50/N); and N can be easily estimated (N = 250). In this analogy, a verb is a squirrel and the two trapping events are equivalent to taking two transcripts from a child. A verb which appears in both transcripts is said to be recaptured and the same calculation used to estimate the size of the active vocabulary for each category of verb.

Both Brainerd and Marcus and colleagues point out that in both the ecological and the linguistic settings, the equal probability assumption may not hold. Some squirrels may be 'trap-shy' or which squirrels are caught may depend on where the traps are placed or how they are designed and so on. Similarly, word types which appear infrequently are likely to be underestimated as they are also 'trap-shy'; which types are uttered may depend on the topics or contexts of the collection of the language samples and so on. For these reasons, biologists have refined the technique by increasing the number of trapping sessions and counting how many squirrels are caught once, twice, three times, and so on. Analogies with *hapax legomena, hapax dislegomena*, the weighted groups of Thomson and Thompson or the frequency ranks of Zipf become obvious. Biostatisticians have developed an algorithm called the Jackknife estimator as a method for producing estimated total population from multiple captures which has been shown to be reliable in circumstances when many squirrels are caught often. Marcus and colleagues collected five transcripts from each of the children in their study, and counted how many verbs were found in five, four, three, two, and one transcript(s) for an individual. As there were a large number of verb types appearing in many of the transcripts, by analogy they judged the multiple mark–recapture approach to be appropriate in its application to language.

The most complete formulation

The mathematical account which brings together most completely the notions we have traced in the studies which have followed Thomson and Thompson is the formulation in terms of population statistics of Sichel (1986). The mathematics needed depends on a fuller knowledge of the properties of certain statistical distributions than we are able to present here. We have set out the history of the ideas and scholarship on which Sichel's analysis is built, however, and will provide a description of the distributions he employs, a justification for their application being appropriate to the character of language samples, and an outline of the logic which leads to the solution.

Like Zipf, Sichel begins by ranking every type in a person's active vocabulary, but ranks them by their probability of occurrence, with the lowest being the first rank and the highest the last. In typical English production this last will be the word *the*, the most frequently used word in the language with a probability of about 0.07. All other types will have a lower probability of occurrence, and, as one word or another must be used to have occurrence, all the probabilities must sum to 1. This means that all the thousands of discrete probabilities are squeezed into the very narrow range, between 0 and 0.07, and being so close to each other can be treated as representing a continuous variable. Replacing the groups of Thomson and Thompson and the frequency of occurrence ranks of Zipf by a continuous probability variable, with the types arranged in rank order along it, provides the first of the three probabilities required and opens the way to an analytic solution.

Analogous to the need for a way to work out how many words were in the groups of Thomson and Thompson and just as Zipf's ranked frequencies needed a rule (the harmonic hypothesis) to determine what proportion of the whole belonged to each rank, Sichel's probability variable requires a distribution function to calculate what proportion of the active vocabulary there is in any particular probability range. The shape of this function is worth some thought. In the mark–recapture analogy, we could speculate that there are a few squirrels that are always getting caught – they live in the tree next to the trap. A few more are trapped often, but most squirrels are seldom captured and there are probably a very few who are hardly ever trapped – the trap-shy living well away from the location of the traps. Similarly, there are likely to be a few words in a person's active vocabulary which are very rarely used at all, while most content words, which make up the bulk of the active vocabulary, are used relatively infrequently and over time appear with much the same probability as each other. There is then a long tail consisting of the fewer and fewer content words that recur more often, down to the everyday types and occasional function words before ending with the relatively few common function words which are continually in use. Here, of course, 'few' is used in relation to the many thousands of words in a person's active vocabulary. This reasoning predicts a distribution curve highly skewed to the lower probability end of the spectrum as shown in Figure 3.1.

The shape of the curve at the right-hand end would indicate that the words which appear there are relatively widely spaced in probability terms compared to the bulk of the words to the left. That the tail is long can be illustrated from as few as the first 60 or so types in the word frequency list compiled by Milton and Hales (1997) from a corpus of about 100,000 words taken from the *Guardian* newspaper. The first (*the*), fifth (*and*), and ninth (*that*) most frequent words appear 6718 ($p \sim 0.067$), 2203 ($p \sim 0.022$) and 1105 ($p \sim 0.011$) times while the 51st (*you*), 55th (*after*), and 59th (*says*) occur 218 ($p \sim 0.0022$), 183 ($p \sim 0.0018$), and 175 ($p \sim 0.0018$) times.

Following a suggestion made by Good (1953) in the context of the population estimates of species, Sichel, in an earlier work (1971) had proposed the 'generalised inverse Gaussian' distribution, also known as the Wald distribution, as suitable to represent this kind of pattern. It has the appropriate properties of extreme skewness close to the origin to represent the large

Figure 3.1 Distribution of words of increasing probability of occurrence as a proportion of the active vocabulary

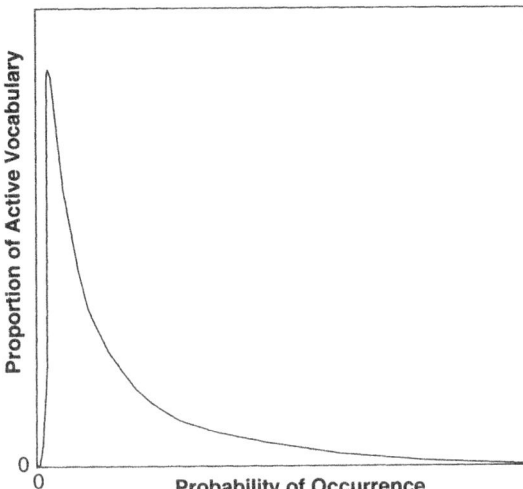

number of content words used infrequently with much the same probability as each other, followed by a falling away in a long tail, which appropriately reflects the decreasing proportion of types which appear relatively often and are more spread out in terms of their occurrence probabilities, that is to say the generalised inverse Gaussian distribution describes the sort of distribution predicted in Figure 3.1.

To complete the formulation (Sichel, 1986), the third probability needed is that of an individual type appearing once, twice, three times ... in a text of length N. This is given by the binomial law, but requires a mixture of binomials to represent all the possible outcomes. Following the same device as Thomson and Thompson, Sichel's analysis uses Poisson's exponential form for the mix of binomials to equate two ways of expressing the probability of a type not being included in a text of N tokens, and solves the resulting equation to produce an expression relating the number of types in a language sample to its length in tokens.

The full solution to the equation includes three parameters, which Sichel calls γ, b, and c and are theoretically invariant. In practice, the first can be set at $\gamma = -0.5$, and in our notation the analysis yields for TTR as a function of N the following two-parameter version:

$$TTR = \frac{2}{Nbc}\left[1 - e^{-b\left(\{1+cN\}^{\frac{1}{2}}-1\right)}\right] \qquad (3.14)$$

where b and c are constants, independent of the size of the language sample.

As Sichel replaces the binomial with the Poisson distribution, it is usually referred to as the 'inverse Gaussian-Poisson' formulation. As well as providing a TTR against N relationship, it permits the theoretical exploration of a number of other indices. In particular, it predicts that the proportion of *hapax legomena* is a decreasing function of text length, but the decrease is extremely slow which Sichel advances as a possible reason for its being observed as near constant by Brainerd (1982b) among others. The prediction for the proportion of *hapax dislegomena*, however, is that it first rises rapidly with increasing N, plateaus, and then falls very slowly towards zero for extremely high token counts. This accords with the near constancy for language samples observed by Michéa and by Sichel himself.

The most significant prediction of Sichel, however, is that Yule's characteristic K must be constant, not a function of text length, and equal to:

$$K = 10^4 \frac{c}{2}(1 + b) \qquad (3.15)$$

which, as K is a measure of repetitiveness, also shows that the higher the diversity, the lower K, b, and c will be.

To test out his theory, Sichel employed a sample of 8045 nouns drawn originally by Yule (1944) from Macaulay's *Essay on Bacon*. Yule had created four independent sub-samples, each of about 2000 tokens, and the combinations of two provide six sub-samples of 4000 or so tokens, while combining them in threes leads to a further four in the order of 6000 tokens each. There is a remarkable consistency within each set of sub-samples, so the means of each set will suffice to illustrate Sichel's results. Table 3.2 gives estimates for selected parameters both as observed in these data and as derived from the theory.

The proportion of *hapax dislegomena*, v_2/V, is the inverse of the 'constant' proposed by Michéa ($M = V/v_2$) to be about 6. Therefore, according to Michéa, these columns should show a constant value of about 0.167. As reported above, Tweedie and Baayen (1998) showed that Michéa's M is not constant with increasing N, but they actually tested it in the form given by Sichel (1975): $S = v_2/V$. The graphical representation of their results for the randomised version of the text of *Alice in Wonderland* (p. 333) is completely in accord with Sichel's analysis, however, showing the rise and gently declining plateau predicted by it. As also noted above, Tweedie and Baayen found K to be constant on this test, so it comes as a surprise that they report both b and c as *not* being constant when their own results demonstrate the veracity of the predictions for K and S based on b and c both being constant.

Just how surprising the inconsistency in Tweedie and Baayen's results is can be seen by considering the TTR versus token curves for differing values of b and c, an investigation which has other significant implications. If we hold one of b or c at an arbitrary value and then plot the curves calculated for differing values of the other, we can see the effect of changing each. Initially

Table 3.2 Theoretical (Sichel's formulation) and mean observed values for TTR, b, c, K and proportions of types for hapax legomena and hapax dislegomena in sub-samples of different sizes from Macaulay's *Essay on Bacon*[*]

Parameter/Index	Mean Sub-Sample Size (Tokens)	Theory	Observed
TTR	2 011.5	0.475	0.465
	4 022.5	0.356	0.351
	6 033.75	0.294	0.292
	8 054	0.255	0.255
b	2 011.5	0.0861	0.0889
	4 022.5	0.0861	0.0915
	6 033.75	0.0861	0.0860
	8 054	0.0861	0.0861
c	2 011.5	0.00365	0.00385
	4 022.5	0.00365	0.00370
	6 033.75	0.00365	0.00370
	8 054	0.00365	0.00365
Proportion of hapax legomena to types (v_1/V)	2 011.5	0.629	0.613
	4 022.5	0.550	0.544
	6 033.75	0.551	0.510
	8 054	0.483	0.483
Proportion of hapax dislegomena to types (v_2/V)	2 011.5	0.170	0.179
	4 022.5	0.173	0.177
	6 033.75	0.173	0.174
	8 054	0.172	0.179
Yule's K	2 011.5	19.8	20.9
	4 022.5	19.8	20.2
	6 033.75	19.8	20.1
	8 054	19.8	19.8

[*] After Sichel (1986, Tables 2-8, pp. 60-6).

this is done in Figure 3.2a and Fig 3.2b by setting both b and c at 0.1, and then by varying first one and then the other to 0.2 and 0.3.

It can be seen that the changes in c (b held constant) bring about immediate large separation among the curves (Figure 3.2a), while similar changes in b (c held constant) make very little difference at low N (Figure 3.2b) but will eventually lead to a significant divergence for large N. It is perfectly possible, then, that two curves with differing values for b and c can cross over at large N.

Values for b and c, then, cannot be calculated adequately from a single point, but values for both *taken together* need to be found from fitting the equation to the whole curve. Tweedie and Baayen give little detail of how they estimated b and c, but the implication of the text is that they were found separately for each of the 20 test points, and this may account for the

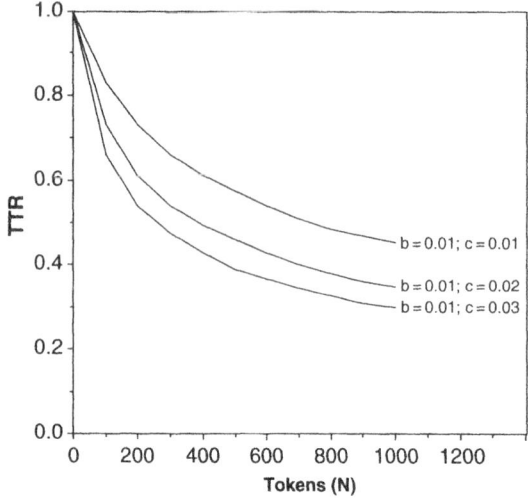

Figure 3.2a Theoretical TTR curves calculated for b held at 0.01 and for c = 0.01, c = 0.02, and c = 0.03

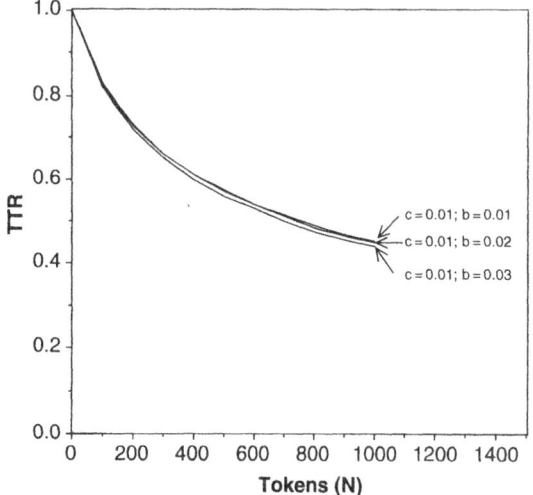

Figure 3.2b Theoretical TTR curves calculated for c held at 0.01 and for b = 0.01, b = 0.02, and b = 0.03

anomalous result. We tested Sichel's equation over the much smaller language samples typically obtained in the study of children's language, by curve fitting to the whole of the TTR versus N graph for each child, and were always able to find a constant pair of values for b and c to give good fits. None the less, having two parameters leaves open the possibility of ambiguity, with differing pairs of values producing equally good fits. Figure 3.2b, however, suggests that for small N, b makes relatively little difference and there ought to be a good approximation for short texts to Sichel's equation, which depends only on c. This is indeed the case. Because c decreases with increasing diversity, we choose to write this approximation for small samples in terms of $\mathcal{D} = 2/c$ as follows:

$$\text{TTR} = \frac{\mathcal{D}}{N}\left[\left(1 + 2\frac{N}{\mathcal{D}}\right)^{\frac{1}{2}} - 1\right] \tag{3.16}$$

We have found that this simplification provides good fits to the TTR relation to token count N, for short texts of a few hundred words. So too did Jarvis (2002), who tested it on 276 transcripts of narrative text of up to 300 or so tokens and found good fits for all but five (a 98 per cent success rate). We choose this formulation in terms of $\mathcal{D}$ because, being inversely related to c, it increases with greater diversity and can therefore be used as a base to make a direct measurement of lexical diversity. The font for $\mathcal{D}$ is used to distinguish it from that measurement, D, which we introduce in the sections below.

A mathematical model for diversity

We begin by considering the general features of plotting a graph of TTR against token count N. Obviously a sample of one token would also contain one type and the TTR for N = 1 will also equal one, and the graph will begin at (1,1). In typical language production, at a certain number of tokens a previously used type will be repeated and that particular incidence of the repeated type will contribute to the token count but not the type count. The type count will therefore fall behind the token count, and it will continue to do so more and more as more and more types are repeated. The TTR will fall below its initial value of one, and continue to fall depending on how many types are being used and how often each is repeated. In the early part of the graph, repeating a type (increasing N by one with no increase in V) will make a large change relative to the small values of V and N, while further along such a difference of one will be small compared to the larger value of N. Consequently, the descending rate of change of V with N will slow down for longer and longer texts. The general trend, then, will be for the graph to fall less and less steeply, and the overall pattern will be a falling curve with negative slope which decreases in absolute value.

If the graph is plotted following the sequence of a transcript, it will wobble about somewhat. If we use the preceding paragraph as an example, the first seven tokens contain seven types and until then the graph will be flat at TTR = 1. On the other hand when we get to '... more and more as more and more ...' in the third sentence, the TTR will fall steeply over this range of seven tokens, which contains only three types. We will put this issue of local variations about the curve to one side for now, however, and for clarity will represent TTR against token graphs by curves following the general shape of

48 *Lexical Diversity and Language Development*

the overall trends. These are 'ideal' curves, then, in the sense that physicists refer to ideal gasses, that is to say they are curves which are the product of theory, but the theory stems from observing real behaviour (Malvern, 2000).

We can now establish a mathematical model for the lexical diversity in language samples. We set up axes with N as the x axis and TTR the y axis. The language samples will be represented by graphs of TTR against N. They will all fall within an area between two extremes. The first extreme represents maximum possible diversity. That is defined as a language sample in which every token is a different type. Although this may seem artificial, it is easy to achieve by simply counting 'one, two, three, four ...' which fits the condition and can go on for ever. Its graph will be TTR = 1 and consists of a straight line parallel to the N axis at TTR = 1. The other extreme of least possible diversity is defined as a language sample in which only one type appears, repeated over and over again. It is harder to exemplify with a sensible illustration (although a parent hearing a child persistently asking 'Why?' may have little difficulty imagining such a sample), but it is mathematically straightforward. The type count would remain fixed at one and the curve would be the TTR = 1/N. The graphs of language samples, then, lie in the plane bounded by these two extremes. Diversity can then be *defined* in the model. The nearer the graph of a language sample is to the line TTR = 1 the greater its lexical diversity; the nearer to the curve TTR = 1/N the lower the lexical diversity (see Figure 3.3).

This model is entirely consistent with the discussion in Chapter 2. A good test is that it provides an explanation for reconciling the conflict between TTRs being not a constant but a function of sample size and the apparent

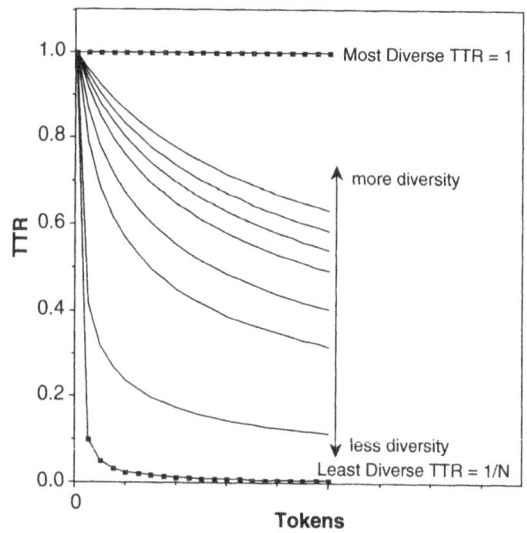

Figure 3.3 A mathematical model of lexical diversity

A Mathematical Model of Lexical Diversity 49

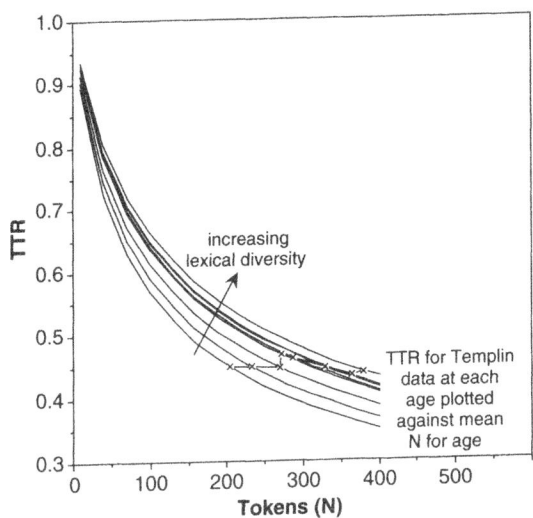

Figure 3.4 Rising curves passing through the points for mean TTRs calculated from Templin's data

constancy noticed by Miller in Templin's seminal work on children. Undoubtedly, TTRs calculated from Templin's figures show the mean TTRs remaining constant at about 0.45 for 50 utterances from children between three and eight years old. They also show that these TTRs are calculated from increasing token counts, as the MLU for the children increases with age. Figure 3.4 plots the points of TTR for the Templin means against N, and also a set of TTR versus token curves passing through these points. The curves rise in the plane for the older children, demonstrating that an increase in the diversity displayed with age, which would be expected intuitively, is perfectly compatible with near constant TTRs drawn from longer and longer samples. Similarly, a play by Shakespeare can show a lower TTR for the whole text, large N, than that for a child's much shorter transcript, small N, while lying on an upper curve representing higher diversity than the child's language sample represented by a lower curve.

Operationalising the model

We can use this model to measure lexical diversity by matching the graph derived from a real language sample to the ideal curves of the model. The diversity of the language sample will be measured by the diversity of the ideal curve which most closely matches it. In order to do this, we need the following:

- a set of ideal curves which lie one above the other and together fill all the permitted space in the plane between $TTR = 1$ and $TTR = 1/N$;

50 *Lexical Diversity and Language Development*

- a mathematical expression to represent the set of 'ideal' curves of the model which distinguishes one from the other by virtue of the location being higher or lower;
- an unambiguous property of this expression to make this distinction and thereby to be used as the measurement of diversity;
- a method of producing graphs to represent real language samples;
- a way of finding the unique best match of the graph for the real sample to one of the set of ideal curves;
- a standardisation which makes use of all the data in the language samples regardless of length and ensures that all users make the measurement in the same way.

A mathematical expression for ideal curves

An appropriate mathematical expression for ideal curves would have a robust theoretical basis, produce graphs of the right general shape, make acceptably accurate fits to graphs from real language production for small N of the order of up to a few hundred tokens, and contain one parameter which defines the height in the plane. As the narratives of this and the previous chapter have shown, over the years the numerous attempts to find a reliable index for lexical diversity have yielded plenty of candidates for an appropriate mathematical expression for ideal curves. Fortunately, most can be disregarded as they have been shown to be flawed or incomplete. Sichel's work is the most complete combination of the insights developed by the various theorists over the years into a single formulation, and, although his full solution contains three parameters, our small sample approximation of it contains only one, $\mathcal{D}$.

From extensive testing we have found good fits between this approximation and curves drawn from short, real language samples of up to a few hundred tokens (see later chapters for examples).

Jarvis (2002) applied our general model (Malvern and Richards, 1997) to investigate $\mathcal{D}$ and four alternatives for goodness of fit to short texts. The four others were:

Related to Herdan's LogTTR
$$TTR = N^{C-1} \tag{3.17}$$

Related to Guiraud's RTTR
$$TTR = \frac{RTTR\sqrt{N}}{N} \tag{3.18}$$

Related to Dugast's Uber
$$TTR = N^{\frac{-1}{U}\log N} \tag{3.19}$$

Related to Orlov/Zipf's Z

$$TTR = \frac{\frac{Z}{\log f_{max} Z} \frac{N}{N-Z} \log \frac{N}{Z}}{N} \quad (3.20)$$

Jarvis's samples were obtained from a narrative writing exercise which produced texts of different lengths up to 300 tokens from 140 Finnish-speaking and 70 Swedish-speaking learners of English and 66 US school students aged ten to 15 years. He tested the five expressions for goodness of fit to graphs of TTR against N calculated first for the whole texts and, second, for just the content words extracted from the texts in order. As is to be expected, neither LogTTR nor RTTR produced expressions that worked at all well. Jarvis found $\mathcal{D}$ and U produced good fits in over 90 per cent of cases on both tests, however, while Z did so for whole texts but not for content words. There was a higher percentage of good fits for whole texts obtained from $\mathcal{D}$ than from U, while U obtained more good fits from transcripts listing only the content words in the original texts.

The tests carried out by Tweedie and Baayen (1998) are of limited relevance here, as they used such huge texts and it is not made clear how b and c were tested separately. Neither c (and by implication, therefore, $\mathcal{D}$), however it was tested, nor U comes out well in their large text tests, although as pointed out above, their results in relation to Michéa's index and Yule's characteristic for randomised text give some support for Sichel's formulation. Given that both $\mathcal{D}$ and U are capable of producing good fits, we prefer on balance to use $\mathcal{D}$; first because it is underpinned by Sichel's formulation, a more complete probabilistic analysis than any other, and, second, because its form permits a remarkable simplification when applied to type–type ratios (see Chapter 8).

The expression for the ideal curves used to make the measurement, then, is as given in Equation 3.16:

$$TTR = \frac{\mathcal{D}}{N}\left[\left(1 + 2\frac{N}{\mathcal{D}}\right)^{\frac{1}{2}} - 1\right] \quad (3.21)$$

It describes a family of curves, which occupy the plane in the model with one curve lying above another to fill the permitted space between $TTR = 1/N$ and $TTR = 1$. How high a curve lies is determined by the value of the parameter $\mathcal{D}$ – the larger $\mathcal{D}$ the higher the curve (see Figure 3.5). That is to say that the bigger the value of $\mathcal{D}$ the greater the diversity and $\mathcal{D}$ itself is the property required as the basis of a measurement of diversity.

Producing the graphs from real data

In some transcripts, the flow of communication causes clusters of the same vocabulary item at certain points. Thomson and Thompson pointed to the

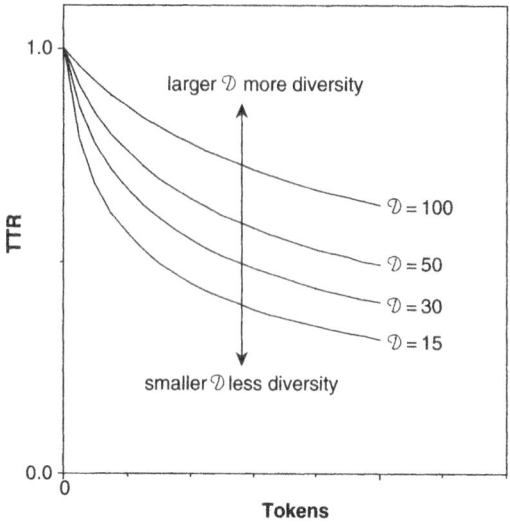

Figure 3.5 Ideal TTR versus token curves showing increasing diversity with increasing $\mathcal{D}$

role of context or topic in the emergence of such clusters, noting that the likelihood of a particular word's appearance would in part depend on '... its relation to the subject matter requiring expression' (Thomson and Thompson, 1915, p. 58 footnote 1). Chotlos (1944) also argued that diversity may in part be related to the number of topics discussed in a sample. Wimmer and Altmann (1999), in their review article on Cossette's *La richesse lexicale et sa mesure* (1994), make the point forcibly with respect to the introduction of new vocabulary with a change of context:

> But at several values of N the V-points [in a curve of cumulative V against N] make a jump, go rapidly up then continue in a line almost parallel to the prolongation of the original line [curve]. These points signal breaks in the text, e.g. beginnings of a new chapter, coffee pauses, intermittent sleep, long breaks used for thinking ...
> (Wimmer and Altmann, 1999, p. 6)

This argues that the points would be better based by determining the TTR at a given token count, say N = 50, by averaging a number of sub-samples of size 50 tokens drawn from throughout the whole sample. Moreover, calculating the points from averages of a number of sub-samples reflects the probabilistic theories on which the ideal curves are based which predict ideal *expected* values for the TTR.

Reasons can be put forward for choosing, as the basis for the method of selecting these sub-samples, either sampling of individual tokens at random, or of strings of words in sequence with the starting points chosen at random. Averaging sequential sub-samples is akin to using a mean segmental TTR to determine each point. Taking the sub-samples at random would go some way to compensate for the effect of clustering, as some would include clusters (and hence lower diversity) and others would not (higher diversity) and as long as they came in roughly equal numbers this difference would tend to be washed out. There would be a decrease in reliability, however, because the variation among sub-samples would increase, and some vocabulary changes and long-range repetition may escape detection if the sub-samples are smaller than the topic sections. In a book on language assessment, a section on 'lexical profiling systems' is likely to repeat those three words as often as another section on 'communicative language testing' would repeat that trio. The TTR for sub-samples from both sections may well give a similar value reflecting frequent repetition of the three types, but may ignore the fact that 'lexical profiling systems' and 'communicative language testing' if taken together actually contribute six types in the whole text. Moreover, if there are two sections on 'lexical profiling systems' separated by the one on 'communicative language testing', all three may well return similar TTRs although the third section adds no more new types to these six.

The argument for sequential sampling is that it preserves the structure of the language, where random sampling of single tokens does not (see Jarvis, 2002; Tweedie and Baayen, 1998). The underlying probabilistic model, however, assumes that there is a distribution of frequencies for the occurrence of words which is such as to permit two or more words to have the same or similar frequency. This automatically takes account of collocations, for example, because the contribution of such structures to the frequencies of their constituent types will be the same for each type and be reflected in the random sampling with equal likelihood. The theoretical underpinning therefore does not require that the word sequence need be preserved in the sampling.

There are, however, two ways of taking random samples of single tokens. The first is *with replacement* – that is having selected a particular token from the text, it is returned to be available for selection again. For example, if the first selection is the word *The* at the start of the previous paragraph, the *The* is then replaced and may be selected again as the second, third, fourth, and so on word in the same sub-sample. The second is *without replacement* – on selection the token is removed from the whole sample and is not available for reselection in the same sub-sample. Here the *The* at the start of the previous paragraph is not replaced and cannot be selected again in the same sub-sample (although another *the* from elsewhere might be).

Thomson and Thompson, and many others addressing the problem of predicting an author's total active vocabulary from the vocabulary stream in the sample, argued for selection with replacement. Their assumption was that the next word to be written can be selected from the whole of the author's active vocabulary – the urn of the urn model being the author's brain, as it were. The selection, then, is of a type and as, in principle, all the types in the author's head are always available for the next token, all types must remain 'in the urn' for every selection. This means that sub-samples could contain the same particular token repeated over and over again, although the likelihood may be very small – as in real texts the word *the* is highly unlikely to be followed by another *the*, but it is not impossible as the final sentence of the previous paragraph was written to demonstrate.

Selection without replacement may be better suited to the task in hand, however, as it is to measure the lexical diversity found in a collected language sample. We are dealing with fixed numbers of tokens and types in the data set, then, and the urn is the language sample. Random sampling *with replacement* permits the same token of a given type to be repeated over and over again up to the size of the sub-sample being selected. For a type whose frequency is less than the size of the sub-sample, this could mean that it is possible to produce a sub-sample containing more examples of it than there are in the sample as a whole. Random sampling without replacement avoids that problem.

Random sampling of individual tokens matches the assumptions underlying the probabilistic model, and *without replacement* seems preferable to *with replacement* as it is a better match to the fixed data of previously collected language samples. Although the probabilities reflect language structures, sampling at the level of tokens does destroy the structure, and for particular applications there may be good reason to require sequential sampling. We can predict, however, that the 'over-repetition' possible in random token sampling with replacement will lead to lower diversity than that found by token sampling without replacement, as too will the clustering effect in sequential sampling. For now, however, we wish to retain all three methods of selecting sub-samples to average for the TTR-points on the graphs derived from real curves, and will investigate them further in terms of their sensitivity to sample size in Chapter 4.

Standardising how the measurement is made

A number of things need to be standardised: the values of N for which the curve is plotted; the number of trials of sub-samples used for the average at each point on the curve; and the method of random selection should all be fixed, so that every researcher makes the measurement in the same way. We have already decided to retain the option of sequential sampling for the time being, as well as sampling by randomly chosen tokens both with and without replacement. At first glance, it seems possible to work out the latter two analytically – that is to say by calculation, without actually having to average a number of sub-samples. Random token choice with replacement is akin to calculating the Theoretical Vocabulary for each point, but as we have seen, this is a somewhat naïve application of binomial probability which assumes a constant and equal-for-all probability. Random selection without replacement is much more complicated, however, and leads to a mixture of binomials.

More significantly, Sichel's theory treats the language sample as just that, a language sample drawn from the underlying probability distributions to be found in the author's active vocabulary – to calculate the number of types in a sub-sample analytically, then, requires *prior* knowledge of b and c in the formulation, or in this case of $\mathcal{D}$. No theory provides a calculation which predicts the *sequence* of types and tokens in sub-samples, and sequential samples have to be simply chosen at random. Standardisation, then, as well as the theoretical objections to using over-simplified calculations, requires that the selection of sub-samples should be carried out by straightforward sampling at random.

The number of trials for each sub-sample should be sufficiently large to approach the expected values, but not large enough to take an inordinate amount of time to assemble and average. This is fundamentally a pragmatic decision, and we found from trials that taking 100 trials for each sub-sample produced sufficiently consistent results in a reasonable time.

Similarly, the points to use to plot the curve were determined by trying out different sub-ranges. Jarvis and Tweedie and Baayen chose to plot their curves over 20 points, separated as near as possible by intervals of N/20 tokens. This has the disadvantage of plotting the curves for transcripts of different length at different points and over different ranges. It is better to standardise the range and points to be the same in every case. Plotting the curve over a standard range still calls on all the data in the full transcript, as the random selection of trials of sub-samples is made from throughout the transcript, and is therefore just as much a reflection of the whole transcript as plotting it over the full range of N. For applications to child language studies, the sub-range has to cover a range large enough to show the pattern of the curve but be over sufficiently small values of N to be derived from sampling from the relatively short transcripts of a few hundred tokens obtainable from children. The 16 points between $N = 35$ and $N = 50$ were found to be suitable, permitting adequate sub-sampling from children's transcripts and providing sufficient separation of the curves for different language samples.

Making the measurement, D, and *vocd*

Clearly, the actual measurement is best done by computer. This requires a program which can read a transcript of the language sample, then plot the TTR versus tokens curve between $N = 35$ and $N = 50$, deriving each point from an average of 100 trials on sub-samples of words of the token size for that point. The program then needs to find the best fit between the ideal curves of theory and the curves drawn from empirical data by a curve-fitting procedure which adjusts the value of the parameter ($\mathcal{D}$) in Equation 3.21 until a match is obtained between the actual curve for the transcript and the closest member of the family of curves represented by the mathematical model. This value of the parameter for best fit, $\mathcal{D}_{best\ fit} = D$, is the index of lexical diversity. D is the measurement. High values of D reflect a high level of lexical diversity and lower diversity produces lower values of D. It should be emphasised that, being based on a probabilistic model which predicts *expected* values, the calculating processes are stochastic, and averaging is intrinsic at all stages.

The program to make the measurement is *vocd*, which was written to our specification by Gerard McKee of the Department of Computer Science at The University of Reading. It was written in 'C' and exists in PC and Macintosh versions, freely available as part of the Computerised Language Analysis (CLAN) suite of programs (available on the Child Language Data Exchange System (CHILDES) web site at http://childes.psy.cmu.edu). A UNIX version is also available. It operates on files of transcripts set out and coded according to the Codes for the Human Analysis of Transcripts (CHAT) system developed by Brian MacWhinney as part of CHILDES (MacWhinney, 2000a, 2000b). Originally devised for first language research, CLAN and CHAT are increasingly being used in other fields such as second language. Examples of CHAT transcripts are contained in Appendices II–IV.

The text-handling features of *vocd* have been modelled on CLAN programs, particularly a program called *freq* whose function is to make frequency counts of words or codes. *Freq* and *vocd* are almost totally compatible with regard to the items they include in word counts by default. As with *freq*, however, the use of various switches and exclude files, in combination with the careful use of CHAT transcription conventions, enables linguistic items to be selected or rejected in a way that corresponds with researchers' theoretical perspective on what should count as a word and what should count as a *different* word. A full description of the text-handling options and documentation for the UNIX version of *vocd*, as well as sample printouts can be found in Appendices V–VII.

In calculating D, *vocd* uses random sampling without replacement of tokens as the *default* mode for plotting the curve of TTR against increasing token size for the transcript under investigation. There is, however, a switch to enable sequential sampling and random sampling with replacement if required. For both methods, each point on the curve is calculated from averaging the TTRs of 100 trials on sub-samples consisting of the number of tokens for that point, drawn at random from throughout the transcripts. The default is for the curve to be drawn and fitted for $N = 35$ to $N = 50$ tokens in steps of one token. The procedure then depends on finding the best fit between the empirical and ideal curves derived theoretically from the small sample approximation to Sichel's equation, by the least square difference method. Extensive testing confirmed that the best-fit procedure was valid and was reliably finding a *unique* minimum at the least square difference. The value of the minimum sum of squared difference is included in the output of *vocd*, as it measures how close the language sample is to the best fitting ideal curve and is an indication of the accuracy of the measurement for the particular text.

Finally, as the points on the curve are averages of random samples, a slightly different value of D is to be expected each time the program is run. Tests showed that with the chosen defaults these differences are relatively small, but consistency was improved by *vocd* calculating D three times by default and giving the average value as output. Figure 3.6 shows a flow diagram for the default version of *vocd*.

As noted above, the software plots the TTR versus token curve from 35 tokens to 50 tokens and each point on the curve is produced by random sampling *without* replacement. The software therefore requires a minimum of 50 tokens to operate. We should point out, however, that the fact that the software will satisfactorily output a value of D from a sample as small as 50 tokens does not guarantee that values obtained from such small samples will be reliable (see the next chapter).

Summary

We have shown in this chapter that diversity also depends on the way types are deployed as well as how many there are in a language sample. Empirically, this leads to graphs of TTR against N, the token count, producing curves which fall from the point (1,1) on a downward path of decreasing slope. Starting with the seminal paper by Thomson and Thompson, a substantial body of scholarship has explored how best to represent such curves mathematically by including the frequency of types in measuring lexical diversity. The account we give here is largely historical, and traces the highlights in the accumulation of ideas which led to an understanding of the combination of probabilities required to analyse the statistical problem of how new and repeated types appear as tokens and are added to the language stream.

The most complete account, which welds all these ideas together, is the 'inverse Gaussian-Poisson' formulation of Sichel. In its complete form it depends on three parameters, but is reducible to an equation for the TTR versus N curves which has only two. For small samples, typically found in child language studies, however, there is a good approximation containing only one parameter, $\mathcal{D}$.

We then introduced a mathematical model for lexical diversity as given by the location of ideal curves for TTR against N, lying one on top of the other so as to fill the space between the graphs of the two obvious extremes of lexical diversity: TTR = 1 (complete diversity) and TTR = 1/N (no diversity).

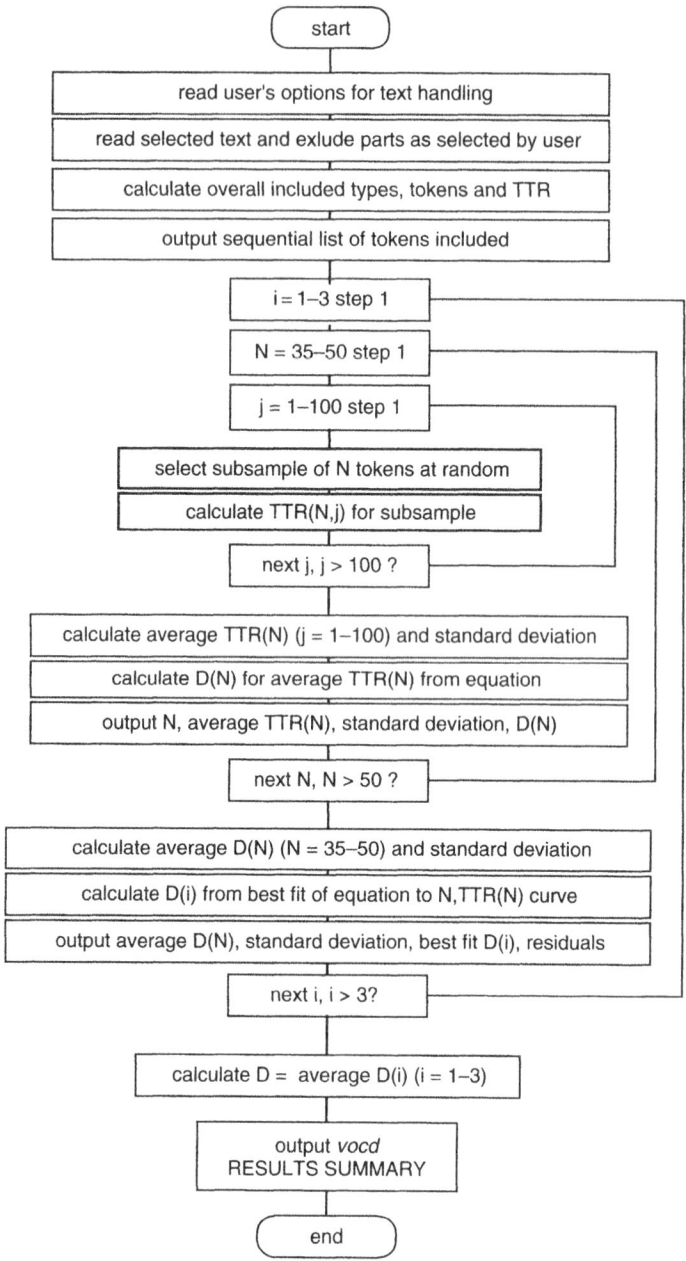

Figure 3.6 Flow chart for *vocd* (default version)

Lexical diversity is defined in the model as the combination of properties, such as range of vocabulary, repetition or relative frequency of the types, which cause a curve for a language sample to be further away from the lower extreme and nearer to the upper one. The model makes it possible to measure diversity of a real language sample by comparing the TTR versus N curve derived from it to the family of ideal curves. It should be noted that both this mathematical model and the general method of utilising it to measure diversity are independent of any particular formulation for the equation of the ideal curves or procedure for plotting the graph from real language.

To make a measurement, however, requires a formula for the ideal curves with a property which specifies their location in the model space and a specific procedure for plotting graphs from real language which matches the theory chosen to describe the ideal curves. Various formulations and procedures were considered to make suitable choices, and the model operationalised using the equation based on $\mathcal{D}$ (Equation 3.21) and sampling at the level either of tokens or of sequences. The *vocd* program, devised to measure lexical diversity based on this way of operationalising the model and having suitable standardisations built in as defaults, was then described.

It is important to understand that the automated procedure results in a measurement, D, which is different in kind to $\mathcal{D}$ the parameter for ideal curves. D is a particular value for best-fit between the ideal curves and those derived from real transcripts over the standard range of points of the TTR versus N curve drawn by a standardised procedure. As we have pointed out, this gives it an advantage over any method of measuring diversity which depends on just one point. We have also shown that because the random sampling uses all the data in the full transcript, it reflects the whole transcript.

This is not the same as saying that D is equal to the value of $\mathcal{D}$ to be found from the single point of the TTR for the transcript as a whole. If it were, measuring it through *vocd* would be a waste of time. The whole purpose of the model is that the measurement must be made over a number of points in order to establish the pattern of fall of the curve, which is what matters, not any particular value on it. In making the measurement, *vocd* essentially knocks the curve from real language into its nearest ideal state, and uses that ideal state to measure real language. This is an entirely familiar process in measurement. A good parallel is the measurement of atomic mass of gaseous elements from a graph of density/pressure at $0°C$ against pressure (see Malvern, 2000). Measurements from real gasses are used to plot points on the graph. The graph for an ideal gas would be a straight line, so the best straight line is fitted. This straight line, which describes the behaviour of the nearest ideal gas, is then extrapolated to zero pressure to find the limiting ratio of density to pressure, from which the atomic mass can be calculated. Until the invention of the mass spectrometer, this method was the most accurate measurement of atomic masses of gaseous elements, even though it depends on a value for density/pressure which can only apply to an ideal gas. It would be impossible to realise the physical conditions for the measuring point in the real world (a gas being a gas at 0°C but at zero pressure and having a measurable ratio of density to pressure).

Similarly, D is a measurement of the real, but in the ideal. The choice of formula and defaults were made to suit the short samples found in child language study, and the standardisations made to ensure all researchers carry out the measurement in the same way. Realising that D is not the same as $\mathcal{D}$, we cannot expect D to substitute for $\mathcal{D}$ in describing the behaviour of real curves at large N. D is a measurement of lexical diversity as defined by the model and standardised in our operationalisation, *not* a predictor of how the curve behaves over the full range of N tokens.

For our purposes, however, what matters is that D provides a robust measure of lexical diversity which is not a function of sample size in the way raw TTR and its simple transformations are. It is based on the most complete development of an extensive canon of theory available, and on a general mathematical model which gives it face validity. We now turn to investigate it further as a measure, and in the next chapter subject it to the usual tests of validity and reliability found in measurement practice.

Part II
Validation of the Model and its Application to Language Corpora

4
Early Child Language 1: the New England Corpus

Chapters 4 and 5 provide examples of the application of *vocd* to two corpora of early child language, beginning here with American transcripts obtained from the CHILDES database (MacWhinney, 2000b) and followed up in Chapter 5 with a British dataset. The analyses of the corpus reported in this chapter aimed initially to try out the software on a real data set, as opposed to artificial transcripts specially constructed for debugging, and to see whether the use of switches to remove repeated words and phrases ('retracings') and to strip words of regular inflections would make the predicted differences to the D-values obtained.

Second, the measure's sensitivity to sample size was investigated together with two further facets of reliability. These are the reliability of the model in producing consistent sets of D-scores from the same data set and the internal consistency of D itself.

Third, having made a case for the construct validity of D in the previous chapter, we set out to assess its criterion-related validity by seeing whether it correlated with age and tried and tested measures from the child language literature. We also conducted analyses of social background and sex differences to see whether the results of these match those of a traditional measure of language development.

Testing *vocd*

During its development the text-handling features of *vocd*, that is to say its ability to conduct an analysis according to the users' requirements as to what counts as a valid word (token) and what is defined as a different word (type), had been tested and debugged using specially constructed dummy transcripts that contained the complete set of valid CHAT codes as defined by the CHILDES manual that was current at that time (MacWhinney, 1995b). These were processed using all possible combinations of switches (see the *vocd* documentation in Appendix V) for features such as speaker selection, conducting analyses on dependent tiers of the transcript, morphemicisation, (stripping off inflections to allow analysis of lexemes or word stems), exclusion of lists of non-words, or removal of self-repetition or 'retracing', and so on. Words listed in the output were checked for anomalies and the type and token count checked against corresponding analyses using the *freq* program, a facility for obtaining word lists and word frequency counts in CLAN (MacWhinney, 2000a).

To test the reliability and validity of D we use the transcripts of the 38 children in the 32-month directory of the New England Corpus (Dale, Bates, Reznick and Morriset, 1989; Snow, 1989) in the CHILDES database. The children are all from English-speaking families and their age at the '32-month' recording actually ranges from 27 to 33 months with a mean of 30.3 months. There are equal numbers of girls and boys, and 17 children are described as working class and 21 as middle class. Data collection took place in the laboratory where mother and child were video-recorded playing with the contents of four boxes in succession. This dataset was chosen because morpheme boundaries had been marked on the transcripts and were considered to be particularly reliable (Brian MacWhinney, personal communication, 1996).

Investigating sensitivity to sample size

We have claimed that by using a mathematical modelling procedure on a standard-sized window of 35 to 50 tokens of the TTR versus token curve, lexical diversity values will no longer be a *function* of text length. The use of the word 'function of' is crucial here, as we do not mean to imply that there is no *relationship* between lexical diversity values and total number of words. In the past, some researchers have investigated the sensitivity of vocabulary richness measures to sample size by computing correlations between measures and the total number of words spoken or written (Hoare, 2000/2001; Afitskaya, 2002; and Dewaele and Pavlenko, 2003 are recent examples). Where this is carried out across the work of a single author (for example by Ménard, 1983), there may be no objection to this procedure. In research into first and second language development, however, we are usually dealing with samples from populations that display considerable individual differences both in volubility and language proficiency. Frequently these two factors are themselves significantly correlated, even though there are conflicting views as to whether these correlations will be positive or negative. On the one hand, Dewaele and Pavlenko (2003) argue that because psycholinguistic research has shown that producing longer words makes higher cognitive demands on the speaker, producing lexically rich language will be at the expense of fluency and, hence, of the quantity of speech produced. Studies of early language development, on the other hand, show that more advanced language users say more and use more diverse language, and this was part of our explanation in Chapter 3 for the stability over time of TTRs calculated from Mildred Templin's data (Templin, 1957). This brings about the possibility of an entirely spurious positive correlation between a vocabulary richness measure and text length that is actually brought about by the common underlying factor of language ability. In the New England Corpus, for example, the correlation between D and the number of words spoken would tell us nothing about D's sensitivity to sample size because we know for these 38 children that the rank order correlation between total number of words and a general measure of language development (MLU) is 0.610 ($n = 38$; $p < 0.001$), and nobody would claim that MLU, as a token/token proportion, is functionally dependent on sample size. Any correlation between a lexical diversity index and the word count may therefore be totally spurious as a test of its sensitivity to sample size.

Other researchers have avoided this trap by looking at cumulative plots of the measure against sample size for individual cases (Richards, 1987; Meara and Bell, 2001). This approach is frequently used with literary texts (see Tweedie and Baayen, 1998). Another approach is to divide all the transcripts into standard sized long and short segments, and compare the average vocabulary richness values obtained from each. Thus, in a study comparing children with specific language impairment (SLI) with two groups of normally developing children, one matched for age and the other for MLU, Owen and Leonard (2002) tested the relationship of three lexical diversity measures with sample size by comparing average values for the first 250 words with the values for 500 words. A slightly more sophisticated and probably more reliable alternative is provided by Hess, Sefton and Landry (1986) who tested five vocabulary diversity measures on 50 utterances elicited from children aged three, four, and five. Hess and colleagues divided their speech samples into four segments of 50 words, two of 100, one each of 150 and 200 words, and a final one consisting of the whole transcript (length varied from 201 to 361 words) and conducted repeated measures ANOVAs for each measure. A very similar method is adopted with older children by Hess, Haug and Landry (1989).

Method

One problem with the above procedures, and particularly where only two lengths of segment are compared, is that in terms of the topics, themes, and situational context we may not be comparing like with like. For example, the whole way in which we conceptualise lexical diversity and how it relates to the quantity of language a speaker produces is placed under considerable strain when we ask ourselves whether controlling for sample size means that someone who covers ten themes in the first half of their transcript and 20 themes in the whole transcript should obtain the same lexical diversity score for each. Our own approach tries to overcome this problem by capitalising on *vocd*'s split-half facility. This gives the option of carrying out a comparison of D for even-numbered or odd-numbered words with the D for the whole transcript. In other words, D for half the words is compared with the D for all the words in a way that minimises local contextual effects or the number of topic changes and focuses on whether, for each of the three methods of sampling words available to *vocd*, the scores are a function of the size of the sample.

The three sampling methods, which were described in Chapter 3, are sequential sampling, random sampling with replacement, and random sampling without replacement. For each method, the New England files were run through *vocd* using the minimum command line to extract the words of the target child, with no tokens excluded, and the following four D values obtained: $D_{\text{all words}}$; $D_{\text{even-numbered words}}$; $D_{\text{odd-numbered words}}$; the mean of $D_{\text{odd-numbered words}}$ and $D_{\text{even-numbered words}}$. In addition, *vocd* always outputs type and token frequencies (see Appendix VI) and TTR s were calculated for the same four odd or even word combinations, for which we expected to find a significant difference between the whole and half-sized samples.

Results

Means and *t*-tests for all four variables are reported in Tables 4.1 to 4.4 below for TTR and each sampling method for *vocd*. As expected, TTR was significantly affected by sample size. All three values for the half transcripts were significantly higher than for the whole transcripts (Table 4.1). The same pattern obtains for sequential sampling (Table 4.2). For random sampling *with* replacement, on the other hand, Table 4.3 shows that all values for half the transcript are significantly *lower*. As can be seen in Table 4.4, and as we

Table 4.1 Mean TTR for different parts of the transcripts ($N = 38$)

	Mean	SD	Significance of Difference from the Mean for all Words	
Even-numbered words	0.510	0.075	$t = 32.56$	$p < 0.001$
Odd-numbered words	0.497	0.080	$t = 29.68$	$p < 0.001$
Mean of odd and even	0.503	0.075	$t = 47.57$	$p < 0.001$
Whole transcript	0.377	0.066		

Table 4.2 Mean D (sequential sampling) for different parts of the transcripts ($N = 38$)

	Mean	SD	Significance of Difference from the Mean for all Words	
Even-numbered words	32.74	14.46	$t = 7.51$	$p < 0.001$
Odd-numbered words	31.37	12.79	$t = 7.87$	$p < 0.001$
Mean of odd and even	32.06	12.56	$t = 12.51$	$p < 0.001$
Whole transcript	23.68	9.74		

Table 4.3 Mean D (random sampling with replacement) for different parts of the transcripts (N = 38)

	Mean	SD	Significance of Difference from the Mean for all Words	
Even-numbered words	29.09	12.36	$t = 9.69$	$p < 0.001$
Odd-numbered words	28.26	11.55	$t = 10.27$	$p < 0.001$
Mean of odd and even	28.67	11.58	$t = 13.67$	$p < 0.001$
Whole transcript	35.72	13.71		

Table 4.4 Mean D (random sampling without replacement) for different parts of the transcripts (N = 38)

	Mean	SD	Significance of Difference from the Mean for all Words	
Even-numbered words	47.54	20.51	$t = 1.03$	$p = 0.310$ ns
Odd-numbered words	45.79	17.88	$t = 0.46$	$p = 0.646$ ns
Mean of odd and even	46.67	18.03	$t = 1.31$	$p = 0.197$ ns
Whole transcript	46.26	17.77		

reported in McKee, Malvern and Richards (2000), there are no differences at all for random sampling without replacement.

In order to gauge the relative sensitivity to sample size for TTR and the three versions of D, we calculated Eta^2 as an estimate of effect size for the comparison between the mean for the whole sample and the mean of the odd and even half samples. These show TTR to have the largest effect ($Eta^2 = 0.872$) followed by random sampling with replacement ($Eta^2 = 0.835$), sequential sampling ($Eta^2 = 0.809$), and, for comparison, random sampling without replacement which is much lower ($Eta^2 = 0.045$).

Inter-correlations between the scores obtained from the three methods of sampling are high (Pearson coefficients are 0.974 between the two random sampling methods, 0.912 between random sampling without replacement and sequential sampling, and 0.854 between random sampling with replacement and sequential sampling). An examination of Tables 4.1 to 4.4, however, shows that not only do the three versions of D differ in their reliability when applied to corpora whose individual language samples vary in size, but that the magnitude of D varies according to the method of sampling used. This is confirmed by a one-way ANOVA ($F(2,111) = 24.30, p < 0.001$), and Scheffé tests show that the three sets of values differ significantly from each other ($ps < 0.01$). The reasons for the differences in sensitivity to sample size and the relative size of D obtained from different methods of sampling from transcripts will be discussed at the end of this chapter. Because random sampling without replacement appears to output the most reliable D-values, all further analyses in this volume will report only this version of D, which is the default method of *vocd*.

Reliability

In this section we investigate two aspects of the reliability of scores obtained from random sampling without replacement. The first is their stability when the same data are run through the software on more than one occasion, and the second is the internal consistency of D.

Stability

As we have pointed out in Chapter 3, any procedure that randomly samples words will give a different result each time. The *vocd* software is designed to minimise these differences by calculating the TTR for each point on the TTR versus token curve from 100 samples and by carrying out the modelling procedure three times and outputting the average D from these (see specimen printout from *vocd* in Appendix VI). Nevertheless, we needed assurance that random sampling would not introduce an unacceptable amount of error into the procedure. In order to check this we re-ran the analysis above, from which we had obtained Ds for random sampling without replacement, using exactly the same *vocd* command line. We then compared the means, ranges, and standard deviations, and examined the test–retest correlation. The descriptive statistics shown in Table 4.5 shows that the difference between the means is not statistically significant ($t = 0.407$; $df = 37$; $p = 0.686$) and suggests that for each child the difference between each pair of scores is minimal. In addition, the rank order of the children is maintained perfectly in the second application, and the Pearson correlation is 1.00.

Internal consistency

The reliability of lexical richness scores has been investigated in a number of ways, depending on the purpose. Meara and Bell (2001) computed a parallel forms reliability coefficient for two discursive essays written less than a week apart by the same students. For children's oral language, Hess and her

Table 4.5 Descriptive statistics for test–retest of D (random sampling without replacement) and the paired differences between each application of *vocd* ($N = 38$)

	Mean	SD	Min.	Max.
1st set of D scores	46.26	17.77	6.86	86.80
2nd set of D scores	46.23	17.88	6.81	87.85
Differences between 1st and 2nd	0.03	0.49	−1.27	1.23

colleagues (Hess et al., 1986; 1989) also treated segments of transcripts consisting of 50 words as parallel forms and computed inter-correlations from these. The Spearman-Brown prophecy formula was then used by Hess and her colleagues (1986) to estimate the number of words required for reliability coefficients of 0.7, 0.8, and 0.9. The process of dividing language samples into equal sized segments on which correlational analyses can be carried out, varying the size of segments so that reliability estimates can be compared from shorter or longer samples, and following up with the Spearman-Brown procedure to estimate the reliability of a larger sample goes back at least as far as Chotlos's (1944) analysis of written scripts, although Chotlos refers to 'split half' rather than 'parallel forms' (or 'alternate forms') reliability.

We also proposed to investigate the internal consistency of D-scores using the split-half method. However, one crucial issue is how the split should be made to ensure that there are no order effects (Scholfield, 1995) and that the two halves really are equivalent (Mehrens and Lehmann, 1978). Most often, the split-half procedure has been applied to tests containing a large number of items where the scores on even-numbered items can be correlated against those for odd-numbered items, but this is not possible for open-ended tasks or naturalistic language data. This was the reason that we had developed the split-half facility for odd and even words in *vocd* that was referred to in the previous section. We therefore correlated the Ds for even- and odd-numbered words that were obtained during investigation into sensitivity to sample size. The result, as we reported in McKee, Malvern and Richards (2000) is a Pearson correlation of 0.763 ($df = 36$; $p < 0.001$).[1] As this is based on a mean number of 158 words across the half-transcripts, it compares favourably with Hess, Sefton and Landry's (1986) estimate that a sample of 350 words is needed for a minimum reliability of 0.70 for TTR-related indices. On the other hand, some caution is necessary where the two halves being correlated are not independent of each other (Scholfield, 1995). This is frequently a problem with language measures derived from unstructured activities and is likely to boost reliability estimates. Nevertheless, applying the Spearman-Brown formula to the above coefficient gives an estimated reliability of 0.866 for just over 300 words and, while this may well be an overestimate, it does give grounds for confidence in the internal consistency of the measure.

Morphemicisation

In Malvern and Richards (2000a) we showed that removing retracings (self-repetitions with, and without, correction) made a significant difference to the values of D obtained from the New England children. As expected, values were higher when retracings were removed. We now study the effect of stripping words of their inflections and compare D-values calculated for inflected forms

Table 4.6 Descriptive statistics for D (random sampling without replacement, retracing and exclude file filtered out) for inflected forms and word stems ($N = 38$)

	Mean	SD	Min.	Max.
Inflections included	46.30	17.99	4.67	85.52
Word stems	39.51	14.12	4.69	63.37

and for just the word stems. Following the CHILDES terminology, we refer to this as 'morphemicisation'. The complete command line for this analysis is:

vocd +t"*CHI" +r6 +s"* -%%" -s@exclude filename.cha

where **vocd** runs the program, **+t"*CHI"** selects the child's tier in the transcript, **+r6** removes retracings, **+s"*-%%"** strips off inflections, and **-s@exclude** removes from the analysis a list of non-words such as hesitation markers.

We would predict that D for the samples with inflections omitted will be lower, as operating only on stems will introduce greater repetition without the differences caused by the inflections. The results are given in Table 4.6.

It can be seen from Table 4.6 that omitting inflections has the predicted effect on the average values for D and this difference is highly significant ($t = 8.32$; $df = 37$; $p < 0.001$). The two measures are highly correlated ($r = 0.980$) but the magnitude of the difference between the inflected forms version and stem forms is far from trivial ($Eta^2 = 0.652$). This can be seen in the table from the difference morphemicisation makes to the maximum value, and it draws attention to the importance of adopting standard procedures if children's lexical diversity is to be compared across different studies or if they are to be assessed against norms.

Criterion-related validity[2]

If D is valid as an index of language development, it should be sensitive to age differences as well as to variation in tried and tested assessment tools. As we reported in Richards and Malvern (2004), we correlated the two versions of D with age and concurrent mean length of utterance (MLU) and with scores from vocabulary checklists completed by mothers using a forerunner of the MacArthur Communicative Development Inventory (CDI) (Fenson, Dale, Reznick, Thal, Bates, Hartung, Pethick and Reilly, 1993) when their children were 14 and 20 months old. We were able to obtain scores for productive vocabulary for 30 of the 38 children at 20 months, and both the production and receptive scores for 34 children at 14 months. Because the data for some of the analyses that follow do not meet the assumptions for parametric tests, we will only report non-parametric statistics. The full set of correlations is contained in Table 4.7.

Table 4.7 Spearman correlations between non-morphemicised and morphemicised versions of D and age and other language measures for the New England Corpus

	D-Inflected Forms			D-Stem Forms		
	rho	N	p	rho	N	p
Age	0.376	38	< 0.01	0.372	38	< 0.05
MLU (morphemes)	0.603	38	< 0.001	0.538	38	< 0.001
CDI productive, 20 months	0.327	30	< 0.05	0.248	30	ns
CDI productive, 14 months	0.302	34	< 0.05	0.302	34	< 0.05
CDI receptive, 14 months	0.276	34	ns	0.285	34	ns

The concurrent correlations between both versions of D and MLU are highly significant and moderately strong. In spite of such limited age variation in the sample (27–33 months), they are also significantly correlated with age, although slightly less so than for MLU (Age × MLU: $rho = 0.408$; $n = 38$; $p < 0.005$). The CDI scores at earlier ages are less strongly related with D, and receptive scores are not significantly related to them at all. Three correlations between D and production scores are statistically significant, but only marginally so. Nevertheless, the overall pattern of results in Table 4.7 is that, if anything, the vocabulary *production* scores rather than the comprehension scores correlate with a vocabulary diversity index that measures productive usage. This suggests that D may be tapping an important facet of spoken language.

Mann-Whitney U tests were used to test for sex and socio-economic status (SES) differences. No sex differences were found for either version of D, but for both versions there was a significant advantage for the middle-class group. For inflected forms, the mean for the middle-class group was 51.22 compared with 40.22 for the working-class children ($U = 108$; $N = 38$; $p < 0.05$). For root forms the corresponding means were 43.21 and 34.93 ($U = 104$; $N = 38$; $p < 0.05$). This pattern is replicated for MLU – as for D there were no sex differences, but like D there were higher scores for the children in the middle-class group ($U = 102$; $N = 38$; $p < 0.05$), thus providing evidence of both convergent and discriminant validity for D.

Discussion

Applying *vocd* to the files of the New England children showed that the measurement responded in predictable ways to the use of switches for omitting retracings and for confining analyses to stems rather than inflected forms. For one version of the model – random sampling without replacement – it gave reassurance that scores were not a function of the number of tokens, that they were stable across a repeated assessment of the same transcripts and showed a high degree of internal consistency.

We compared the magnitude of D-values and whether they were a function of sample size for two possible sampling methods for *vocd* in addition to the version that has since become the default, that is to say random sampling without replacement. There were significant differences between the mean D for sequential sampling and for random sampling with and without replacement. Random sampling without replacement was the only method that showed no relationship with the number of tokens in the sample. The reason for these differences merits some discussion and we will begin with a description of how the TTR versus token curve is plotted in each procedure.

The sequential sampling model fits the segment of the empirical TTR versus token curve between 35 and 50 tokens plotted at increments of one token. Each point of the curve is the mean TTR for the maximum number of segments of consecutive words obtainable for that point. For example, in a transcript of 240 words the final point of the curve (50 tokens) would be represented by the mean TTR for four consecutive segments of 50 tokens. The remaining 40 tokens would be discarded. Unlike random sampling, this method can be argued to maintain the integrity of the text. On the other hand, as discussed in Chapter 3, it is distorted by the local clustering of content words. See Baayen (1996) for an interesting account of the effect on the cumulative increase of types in a language sample caused by the tendency of the same type to appear in clusters within a text, which he attributes to 'topic cohesion in discourse'. Here, we note that sequential sampling is more likely to include in its smaller sub-samples the greater repetition caused by clustering and therefore produce smaller Ds than random sampling, which is confirmed by comparing values for the whole transcript in Tables 4.2 with those in Tables 4.3 and 4.4. On the other hand, dividing the transcript by the odd and even method is likely to split up some of the clusters and result in higher Ds for the two half (odd or even) transcripts compared to D for the whole transcript as is shown in Table 4.2.

The two methods of random sampling also confine the curve-fitting procedure described in Chapter 3 to a window of 35 to 50 tokens and all 16 of the possible points are plotted. This window represents the portion of the curve for which the approximation holds (McKee et al., 2000) and its use as a standard guards against poor fits if these limits are exceeded. Each point is calculated from the average TTR for 100 random samples drawn from the whole transcript. The only difference between them is how each of these samples is obtained. 'With replacement' means that a word already sampled is available to be sampled again. This can have two effects. First, it will depress the value for D because re-sampling the same word will reduce the number of word *types* that go into each TTR. Second, because random sampling uses words from all of the transcript, the probability of re-sampling is greater in shorter transcripts and longer transcripts will output higher Ds, which is exactly what is found in Table 4.3.

As far as D's validity as a general developmental measure and an index of early language progress is concerned, we have provided some initial supporting evidence. This includes D's correlation with age over a relatively restricted range, even though D actually correlates with age slightly less well than MLU. Its relationship with *language* development is shown by concurrent correlations with a well-validated measure such as MLU. The latter are highly significant and moderately strong. Correlations with earlier vocabulary checklist scores are only marginally significant and considerably weaker (as one might expect with measures taken 10–16 months earlier) or non-significant. But even here the pattern is interpretable, with three out of four correlations with *productive* vocabulary being significant, while both those with *receptive* scores are non-significant – an issue that will be pursued further in the next chapter. In addition, in respect of sex and SES differences the pattern of results for D is the same as for other concurrent language measures across the two corpora.

Conclusion

This chapter has provided some evidence for the reliability and validity of D-scores as an index of expressive vocabulary obtained from one method of sampling – random sampling without replacement. This method is now the default in *vocd* and in subsequent chapters this is the only form of D that will be reported. We have also shown that the use of certain switches that affect the inclusion and exclusion of word types and tokens make statistically significant and non-trivial differences to the magnitude of values even though they may be strongly inter-correlated. This is particularly true of the morphemicisation switch. Clearly, it makes sense to omit non-valid words through an 'exclude file' and to filter out retracing but, in addition, conducting analyses of young children's language on inflected forms would seem to confound the development of morphology with vocabulary diversity. In the inflected forms version of D there will be an *apparent* increase in lexical diversity once productivity of inflections enables children to apply different inflectional morphemes to a wider range of verb stems. That is something that will be explored in greater depth in Chapters 5 and 7, but for the study of children's early language development we would recommend the analysis of stem forms rather than inflected forms as a diagnostically 'purer' measure of vocabulary and for ease of comparison of results across different researchers.

Finally, our comparison of half-sized and complete transcripts suggests that Ds obtained from random sampling without replacement are not a function of sample size. This result has recently been replicated for D by

Silverman and Ratner (2002) on a sample of 30 stutterers and non-stutterers aged 35 months, but using utterances rather than words as the basis for the split-half. Neither Ds for odd-numbered nor even-numbered utterances differed from Ds for the whole sample. These researchers believe that:

> Analyses of the effect of sample length, performed by comparing half samples to whole samples, appear to suggest that *D* is not sample size sensitive.... As such, *vocd* would seem a reasonable solution to the use of *TTR* and *NDW*, both of which can be sensitive to sample size variation.
> (Silverman and Ratner, 2002, p. 301)

The same result, again using Ds for odd and even utterances compared with Ds for the whole language sample, was obtained for aphasic patients by Wright, Silverman and Newhoff (2003). Nevertheless, as we stressed above, this does not mean that there is no relationship with sample size at all. This is true in two respects. First, for more advanced speakers, a larger vocabulary and greater range of usage often goes hand in hand with greater volubility. Second, and perhaps more importantly, a greater quantity of speech is likely to contain more changes of theme and extra-linguistic context and will contain a wider range of lexis for that reason. By splitting the transcript between even- and odd-numbered words and comparing these with the whole transcript in our investigation into sample size effects, we effectively removed this factor.

By contrast, Owen and Leonard (2002) investigated the effects of sample size by comparing results for the first half of their samples to those for the whole. That is, they calculated D, TTR, and NDW for the first 250 tokens as well as for the whole 500 words in the transcripts they obtained from 41 children with SLI and 78 children developing normally. As is entirely to be expected, there were statistically significant differences in the TTRs and NDWs found for the half and whole transcripts. But, as this method of obtaining a small and a large sample does not control for the greater number of changes in topic likely in the larger sample, they also found a significant difference in the two Ds. None the less, they report that it was 'small to medium' as opposed to 'very large' for TTR and NDW (Owen and Leonard, 2002, p. 934) and conclude that:

> Because D seems as sensitive to developmental differences as other measures and it is not as heavily influenced by sample size, it deserves careful consideration as a tool in research and clinical settings.
> (p. 936)

The issue of the relationship between contexts, topics, and themes, and diversity indices strikes at the heart of our conceptualisation of what lexical diversity actually is. If we imagine two transcripts of equal length from children of equal language ability where one contains changes of speaker and other features of the extra-linguistic context such as the toys children play with, we would expect this to be reflected in their lexical diversity scores. For this reason, we concur with Owen and Leonard when they recommend 'experimental control of the topics included in the child's speech' during data collection and assessment (p. 936).

5
Early Child Language 2: the Bristol Corpus

The previous chapter used an American corpus of language data from children aged between 27 and 32 months to carry out an initial validation of procedures used in the *vocd* software and to assess the criterion-related validity of the measure D. We also examined the relationship between sample size and D-values and tested the reliability of D.

In this chapter we continue our focus on monolingual early child language development, but this time we use British data, the Bristol Corpus (Wells, 1985), that enables us to adopt a longitudinal perspective over a lengthy period. This allows further assessments of construct validity at regular intervals and the investigation of relatively long-term developmental trends in lexical diversity. It also enables us to find out whether D has any predictive validity of measures taken when the children were in the early years of secondary school. The two versions of D calculated from stems and inflected forms that were compared in Chapter 4 are now supplemented by a third version calculated from root forms or lemmas. Comparisons will be made between the Bristol and the New England children at a comparable age. Finally, the analyses will provide indicative norms, that is to say, an indication of the mean values of D together with the ranges and standard deviations that might be expected at different ages.

The Bristol Corpus

For well over a decade during the 1970s and 1980s, Gordon Wells directed a normative study of 128 pre-school children in the city of Bristol in the west of England (Wells, 1985). Two groups of children were studied longitudinally from the age of 15 months and 39 months respectively. Families were representative of the local urban population in terms of social background, sex, and the children's month of birth. However, children whose parents did not speak English as their first language, those in full-time day care, multiple births, and children with known handicaps were not included.

In the younger cohort of children ten recordings were made between the ages of 15 and 42 months. In order to obtain naturalistic, spontaneous speech data the children were recorded in their homes without the presence of an observer. This was made possible by the use of radio microphones with sufficient range to allow the children to move freely around the house and its immediate environs. The microphones were linked to a concealed tape-recorder that was pre-programmed to take 24 samples of 90 seconds' duration between the hours of 9 a.m. and 6 p.m., the aim being to obtain a minimum of 110 utterances in each recording. In theory, neither the children nor their parents knew precisely when they were being recorded.

For the current study we used the transcripts of the 32 children in the younger cohort whose files are contained in the CHILDES database (Mac-Whinney, 2000b). For these children there are nine transcripts in CHAT format, at three-monthly intervals from 18 months to 42 months. Only four transcripts out of a possible 288 are missing. For 15 children there is a further transcript made on transfer to school at five years. An extract from the transcript of one child, Jonathan, at 42 months is contained in Appendix II.

The 128 families in the original Bristol sample had been selected to fall equally into four family background groups. This was done on the basis of an index that combined scores for both the occupation and education of the mother and the father. Details of these scores and how they were combined are given in Wells (1985, p. 21–3). The distribution of our sample by sex and family background is shown in Table 5.1.

It is clear that the Bristol Corpus has many advantages for the aims outlined above. These are the representative sample of children, the naturalistic recordings obtained in the home without the presence of researchers, the longitudinal design and regular sampling over an extended period, and the lack of missing data. Nevertheless, the use of 24 pseudo-random naturalistic speech samples lasting 90 seconds has implications for the quantity of language obtained from some children. While these samples undoubtedly resulted in extremely rich data and more natural behaviour from both children and family members, there are some samples in which data are

Table 5.1 Distribution of sample by sex and family background

Family background	Sex		Total
	Girls	Boys	
Group 1 (highest)	4	4	8
Group 2	5	2	7
Group 3	3	4	7
Group 4 (lowest)	4	6	10
Total	16	16	32

extremely sparse. As will be shown below, this meant that reliable values for lexical diversity could not always be calculated. At the same time, a research design in which there is no control for situational context, activities, and the participants in the interaction can result in a wider range of contextual features and conversational topics than is usual in most child language research, and this is likely to impact on the range of vocabulary used. Values for D will therefore need to be interpreted accordingly.

Measures from the Bristol project

A further advantage of using Gordon Wells's data is the availability of language measures used in the Bristol project that can be correlated with D in order to investigate two facets of criterion-related validity: concurrent and predictive validity. The first measure is the Mean Length of Structured Utterances (MLUS) developed by Wells as an alternative to Brown's (1973) MLU. Wells excluded all 'unstructured utterances', defined as 'all utterances which have no explicitly mentioned topic' (Wells, 1975, p. 65). They comprise single word or idiomatic affirmative or negative responses ('yes', 'all right', 'OK', 'no'), idiomatic utterances and rote-learned chunks ('how do you do?'), textual quotation ('Tishoo, tishoo, all fall down'), routine formulae ('hello', 'pardon', 'please', 'peekaboo'), and exclamations ('ouch', 'Good Heavens').

In the current project we have chosen to use Wells's MLUS scores in preference to calculating new MLUs in CLAN because the original project team was meticulous in checking their reliability and MLUS has been well validated and favourably compared with the more traditional MLU (see Wells, 1985, pp. 120–5). One potential disadvantage that, as far as we are aware, has received little or no attention, is that, particularly in early recordings, some children who produce many unstructured utterances will produce no structured ones. Their MLUS is therefore zero, and this can distort distributions across the sample of children. Since the analyses reported below use non-parametric statistics such statistical problems are circumvented.

The second measure adopted from the Bristol study consists of the levels attained by the children on the Bristol Language Development Scales (BLADES) (Gutfreund, Harrison and Wells, 1989). BLADES contains scales of syntactic, semantic and pragmatic development, each divided into ten levels of attainment, and these profiles can be combined into a single ordinal measure. The items included in each scale and their relative language level are derived from an analysis of the 60 younger children in the younger cohort of the Bristol study. Criteria for the inclusion of items included their saliency (the ease with which they could be identified in spontaneous speech), frequency (items should occur frequently once they emerge in child speech), and, most importantly, order of emergence (items at each level should be strongly and statistically significantly ordered in relation to each other) (Wells, 1985). Although the correlations between scale scores and MLUS were moderate to strong in the Bristol study ($r = 0.69$ for the 60 younger children at 42 months) (Wells, 1985, p. 332), the scale appears to continue to discriminate between children at stages where MLUS is subject to ceiling effects (Wells, 1985).

The third measure we borrowed consists of the children's scores on the English Picture Vocabulary Test (EPVT) (Brimer and Dunn, 1963). EPVT is a standardised test of receptive vocabulary that was administered at the age of 39 months to the younger cohort and at five years to the older cohort. Here the correlation between the standardised EPVT scores and lexical diversity at 39 months will be examined.

Finally, in a study of the antecedents of foreign language aptitude, Skehan (1989, 1990) investigated relationships between early first language variables and a battery of measures of foreign language aptitude and attainment that were administered when the Bristol children were in the early years of secondary school. Skehan's results show that, for the younger cohort of children, first language variables such as MLUS and BLADES at 42 months, cumulative range of adjectives and determiners, sentence comprehension, and the EPVT at 39 months consistently predict foreign language aptitude scores on the battery of tests administered at the children's schools at 13–14 years (see Skehan, 1990, p. 94, Table 1). Even though receptive vocabulary is included in the analysis, what is lacking is any index of vocabulary *production*.[1] Here we test the predictive validity of D by computing correlations with each of the six aptitude tests used by Skehan. The aptitude battery consisted of:

AH2: A test of general verbal intelligence (Heim, Watts and Simmonds, 1975).

MLAT1: Modern Language Aptitude Test (Elementary), Part 1, Hidden Words (Carroll and Sapon, 1965). This test claims to tap into a combination of first language vocabulary knowledge and sound–symbol association (phonemic coding ability) by presenting misspelled English words followed by four possible meanings from which the correct one has to be selected.

MLAT2: Modern Language Aptitude Test (Elementary), Part 2, Matching Words (Carroll and Sapon, 1965). This is a test of sensitivity to the grammatical function of words. A sample sentence contains one word in upper case. The respondent has to select the word in another sentence that has the same function.

York Language Aptitude Test (Green, 1975a, 1975b). This tests the ability to induce grammatical rules from sample phrases and sentences presented in Swedish and to apply them to new linguistic contexts.

PLAB5: The Pimsleur Language Aptitude Battery (Pimsleur, 1966), Part 5, Sound Discrimination. Respondents are taught three words in Ewe, a language of the Niger-Congo family (Crystal, 1987), from a tape recording. They then have to identify which of the three words is contained in full sentences also presented from a tape.

PLAB6: The Pimsleur Language Aptitude Battery (Pimsleur, 1966), Part 6, Sound–Symbol Association. Nonsense words are presented on tape and the respondent has to identify which of four possible spellings they match.

This battery has been shown to have good powers of prediction of success in foreign language learning. In Skehan's study the tests correlated significantly, and in some cases strongly, with subsequent attainment tests in listening, speaking, reading, and writing in French or German for a subset of 23 children. The only exceptions were PLAB5, which correlated with none of the four skills, and PLAB6 which failed to correlate significantly with speaking (Skehan, 1990, p. 95, Table 2). For our investigation, scores were available from all six of the above tests for 29 out of the 32 children.

Method

The preparation of transcripts

In any investigation of lexical diversity it is essential that there is compatibility between the software, the transcription system, and the researchers' definition of what counts as a word and what is defined as a *different* word. In this case, even a cursory inspection of the files made it clear that to run them through *vocd* in their raw form would lead to so many anomalies that the validity of the measure would be compromised. After scrutinising all transcripts and obtaining complete word lists by running them through the *freq* program in CLAN (MacWhinney, 2000a) the transcripts were edited in four ways. First, inconsistencies with spelling ('doggy' versus 'doggie') and phonetic variants of the same word (for example, 'yes', 'yeah') were standardised using CHAT's text replacement facility, so that they would *not* be counted as different words. Second, homographs ('may': the month of May versus the modal verb) were tagged so that they *would* be treated as different words. Third, all 'retracing', that is to say, self-repetition of words and phrases, including repetition with self-correction was bracketed and coded so it could be excluded from analyses using the **+r6** switch in *vocd* (see the documentation for *vocd* in Appendix V). Finally, boundaries for inflectional morphemes were marked. In addition, the word lists produced by *freq* had revealed a large number of non-words that needed to be omitted. These included laughter, exclamations, hesitation/pause markers, and onomatopoeia with no referential value. All such items were listed in an 'exclude file' and filtered out by *vocd*.

The calculation of D

Values for D were obtained for each child on each occasion using the following as the command line:

vocd +t"*ABI" -s@excl.txt +r6 abigail04.cha

where *vocd* executes the program, **+t"*ABI"** selects the child speaker tier of the transcript (in this case, Abigail), **-s@excl.txt** invokes the exclude file, **+r6** filters out self-repetition, and **abigail04.cha** is the child's fourth transcript in CHAT format.

Three versions of D were obtained, the first two of which correspond with those used in the previous chapter. The first took the nouns and verbs in the files at their face value, that is to say, in their fully transcribed form. Therefore, 'fall', 'falls' (transcribed as 'fall-s') and 'fell' (transcribed as 'fall&ed') counted as three tokens and three types. We will refer to this version as 'D (inflected forms)'. The second run used the **+s"*-%%"** switch to strip off regular inflections. In the above example with 'fall', this leaves three tokens and two types. This version will be referred to as 'D (stem forms)'. The third analysis employed an additional switch (**+s"*&%%"**) which reduced irregular verbs and nouns to their root form, giving us three tokens and one type for the example above. This version will be referred to as 'D (root forms)'. Since inflected forms give rise to the most word types from a given number of tokens this will give rise to the highest values. Conversely, the D (root forms) gives the least number of word types from the same token count and will produce the lowest. There should be a clear differentiation therefore between the three versions except during stages of development where there is little or no evidence of inflectional morphology.

Results

The three versions of D

It was noted above that, for all the advantages of the Bristol data collection procedures, some samples were rather sparse. Because *vocd* carries out its curve-fitting procedure on a curve segment of 35–50 tokens, values for D could not be obtained for children who produced less than 50 valid words. The effect of this in reducing the overall sample size can be seen from the ns in Table 5.2. Wells (1985, pp. 111–13) showed that the amount of speech produced by the children increased over time, and did so dramatically between the ages of 15 and 30 months (Wells, 1985, p. 112, Figure 3.1). Consequently, we would expect the greatest loss of data to be in the earliest recordings, and this is in fact the case, with the samples at 18 and 21 months being reduced to 18 and 20 children respectively. Inevitably, it tends to be the children who are linguistically least developed who produce the fewest

82 Lexical Diversity and Language Development

Table 5.2 Descriptive statistics for D (stem forms) at each age

Age (months)	N	Mean	SD	Median	Min.	Max.
18	18	14.80	10.31	13.60	1.48	36.99
21	20	21.49	16.70	19.09	2.60	67.24
24	28	27.44	20.52	25.41	2.50	84.64
27	29	34.77	17.70	31.16	7.48	65.76
30	29	41.53	16.93	45.59	4.05	69.67
33	29	43.67	15.45	45.47	10.38	73.88
36	29	47.83	13.97	47.14	13.26	69.95
39	30	49.48	15.41	49.08	11.22	80.78
42	29	53.12	13.55	53.80	10.57	73.54
60	15	64.02	8.46	63.48	50.83	83.30

words,[2] so it is likely that at these ages the mean values for D are an overestimate of the mean for the population.

Figure 5.1 plots the mean for the three versions of D against age. For all three measures, a Friedman analysis of variance by ranks (Siegel and Castellan, 1988) shows a highly significant effect for age (inflected forms: Chi-square = 51.06, $df = 9$, $p < 0.001$; stem forms: Chi-square = 51.06, $df = 9$, $p < 0.001$; root forms: Chi-square = 49.78, $df = 9$, $p < 0.001$). Figure 5.1

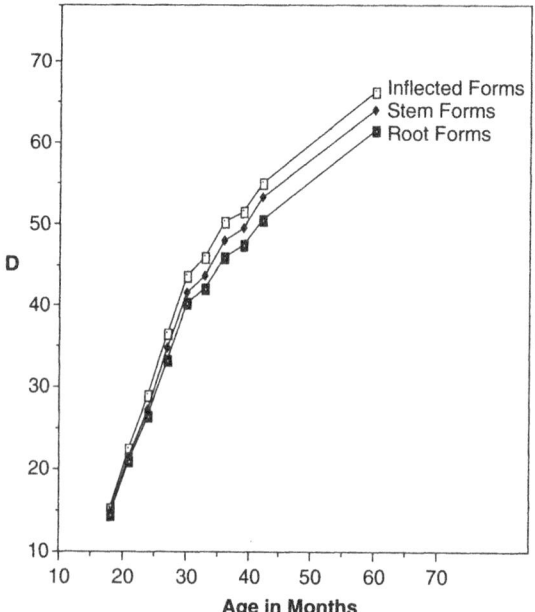

Figure 5.1 Mean D for inflected forms, stem forms, and root forms plotted against age

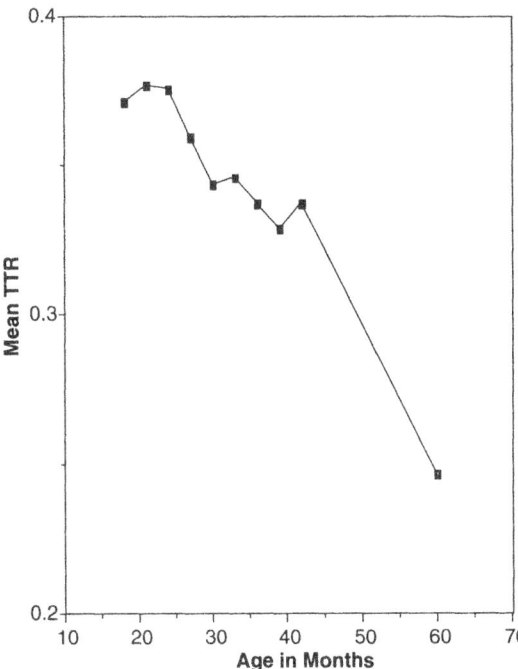

Figure 5.2 TTR plotted against age

demonstrates a consistent upward trajectory for all three versions, and the curves for all three follow a common pattern with an early sharp rise from 18 to 30 months, followed by a continuing steady increase. Interestingly, a corresponding plot for the TTR (Figure 5.2) shows not just that it fails as a developmental measure but that it actually shows a strong tendency to decrease over time. Any real gains in vocabulary richness have been totally overwhelmed by the increasing size of language samples as children get older, vividly demonstrating the flaw in calculating TTRs from samples standardised by the length of recording.

The relative position of the three curves in Figure 5.1 bears out the expectations above, with the inflected forms being highest, and the root forms the lowest. These differences are barely discernible at 18 months and are relatively small at 21 months when little inflectional morphology is apparent. Over time, however, the gap between the three versions widens as an increasing repertoire of inflections is applied to a broader range of verbs and nouns. A Wilcoxon matched pairs signed ranks test was used at each age to test whether the three measures differed significantly from each other. As might be expected, there were no differences at 18 months and the difference between the stem form and the root form was not significant at 21 months. Otherwise all differences between all three versions were highly significant at $p < 0.001$.

The widening gap between these versions of D and its relationship with morphology suggests that difference scores, particularly between inflected forms and stem forms may themselves provide a valid index of early grammatical development and this is a theme that is pursued further in Chapter 7. Nevertheless, and despite the differences in mean values, the developmental trajectories of the three versions are sufficiently similar for us to question whether they complement each other with worthwhile information about the development of lexical diversity. That they do not is confirmed by the size of their inter-correlations. For the data pooled across subjects and occasions these approach unity (inflected forms x stem forms: *rho* = 0.997; inflected forms x root forms: *rho* = 0.996; stem forms x root forms: *rho* = 0.997). When inter-correlations are computed separately at each age, these range from 0.971 to 0.998. Inter-correlations for individual children across recordings are all above 0.9, except for two children who provided too few data points and one child whose correlation between stem forms and root forms was 0.886. Because of the magnitude and consistency of the relationship between the three versions of D, only one (stem forms) will feature in the rest of this chapter. Stem forms is chosen as the version least likely to confound lexical diversity and the development of morphology.

D (stem forms)

Descriptive statistics

Table 5.2 shows descriptive statistics for stem forms at each age. The steady increase in mean values is accompanied by corresponding and comparable increases in the median except between 30 and 33 months. Standard deviations initially rise and then fall, with the lowest value occurring at 60 months. Minimum and maximum values also tend to increase over time although there is a surprisingly high maximum value at 24 months. The pattern of development is clarified in Figure 5.3, where the average D (stems) together with percentile ranks is plotted against age.

When considering the external validity of the above values it must be remembered that lexical diversity is likely to be influenced by a number of factors such as the number of topic changes and that these in turn will be influenced by contextual factors such as the physical surroundings, nature and variety of activities, and the number and age of the participants in the interactions. In the Bristol study these were deliberately left uncontrolled, the aim being to sample a typical day in the life of each child. This is a factor that is likely to contribute to the high ranges of scores and may result in relatively high values compared with more constrained laboratory or clinical contexts. It is useful, therefore, to compare scores at 30 months with those from the 38 children (mean age 30.3 months) in the 32-month directory of the New England Corpus (Dale et al., 1989; Snow, 1989) reported in Chapter 4. Recall that this sample consists of equal numbers of boys and girls of

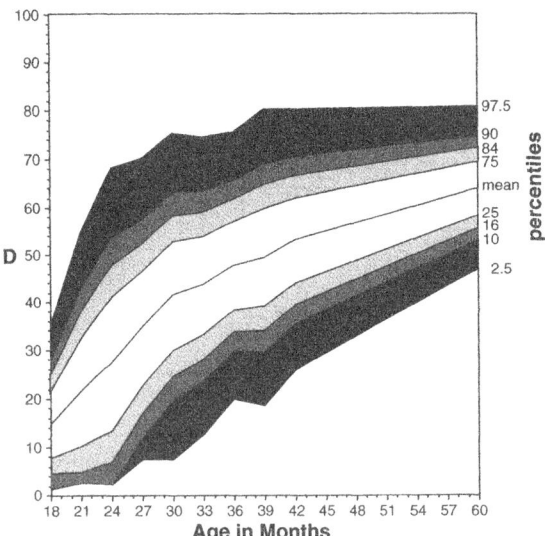

Figure 5.3 Indicative values for D (stem forms)

which 17 are working class and 21 middle class. The recordings took place in a laboratory and they sample parent and child playing with the contents of four boxes presented in succession. Recall also that the version of D used in Chapter 4 is also D (stems). Interestingly, despite the differences in geographical location and context, the means for the two samples at 30 months are very close, and the other descriptive statistics are at least comparable (New England Mean = 39.51; SD = 14.12; Median = 41.80; Min. = 4.69; Max. = 63.37). Differences tend towards slightly higher average scores and greater range in the Bristol sample but a Mann-Whitney test showed no difference between the two samples ($U = 500.0$; $N = 67$; $p = 0.5$).

Developmental trends

The Friedman tests carried out above show significant differences but this does not mean that there is a significant trend overall. The significance of the upward tendency in values for D was tested using the Page test for ordered alternatives (Page, 1963). Page's test is a non-parametric test of trends in which scores are ranked across conditions (in this case occasions of recording) for each subject. Page's L statistic is based on the sum of ranks for each occasion and its significance is related to the number of subjects and conditions. For large samples and/or a large number of conditions a z-score (z_L) can be calculated whose significance is determined by reference to the normal distribution (Siegel and Castellan, 1988). In this case, the test was conducted on the first nine recordings only. This was because of the longer interval between recordings nine and ten and the small sample size at recording ten. In handling missing data, a highly conservative method was used whereby each missing data point was replaced by the median rank of 5 across the nine occasions. This tends to bias the analysis against obtaining a significant result because most of the missing data was in recordings one and two (ranks one and two). In spite of this, the result shows a statistically significant trend across recordings ($L = 7405$; $k = 9$; $N = 32$; $z_L = 1.708$; $p < 0.05$). To see to what extent this trend held true for individual children we computed Spearman rank order correlations for each child separately between D and age. In spite of missing data and the small N, the values for Spearman's *rho* were statistically significant for 26 out of the 30 children who supplied sufficient data points to compute correlations.

Criterion-related validity
Correlations between D (stem forms) and other language measures

In order to assess *concurrent* criterion-related validity, rank order correlations were computed between D and MLUS, Bristol Scale scores, and the EPVT at each age. These will be reported in turn.

Wells's MLUS scores at 60 months were not available to us, but the overall correlation between D and MLUS for the children's data pooled across the first nine occasions is 0.752 ($N = 241$; $p < 0.001$). Separate correlations at each age are shown in Table 5.3. After the age of 18 months these are, in most cases, moderate to strong and are highly significant. On the other hand, the correlation at 60 months between D and a version of MLU calculated using CLAN was close to zero (*rho* = −0.129; $N = 15$; ns). Correlations between D and MLUS for individual children across recordings were statistically significant for 24 out of the 30 children for whom there were enough data points for a correlational analysis.

Table 5.3 Rank order correlations between D (stem forms) and other language measures at each age

Age (months)	MLUS	Scale Score	N
18	0.340	0.381	18
21	0.585**	0.636***	20
24	0.673***	0.738***	28
27	0.689***	0.692***	29
30	0.755***	0.747***	29
33	0.473**	0.546***	29
36	0.333*	0.422*	29
39	0.558***	0.615***	30
42	0.544***	0.255	29

*$p < 0.05$; ** $p < 0.01$; *** $p < 0.001$

Bristol Scale scores were not available at 60 months, but the overall correlation between D and the scale for the data pooled across the first nine occasions is 0.765 ($N = 241$; $p < 0.001$). Separate correlations at each age are shown in Table 5.3. These follow a similar pattern to MLUS except at 42 months where the result is not significant. As with MLUS, 24 out of 30 correlations for individual children are statistically significant.

The correlation between D and the standardised EPVT scores at 39 months was also computed. This was weak and non-significant ($rho = 0.218$; $N = 26$; ns).

Finally, in Chapter 4 we found that the presence or absence of sex and social class differences in the New England children's D scores was matched by the results for MLU. In this chapter we wished to see whether any group differences for sex and family background in the D values of the Bristol children were mirrored in their scores on MLUS, BLADES, and EPVT. Mann-Whitney U tests and the Kruskal-Wallis one-way analysis of variance were used to test for sex and family background respectively in D and BLADES. Independent t-tests and one-way ANOVAs were conducted for MLUS and the standardised EPVT scores. There were no differences between boys and girls on any variable. Only one significant result was obtained for family background, and that was an effect for EPVT receptive vocabulary scores ($F(3,23) = 3.86$; $p < 0.025$; $Eta^2 = 0.335$). The absence of sex and family background differences for D means that it is not necessary to report trends and indicative norms, or repeat validity analyses separately for each group.

Stability of scores over time and predictive validity

Values for D were available for children at ten different ages, but to correlate all of these with each of the six language aptitude measures would produce a large set of results that would be difficult to interpret and would be likely to include results that were statistically significant by chance. Instead, we opted to combine the D values from different recordings for each child, and to do so in a way that maximised the reliability of the final scale. A precedent for doing this with the Bristol data is a study by Croll (1995) that used both the younger and older cohorts to investigate the relationship between early language measures (MLUS and EPVT), family background, and performance in school examinations at the age of 16 years. For MLUS, Croll standardised the scores from each occasion of recording as z scores and used the mean z score as the index for each child. Reliability was measured by Cronbach's coefficient alpha (Cronbach, 1951), an index frequently applied to educational and psychological tests that consist of items that are not scored dichotomously (Mehrens and Lehmann, 1978).

In Croll's study, alpha was 0.79 for the older cohort ($N = 53$) and 0.86 for the younger cohort ($N = 48$) (Croll, 1995, pp. 16–17). We adopted a similar procedure to Croll, but first of all we needed to replace missing values. This was carried out by using the mean for each occasion. This method of replacing missing values has both disadvantages and advantages – on the one hand, it reduces the variance and may distort the distribution. On the other hand, it is objective and conservative, the reduction in variance tending to attenuate correlations (Duffy and Jacobson, 2001). We then computed z scores at each age and used alpha to assess reliability. The alpha coefficient normally measures the internal consistency, equivalence or homogeneity of the items in a test. It could be argued, however, that reliability needs to be conceptualised slightly differently here since there is an element of stability of scores over time, something normally measured by a test-retest coefficient (Satterly, 1989). Perhaps the best analogy for the use of alpha here is that the combined assessment of D at ten age points is similar to a test containing ten items that measure the same latent trait but vary in difficulty (Croll, personal communication). Unlike Croll, however, we reduced the number of variables, that is to say age points, to obtain the highest possible reliability before calculating the mean z score for the remaining recordings.

As column 1 of Table 5.4 shows, the alpha coefficient when all ten recordings are included is 0.800, which is very close to Croll's value for MLUS for the older cohort, but is rather lower than for the younger group. We were particularly concerned about the reliability of the first recordings and at five years because of the amount of missing data. Table 5.4 also shows the item-total correlation for each point, that is to say the correlation between the standardised scores for a particular age and the combined scale. These are of interest, not just because they indicate occasions that may need to be omitted from the overall D scale, but because of the information they provide about the relative reliability of the separate D scores at different ages.

Table 5.4 Item–total correlations and alpha coefficients for standardised D scores

Age in Months	Item-Total Correlations			
	Scale Including All 10 Age Points	Scale Excluding 5 Years Only	Scale Excluding 18 Months Only	Scale Excluding 18 Months and 5 Years
18	0.310	0.295	–	–
21	0.514	0.527	0.450	0.459
24	0.566	0.579	0.503	0.511
27	0.558	0.542	0.535	0.515
30	0.798	0.815	0.820	0.837
33	0.559	0.623	0.570	0.638
36	0.553	0.524	0.620	0.590
39	0.353	0.368	0.397	0.416
42	0.380	0.363	0.409	0.391
60	0.181	–	0.165	–
Alpha	0.800	0.815	0.801	0.822

Table 5.5 Pearson correlations between D (21–42 months) and later language aptitude tests

Aptitude Measure	r	N	p (1-Tailed)
Verbal reasoning (AH2)	0.242	29	ns
MLAT Part 1 (hidden words)	0.078	29	ns
MLAT Part 2 (grammatical sensitivity)	0.089	29	ns
York Test (inductive rule learning)	0.117	29	ns
PLAB Part 5 (sound discrimination)	0.439	29	<0.01
PLAB Part 6 (sound–symbol association)	0.636	29	<0.001

Column 1 in Table 5.4 shows the item–total correlations for all ten recordings and seems to confirm doubts about D at 60 months. This is the only correlation that is not statistically significant. Omitting this occasion from the scale results in a slight increase in reliability to 0.815 (see column 2) but it can be seen that the correlation at 18 months is also particularly weak and only marginally significant. Removing the 18 months and including 60 months offers little advantage in terms of reliability over the original scale with ten sets of scores. This can be seen in column 3 where alpha is 0.801. The highest alpha (0.822) is obtained by removing both the 18- and 60-month scores and this can be observed in column 4.

The final D measure that was used for correlations with the aptitude tests therefore consisted of the mean z scores between the ages of 21 and 42 months. The results are shown in Table 5.5, where it can be seen that there are highly significant correlations with the two Pimsleur tests (PLAB5 and PLAB6). Otherwise, no results even approach significance and three correlations are close to zero. The importance of this finding will be discussed below.

Discussion

This chapter has reported indicative values for D and provided further evidence of the reliability of the procedures that produce it and of the validity of the measure itself. Three versions of D, based on unedited forms, stem forms, and root forms were compared and, while their means differed reliably and in the expected direction, they were found to have a very similar developmental trajectory and to be very highly inter-correlated. Nevertheless, the widening differences between the measures over time are a clear reflection of the children's morphological development, or, more precisely, the application of an increasing range of inflectional morphemes to a widening range of stems, however this may be interpreted. This is a theme that we will pursue further in Chapter 7.

Because of such high inter-correlations, further analyses were based on stem forms only. This can be regarded as the 'purest' of the three measures in as far as it depends primarily on lexical diversity without confounding with morphological development. We presented descriptive statistics for a sample of children representative of an urban population in south-west England and demonstrated a significant developmental trend overall and significant correlations with age for 26 out of 30 children. This contrasts sharply with a downward trend for TTR. These analyses provide a graphic illustration of how true gains in vocabulary development can be so swamped by age-related increases in the quantity of speech produced in a set time period that children with low lexical diversity receive high TTR scores and vice versa.

With regard to the external validity of the D values, we acknowledge that missing data from children who produced little speech means that at the first two age points (18 and 21 months) the average scores may be higher than the true mean for the population. We were also concerned about the influence of context on lexical diversity scores. The uncontrolled situational context in the Bristol study may have given rise to higher scores than laboratory or clinical situations, where more constrained activities reduce the number of topic changes and hence the diversity of vocabulary. Nevertheless, a comparison with children in the New England Corpus at 30 months showed average scores that, while indeed slightly higher for the Bristol children, were not significantly different. Nevertheless, this result should perhaps be treated cautiously in the light of a recent publication by Hamilton, Plunkett and Schafer (2000) that compares results from their Oxford Communicative Development Inventories (CDI) on British children with those of the MacArthur CDI (Fenson et al., 1993). Their comparison shows up large and consistent differences in favour of US children between 1;0 and 2;1 for both productive and receptive vocabulary. These differences were totally unexpected and are unexplained, and one must be careful in their interpretation, but if Hamilton and colleagues' findings reflect a real difference between populations in the two countries it is possible that the method of data collection in the Bristol study assisted the British children to obtain D scores that were comparable to those of the New England children at the same age. This, of course, leads to another caveat – whereas the Bristol children were all recorded at 30 months, or very close to it, for New England 30 months is the average age of children who varied from 27 to 32 months. In any case, it must be stressed that further research is needed into the effect of contextual factors on the measurement of lexical diversity.

We also investigated the extent to which D (stem forms) correlated with other language measures at different ages and, wherever possible, across ages for individual children. With MLUS there are highly significant, moderate to strong correlations with D at most ages and significant correlations for most individual children. The exceptions are at 18 months and five years. Naturally, these are the ages with the smallest sample of children, which reduces the power of the study to detect significant effects, but, as can be seen from

Table 5.2, they are also the ages at which D has the lowest range and standard deviation. In addition, they are the occasions with the lowest item–total correlations for the combined scale for D across all ten ages, and an inspection of Table 5.5 suggests that the lack of significant correlations, at least at 18 months is due to something other than the sample size. This is indicated by the relatively high item–total correlation at 21 months when the sample size was hardly larger than at 18 months. So it is possible that D is simply less reliable at 18 months,[3] although the corresponding sets of MLU scores also have the lowest ranges and standard deviations at these ages, which may be another factor that attenuated the correlations. It should be noted that at five years we are not really comparing like with like because Wells's scores were not available and we used an MLU calculated from CLAN, which is likely to produce lower, and probably less reliable, values than MLUS. Nevertheless, it does seem likely that by this age MLU is unable to discriminate reliably between children. This is borne out by Wells's combined analysis of his older and younger cohorts (Wells, 1985, p. 123, Table 3.3) which strongly suggests that both MLUS and Brown's (1973) MLU cease to show developmental trends by 54 months.

A very similar pattern is found for correlations between D and the Bristol scale – these are statistically significant for the majority of individual children and are highly significant and moderate to strong in magnitude on most occasions of recording. Again, there is no significant correlation at 18 months, but in addition to the points made above, an examination of the frequency distribution of scale scores for the 18 children who went into this analysis shows that eight were tied on Level 2 and five were tied on Level 3. It seems that for this sub-sample of the Bristol cohorts the scale fails to discriminate well at such an early age. The other age at which D failed to correlate with the scale was 42 months, in spite of the larger sample of 29. D correlates well with MLUS at this point, so the reason seems likely to lie in the distribution of scale scores rather than with D. The fact that 22 out of the 29 children are clustered at Levels 7 and 8 of the scale supports this interpretation.

It may seem surprising that there was no correlation with the EPVT as, unlike MLUS and the Bristol scale, this is specifically targeted towards vocabulary. On the other hand, D measures how diversely one's vocabulary resources are *deployed* and may be more related to productive language than assessments of receptive vocabulary like EPVT. This is supported by the analysis of the New England data reported in Chapter 4. A weak but statistically significant correlation was found between D at 30 months and MacArthur Communicative Development Inventory (CDI) (Fenson et al., 1993) production scores at 14 months, but there was no correlation with receptive vocabulary. Interestingly, Silverman and Ratner (2002) in a study of 15 children who stutter and 15 fluent peers also found that D correlated significantly ($r = 0.48; p = 0.01$) with the *Expressive One-Word*

Picture Vocabulary Test – Revised but not with the *Peabody Picture Vocabulary Test*, a standardised test of receptive vocabulary ($r = 0.33$; $p = 0.08$). A supplementary reason for the lack of any relationship between D and EPVT in the Bristol sample, however, may lie in the contrasting situations in which the data were collected – spontaneous speech sampling versus a relatively formal testing situation. Wells (1985, p. 333) found that correlations between measures of spontaneous speech and EPVT were relatively low at both 42 and 60 months for the Bristol cohorts and he comments on the greater likelihood of children in the lower family background group being more ill at ease in the testing situation. This view is supported by a higher correlation between family background and EPVT than with spontaneous speech measures (Wells, 1985, p. 459), and the fact that in our own analyses of family background differences the only significant result was for the EPVT.

At this point it is worth repeating that the lack of sex and family background differences in the analysis of D matched the results from MLUS and BLADES. In other words, it behaved the same as the other measures derived from spontaneous speech rather than formal testing. This is not inconsistent with Wells's results for the whole of the younger Bristol cohort. First, Wells and his colleagues found no reliable differences between boys and girls on any spontaneous speech measures (Wells, 1985, p. 345). Second, with regard to family background effects in the larger and slightly more heterogeneous sample, Wells has argued that these are relatively weak and that any significant results he did obtain were carried by children at the extremes of the distribution on both family background and language variables (Wells, 1985, p. 346–50). In addition, in a sample of 48 of the younger children Croll (1995) found no relationship between MLUS and family background and only a weak relationship for 53 children in the older cohort.

With regard to predictive validity we found that a composite measure of vocabulary diversity from the ages of 21 months to 42 months correlated highly significantly and at a moderately strong level with the two tests in the Pimsleur Language Aptitude Battery taken by the children at 13–14 years. We had expected that the strongest correlations would be with factors of aptitude that were sensitive to the processes of vocabulary learning such as sound–symbol association rather than grammar. To a certain extent this was borne out by the results – correlations with grammatical sensitivity and grammatical rule induction were close to zero, and the correlation with verbal reasoning, though positive, was non-significant. One result that may seem surprising at first is the significant correlation with PLAB5, a test that is labelled 'sound discrimination'. On closer examination, however, PLAB5 requires considerably more than the ability to discriminate between sounds. In fact the sequence involved in producing the correct answer includes several processes that would be required for the acquisition of first language vocabulary, as can be seen from the following breakdown of the stages required to produce a correct response:

1 hearing three unknown Ewe words in a tape recording that differ only in their final consonant and being able to discriminate between them;
2 associating the phonological representation of each word with the meaning (also presented from the tape);
3 hearing the target words in Ewe sentences, segmenting, and correctly identifying the target word;
4 retaining the target word in memory and supplying its meaning.

What is perhaps more difficult to explain is that there was such a strong correlation with PLAB6 (sound–symbol association) and none at all with MLAT Part 2 (hidden words) when both require the sounds to be linked with symbols and where MLAT2 is claimed to measure native language vocabulary (Skehan, 1990). Again, it is worth looking at exactly what the children had to do for each task. In the MLAT hidden words task they had to read a misspelled word (for example, 'rnj') and match it with one of four possible meanings ('shelter', 'washcloth', 'a kind of fruit', 'spy'). PLAB6, on the other hand, presented nonsense words from a tape and required children to match the sounds they heard to one of four alternative written representations (for example, 'krimsloder', 'krilsmoder', 'klimsroder', 'klidsmoder'). Therefore, MLAT2 starts with phonemic coding of the target word and the four alternatives but awareness of the possible semantic representations may modify the original phonological representation. By contrast, PLAB6 begins with a stable phonological representation that is held in memory until it is matched with the correct symbol. Although both processes necessitate reading, MLAT appears to be much more heavily dependent on skills related to literacy, whereas PLAB6 is a more straightforward matching task. It may be no coincidence, therefore, that the two measures that are predicted by D are those where the stimuli are presented aurally. In commenting on the correlations between aptitude and early language measures Skehan (1990) notes that the two PLAB tests were least well predicted by the early language measures. Since the latter contained no measure of vocabulary *production*, it is not inconceivable that D provides a useful supplement to Skehan's measures. What is also interesting is that where the PLAB tests did show significant relationships in Skehan's study, it tended to be with sentence comprehension and vocabulary.

Conclusion

In this chapter we have supplied further evidence of the criterion-related validity of one version of D as a measure of expressive vocabulary in terms of both concurrent and predictive validity. We have also shown its relationship with age, and demonstrated the stability of children's scores over time, and particularly between 21 and 42 months, by means of a reliability analysis using alpha coefficients. Finally, we have provided some indication of the averages, variance and ranges of values to be expected in the spontaneous speech of young children between the ages of 18 months and five years. While data from such a small sample certainly cannot be regarded as norms, they can serve as a valuable reference point for those wishing to use D as an index of early lexical diversity.

6
Lexical Diversity and the Investigation of Accommodation in Foreign Language Proficiency Interviews[1]

In this chapter we continue to investigate the validity of D as a measure of lexical diversity and will demonstrate its application as a solution to a measurement problem in a new context: a study of oral language assessment procedures using data from teenagers learning a foreign language. Previous research into language proficiency interviews by Richards and Malvern (2000) found that the aspect of teachers' language in oral interviews that adapted most to the ability of their students was lexical diversity. The analysis reported here focuses on this finding in greater depth using the new measure, D, rather than the mean segmental type–token ratio (MSTTR) that had been used in the previous analysis. We will investigate the relationship between D and other measures of foreign language proficiency and compare the Ds of students and teachers as well as computing correlations between teachers' D and measures of the students' proficiency to judge the extent to which the teachers finely tune their own language to the language level of individual students.

Background: the oral interview

There has been much discussion of the validity of the oral interview as a means of assessing second language proficiency. A major factor in these discussions is the extent to which, both in theory and practice, the interview resembles natural conversation (see He and Young, 1998, for an introduction and overview of the issues). Van Lier (1989) claimed that the language proficiency interview lacked features of real conversation because of the power differential between participants and the fact that the elicitation of language had the highest priority. Later research into oral interviews suggested that, while they do indeed show structural similarities to conversations (Lazaraton, 1992) or are even 'authentic instances of talk-in-interaction' (Moder and Halleck, 1998, p. 144), there is an asymmetry of control over, and contribution to, the interaction (Young and Milanovic, 1992). For example, it is the testees who show greater conversational contingency or 'reactiveness' to their interlocutor, and the testers who show more goal orientation (Young and Milanovic, 1992). The interviewers have greater influence over the choice of topic (Johnson and Tyler, 1998; Moder and Halleck, 1998) and the management of turn-taking differs from natural conversations (Lazaraton, 1992; Johnson and Tyler, 1998; Moder and Halleck, 1998).

By contrast, some researchers have turned their attention to accommodation in language proficiency interviews as a feature of authentic conversation. Accommodation theory attempts to account for processes by which the speech of participants in linguistic interaction converges or diverges in a systematic way – that is to say, how the speech of one person becomes more similar to, or different from, that of a conversational partner. Convergent accommodation can be the result of a desire for social approval or the need to improve the efficiency of communication (see Thakerar, Giles and Cheshire, 1982). It can therefore be seen as encompassing the simplification and discourse adjustments made to young children acquiring their first language in the so-called 'motherese' or 'child-directed speech' register (see Pine, 1994, for an overview). This would include the 'fine-tuning hypothesis' (e.g. Cross, 1977) whereby maternal language is claimed to be optimally matched to the child's stage of linguistic and communicative development. In second language research accommodative processes in conversations between native speakers and non-native speakers and in language classrooms have been identified as 'foreigner talk' or 'language teacher talk' (see Wesche, 1994; Gass and Varonis, 1985).

Foreigner talk modifications have also been found to be a characteristic of language proficiency interviews (Ross, 1992; Ross and Berwick, 1992; Lazaraton, 1996). Lazaraton (1996) argues that the kinds of linguistic and interactional support she identified in interviews are indeed features of conversations, but that in the context of the test, their impact on candidates' ratings is unclear. Little is known about the factors in the candidate that trigger such adjustments in the tester. Ross (1992) and Ross and Berwick (1992) were able to demonstrate that the frequency and extent of accommodation was related, that is to say, (finely) tuned to the proficiency level of the interviewees. These authors suggested that the degree of interviewer accommodation could be used as an additional dimension in the assessment of candidates. Furthermore, they argued that major threats to the validity of the interview test would be, first, a lack of appropriate accommodation to the proficiency of students on the part of the teacher-examiner and, second, over-accommodation which fails to allow candidates to demonstrate the full extent of their proficiency.

It is notable that much of the research referred to above has been conducted in contexts where examiners were native speakers of the target language, usually English. It is frequently the case, however, that for many other languages taught in the educational systems of a large number of countries, the teacher-examiners themselves learnt the target language as a foreign language and that there is huge variation in their L2 proficiency. In an earlier study into discourse and linguistic accommodation in oral interviews with 34 teenage learners of French, Richards and Malvern (2000) investigated whether teachers who were *not* native speakers would accommodate their language to the foreign language proficiency of their students. They found that, while on some teacher variables such as various kinds of teacher repetition of the students' utterances, accommodation to *individual* students does occur, other aspects of the teachers' language are more grossly tuned to the general level of ability of the language class. One particularly large effect involved the lexical diversity of teachers. Of all the measures of teachers' language, it was their vocabulary diversity that was most strongly related to the average ability of the class they taught. In fact, 60 per cent of the variance in teachers' vocabulary diversity was explained by the language class to which the students belonged.

As might be expected at this age, there was wide variation in the quantity of speech produced by the students in the Richards and Malvern (2000) study and the problem of calculating lexical diversity from varying sample sizes was addressed by using the mean segmental type–token ratio (MSTTR), an index that has already been referred to in Chapter 2 and appears to have been originally recommended by Johnson (1944). Since then it has been used in many different kinds of linguistic investigation, including normal spoken language (Fairbanks, 1944), students' L1 writing (Mann, 1944), schizophrenia (Manschreck et al., 1981), aphasiology (Wachal and Spreen, 1973), historical documents (Carpenter and Hersh, 1985), and foreign language learning (Meara, 1978). MSTTR is the average TTR for successive segments of text containing a standard number of word tokens. For the teachers in the oral interview study their transcripts were divided into segments of 100 words (MSTTR-100). Many of the students, however, contributed fewer than 100 words to their five-minute conversation, and their standard segment size had to be set as low as 30 words (MSTTR-30) in order that those who said the least could still be included in the analysis.

There are two clear advantages to MSTTR: it removes the problem of variation in sample size and it also wastes less data and is likely to ensure higher reliability than if all analyses were performed on a standard number of words achieved by reducing all transcripts to the length of the shortest. Nevertheless, at least five problems remain. First, MSTTRs calculated from different sizes of standard segment are not directly comparable, because larger segments will tend to give lower TTRs. Second, very short segments (even those of 100 tokens) are likely to distort results because they are not sensitive to repetition of words beyond the boundary of their own segment.[2] Third, transcripts do not usually divide exactly into standard-sized segments. This results in at least some loss of data. Fourth, the relationship between number of types and number of tokens for any individual sample of speech or writing is a dynamic one. That is to say, an MSTTR value represents only a single point on a curve representing the way in which TTR falls with increasing token size for that sample. Finally, it is worth noting that in the Richards and Malvern (2000) study the variation in MSTTR for both teachers and students was very small compared with other measures, raising the possibility that this might have attenuated correlations.

The measure D overcomes these disadvantages. Like MSTTR it is not a function of sample size, thus allowing valid comparisons between speakers or writers who produce varying quantities of linguistic data. In addition, because *vocd* takes numerous random samples from the whole of a transcript, it takes account of both long-distance and short-distance repetition, and no data remain unused. Finally, it is more informative because it is representative of the whole of the TTR versus token curve rather than just a single point on it.

The development of *vocd* now makes it possible to obtain D values directly from the original transcripts of the 34 learners of French as a foreign language and from their teachers. These analyses have two purposes. First, they allow the properties of D to be explored and further validated on a new type of data. Second, we would predict that D provides a more powerful tool than MSTTR to investigate whether or not non-native speaking teacher-examiners accommodate their lexical diversity to *individual* students, and whether in the Richards and Malvern (2000) study MSTTR simply lacked the sensitivity to detect this.

Method

The data are derived from the audio-tapes of 34 British secondary school students taking their oral examination in French for the General Certificate of Secondary Education (GCSE). The GCSE is a national examination taken by school students in Britain at the age of 16. Our focus is on the oral interviews, described in the documentation of the examining group that oversaw the tests as 'free conversation', although the tapes contain other oral tasks such as role-plays. The interviews averaged just over five minutes in length, and had been conducted by two teachers of French, both of whom tested their own students. Unlike many other summative oral language tests conducted at key points in students' education, the GCSE regulations require that candidates are both tested, and their performance simultaneously scored, not by a stranger, but by their own class teacher. While this, inevitably, reduces the generalisability of the research reported here, the fact that this procedure exists in a national examination system makes it an important context for investigation.

The teachers had learnt French as a foreign language but were experienced and well qualified, and both had a successful record of preparing students for the GCSE examination and of conducting and assessing the oral interview. As noted above, each teacher examined the students in his or her own French class. The interviews were transcribed in CHAT format (MacWhinney, 2000a) by a native French speaker (Francine Chambers) who was also an experienced teacher of French to English-speaking children of this age. They were all subsequently retranscribed by Brian Richards. Discrepancies were resolved with the assistance of a near-native speaker of French who was also an experienced teacher of French as a foreign language in Britain. A final check of all transcription and CHAT coding was carried out by an undergraduate student of French. Where discrepancies could not be resolved, the utterance or word was coded as 'unintelligible' and excluded from the data. In addition to allowing analysis by *vocd*, CHAT format also enabled further computer-assisted analyses to be carried out by the other CLAN programs of the CHILDES project (MacWhinney, 2000a). The 34 transcripts are available to other researchers by selecting 'reading.zip' in the TalkBank database (http://talkbank.org/data/SLA) where accompanying documentation is also available. An example of a complete transcript is provided in Appendix III.

The students

The 34 school students attended a non-selective ('comprehensive') 11–18 secondary school in the state sector located in a working-class area of a small town in the south-west of the UK. They had been learning French for five years, receiving four 35-minute lessons per week. In theory, the weakest students were not included in this sample – their teachers had entered them all for the more advanced ('higher level') version of the GCSE examination rather than the 'basic level', and their final combined grades for French, which included scores for listening, speaking, reading, and writing, ranged from 'A' to 'E' with no students obtaining the lowest pass grades of 'F' and 'G'. Nevertheless, their proficiency varied widely, ranging from students who made very little contribution to the conversation to one who performed at a level comparable with a native-speaker.[3] An impression of the general standard can be gleaned from the sample transcript in Appendix II which is of the student with the median score for the oral test and whose score is also closest to the mean for the total marks in the final examination. As noted above, the lowest number of words spoken in what, according to the regulations, was intended to be a five-minute conversation was a mere 35 and in practice the length of the conversation varied between three and 12 minutes. An indication of the huge variation between the students in the quantity of speech they produced is given in Table 6.1 by the standard deviation for the number of words they spoke (166.5 for a mean of 183.6 words). The range was from 35 to 808 words. The student who performed at near native-speaker level scored the maximum possible number of points for listening, speaking, reading, and writing in the GCSE examination. He also obtained extreme values on various other measures and for this reason, and because of the restricted range of some of the student measures reported below, non-parametric statistics are used for all statistical tests in which he is

Table 6.1 Student variables ($N = 34$)

Student Measure	Mean	SD
Number of words	183.6	166.5
Number of different words	85.1	56.2
MSTTR-30	22.8	1.7
Mean length of utterance (MLU words)	4.6	2.1
Utterances per turn (MLT)	1.1	0.1
Percentage unintelligible words	0.02	0.02
Words per minute	29.8	16.8
Type–token ratio (TTR)	0.5	0.1
GCSE examination results		
Score for oral examination (out of 7)	4.1	1.3
GCSE points (out of 28)	18.1	4.6
Mean ratings from 24 teachers of French		
Range of vocabulary (0–7)	2.8	1.7
Fluency (0–7)	2.7	1.6
Complexity of structure (0–7)	2.2	1.5
Content (0–3)	1.5	0.8
Accuracy (0–3)	1.2	0.6
Pronunciation (0–3)	1.3	0.6

included. Twelve students were interviewed by Teacher A and 22 by Teacher B. The school operates a policy of grouping students according to ability from the first year of foreign language study, with the regular possibility of promotion or demotion into lower or higher ability groups. Students had been assigned to Teacher A's or Teacher B's class on this basis.

Student variables

Three categories of student variable and their means and standard deviations are listed in Table 6.1. First, there are the objective measures obtained directly from the transcripts. These are: total number of words (TNW), number of different words (NDW), and MSTTR-30 as measures of lexical diversity with TTR included for the sake of comparison; mean length of utterance in words (MLU) as a measure of utterance complexity; mean number of utterances per turn (MLT) to indicate the degree of participation in the dialogue; a measure of intelligibility; and the mean number of words per minute (WPM) as an indicator of fluency. The objective measures were extracted either entirely automatically (as with TNW, NDW, TTR, MLU, and MLT) using the CLAN software, or with the assistance of CLAN (MSTTR-30, WPM, and percentage of unintelligible words). The second group of variables consists of the final results of the GCSE examination itself. The examining group had converted the students' scores on each of the four skills to a mark out of seven. Here we report the score out of seven for the oral examination and the total examination score out of 28.

Third, six further measures were obtained from the mean ratings of the tape recordings by 24 experienced teachers of French who carried out assessments on two occasions one month apart. Range of Vocabulary, Fluency, and Complexity of Structure were rated on eight-point scales (0–7) and Content, Accuracy, and Pronunciation on four-point scales (0–3). These measures were chosen because at that time they were all included in the oral examination criteria for the various GCSE examination groups (Chambers and Richards, 1992) and had been applied in a wider investigation into the reliability of oral assessment in modern foreign languages (Chambers and Richards, 1993, 1995; Richards and Chambers, 1996). Further details of the scales and the procedures used can be found in Richards and Chambers (1996).

In addition, using *vocd*, values of D were obtained for both the teachers (one D value for each student they tested, totalling 34 Ds) and for the students. As an illustration of the *vocd* command line, the following was used for the teachers:

vocd +t"*TEA" -s@ttrexclu +r6 -s"[+ bch]" w01.cha

where:

vocd	executed the program;
+t"*TEA"	limited the analysis to the teacher's speaker tier;
-s@ttrexclu	filtered out a list of unwanted items such as English and, sometimes, German words, pause markers and laughter that were held in an exclude file called "ttrexclu";
+r6	removed retracings (self-repetitions);
-s"[+ bch]"	filtered out the content of utterances coded as 'back channels';
w01.cha	was the filename for the first oral interview.

The exclusion of teachers' back channels deserves some explanation. Our definition of 'back channel' is that they are contributions that consist of nothing more than 'oui', 'mm', 'mm hmm', and similar utterances and function to signal continuing interest, attention or understanding (see Schegloff, 1982, p. 78). Our teachers, and all the other UK teacher-examiners whose tapes we have listened to, utter large quantities of these, presumably in order to give encouragement to their students in the stressful situation of a public examination. This can be observed in the sample transcript in Appendix II. To include back channels in our analyses would have two undesirable effects. First, it would substantially depress the lexical diversity scores for the teachers. Second, they would be counted as conversational turns, and would have distorted the students' MLT calculations by artificially reducing turn length.

Seven students produced fewer than 50 word tokens in their oral interview and for these no D values could be calculated. Sample size for analyses involving the students' D is therefore limited to 27. For all other analyses the sample is 34. For the 27 students the mean value for D is 56.9 ($SD = 16.3$); for the 34 Ds calculated for the two teachers, the mean value for D is 44.9 ($SD = 9.6$). The comparison between student and teacher Ds will be discussed below, but first we address the convergent and divergent (discriminant) validity of D by examining the correlation between student Ds and other measures of their language.

Results

The students

Rank order correlations between students' D and other student variables are presented in Table 6.2. We had predicted that, as a measure of vocabulary diversity, D would correlate most strongly with the other vocabulary measures except for the overall TTR, since this is unlikely to be valid when sizes of language sample vary as much as they do in this sample. In Table 6.2 it can be seen that this is indeed the case: the correlation with MSTTR-30

Table 6.2 Spearman rank order correlations between D and other measures for all students for whom D was calculable ($N = 27$)

Student Measure	rho
Measures taken from transcripts	
Number of words	0.18
Number of different words	0.35*
MSTTR-30	0.59**
Mean length of utterance (MLU words)	0.23
Utterances per turn (MLT)	0.09
Percentage unintelligible words	0.02
Words per minute	0.23
Type–token ratio (TTR)	0.20
GCSE examination results	
Score for oral examination (out of 7)	0.34*
GCSE points (out of 28)	0.31
Mean ratings from 24 teachers of French	
Range of vocabulary	0.31
Fluency	0.33*
Complexity of structure	0.31
Content	0.30
Accuracy	0.31
Pronunciation	0.23

*$p < 0.05$; **$p < 0.01$ (one-tailed tests)

stands apart even from other significant correlations as the most powerful in the set, the other significant relationships being with the number of different words, the oral score, and fluency. Importantly, D correlates with the number of *different* words rather than with the total number of words even though, as pointed out in Chapter 4, it is often the case that speakers (or writers) who score higher on various measures of language proficiency will often produce a greater quantity of language.[4] These results provide further evidence of D's validity: it is particularly sensitive to vocabulary and, to a lesser extent, to broader aspects of language proficiency. As expected, there is no significant correlation with overall TTR and this measure will be excluded from all further analyses.

A more surprising result is the lack of any significant correlation between D and teachers' ratings of Range of Vocabulary. Even though the value for *rho* (0.31) is positive and approaches significance it is very weak compared with the correlation between D and MSTTR-30 (0.59). This raises the question of the validity of the impressionistic ratings by the teachers. To investigate this further, the full matrix of Spearman inter-correlations between the ratings of the 24 teachers of French was inspected. It can be seen from Table 6.3 that Range of Vocabulary correlates extremely highly with the other scales; all the inter-correlations in the matrix are above 0.900. The highest figure is between Range of Vocabulary and Content at 0.996. Unlike the more objective measures, therefore, the teachers' ratings do not discriminate between vocabulary deployment and other areas of proficiency. The rating of Range of Vocabulary is likely to be heavily contaminated by halo effects.

This result may also reflect the sheer difficulty of the task of rating Range of Vocabulary while listening to a tape recording. Whereas values of D are adjusted for length of conversation, it is unlikely that teacher raters would even attempt to do this. Instead, they are likely to respond to other aspects of lexical richness such as the use of complex or advanced vocabulary, low-frequency words, or, at least, words which are less common in the foreign

Table 6.3 Spearman rank order inter-correlations between the subjective ratings provided by 24 teachers of French ($N = 34$)

Scale	1	2	3	4	5	6
1 Range of vocabulary	–					
2 Fluency	0.987**	–				
3 Complexity of structure	0.988**	0.977**	–			
4 Content	0.996**	0.985**	0.982**	–		
5 Accuracy	0.974**	0.970**	0.979**	0.970**	–	
6 Pronunciation	0.922**	0.918**	0.920**	0.911**	0.946**	–

** $p < 0.01$ (one-tailed tests)

language classroom. To throw further light on this finding one additional correlation was computed – that between Range of Vocabulary and student MSTTR-30. Interestingly, this is close to zero ($rho = -0.08$). Such results raise the wider issue of the extent to which raters are able to assess particular aspects of performance independently from each other, even using analytical as opposed to holistic rating scales.

The relationship between teacher D and student measures

The aim of the next analysis was, first, to compare D values of students and teachers and, second, to assess whether the teachers' deployment of vocabulary was finely tuned to the language proficiency of the students. A positive correlation between teachers' D and student variables would be indicative of accommodation strategies.

The comparison between the average D for teachers and students is revealing and suggests over-accommodation. The mean and standard deviation of the 34 Ds of the teachers and for the 27 student Ds reported above showed a *lower* lexical diversity and less variance for the teachers (Mean D = 44.9; SD = 9.6; N = 27) than for the students (Mean D = 56.9; SD = 16.3; N = 27). Even with the extreme case excluded, and confining the analysis to the remaining 26 teacher and student scores for whom D could be calculated, the average for the students (Mean = 55.1; SD = 13.8; N = 26) is still *higher* than for the teachers (Mean = 46.7; SD = 7.5; N = 26). This difference is statistically significant on a paired samples t-test: $t = 2.92$; $df = 25$; $p < 0.01$. D values are also higher for the students than the teacher in each class when analysed separately, although statistical significance can only be shown for the 22 students of Teacher B (the larger group).[5] It should be noted that the reason that, on average, the D for teachers is lower than the D for students does *not* lie in teachers giving students the floor in order to get them to talk. This is demonstrated by the fact that the mean and median number of words in the transcripts is substantially *higher* for the teachers (Mean = 295.112; Median = 285) than for the students (Mean = 183.56; Median = 153.5), even when the extreme case is included. The way D is computed would adjust for quantity of speech so this appears to be a genuine simplification of lexis by the teachers that is independent of their dominance of the conversation.

It is also interesting that the range for D (29.6–77.8) and the standard deviation (13.8) are also higher for the students than for the teachers (29.9–63.9 and 7.5). So the teachers are both operating at a lower level and within a narrower band of variation. A Spearman rank order correlation between the two sets of Ds is not significant ($rho = 0.24$; $N = 27$; ns). Correlations computed separately between each teacher and his/her students are also non-significant. There is therefore no evidence of accommodation in teachers' lexical diversity in response to variation in individual student D.

By contrast, teachers' Ds do enter into significant, positive correlations with 12 out of the 14 remaining measures of the 34 students' language, the two exceptions being MSTTR-30 and percentage of unintelligible words. These are shown in Table 6.4. At first sight it would appear, therefore, that the teachers, in spite of a general tendency to over-accommodate, are using greater lexical diversity with students whose language is more proficient, thus engaging in a form of fine-tuning to the individual.

On the other hand, the above interpretation would only be correct if an analysis of each teacher separately indicated effects that were consistent with their pooled data. Separate correlations for the Ds of Teacher A and Teacher B with the language measures of their students show that this is, in fact, far from being the case. These two sets of correlations are shown in Table 6.5. Teacher A shows no evidence of accommodation in the predicted direction at all. There is only one significant correlation and that is a *negative* relationship between Teacher D and GCSE points, suggesting that the teacher uses greater diversity with weaker students. Although unexpected, this finding might be accounted for by other processes of discourse accommodation such as the need for the teacher to reformulate questions, provide synonyms or paraphrases for weaker candidates, or to change topic more frequently if students provide little or no response. A similar lack of relationships is found for Teacher B for whom the

Table 6.4 Spearman rank order correlations between teachers' D and measures of students' language ($N = 34$)

Student Measure	rho
Measures taken from transcripts	
Number of words	0.53 **
MSTTR-30	0.11
Mean length of utterance (MLU words)	0.53 **
Utterances per turn (MLT)	0.53 **
Percentage unintelligible words	0.01
Words per minute	0.54 **
GCSE examination results	
Score for oral examination (out of 7)	0.50 **
GCSE points (out of 28)	0.59 **
Mean ratings from 24 teachers of French	
Range of vocabulary	0.50 **
Fluency	0.46 **
Complexity of structure	0.46 **
Content	0.49 **
Accuracy	0.47 **
Pronunciation	0.42 **

** $p < 0.01$ (one-tailed tests)

Table 6.5 Spearman rank order correlations between measures of students' language and Teacher A ($n = 12$) and Teacher B ($n = 22$)

Student Measure	rho with Teacher A ($n = 12$)	rho with Teacher B ($n = 22$)
Measures taken from transcripts		
Number of words	−0.13	−0.08
MSTTR-30	0.47	0.26
Mean length of utterance (MLU words)	−0.18	−0.04
Utterances per turn (MLT)	0.48	−0.23
Percentage unintelligible words	0.48	0.01
Words per minute	0.12	−0.21
GCSE examination results		
Score for oral examination (out of 7)	−0.22	−0.10
GCSE points (out of 28)	−0.57*	−0.03
Mean ratings from 24 teachers of French		
Range of vocabulary	0.02	−0.22
Fluency	−0.04	−0.28
Complexity of structure	−0.01	−0.30
Content	−0.01	−0.26
Accuracy	−0.06	−0.26
Pronunciation	−0.05	−0.24

*$p < 0.05$ (one-tailed tests)

correlations are very weak and predominantly negative. None is statistically significant.

The striking result that there is a positive correlation for pooled data and yet no relationship or even a tendency towards a negative relationship when the analysis is performed for each teacher separately was investigated further by considering the difference in ability between the two classes. As noted above, the students had been grouped into classes on the basis of previous achievement in French. The effect of this can be demonstrated by concentrating on the strongest correlation in the pooled data, that between the Teachers' average D and students' total number of GCSE points ($rho = 0.59$). Figure 6.1 shows a scatterplot of this correlation in which the two teachers are indicated separately. From this it can be seen that Teacher A's students score lower in the GCSE French examination than those of Teacher B. The median number of GCSE points for Teacher A's students is 13 compared with 20.5 for those of Teacher B and this difference is statistically significant on a Mann-Whitney U test ($U = 4.00$; $N = 34$; $p < 0.001$). Similarly, the median D for Teacher A is 35.1 compared with 50.2 for teacher B. This difference is also significant ($U = 10$; $N = 34$; $p < 0.001$). The separation between the two groups can be seen even more starkly in Figure 6.2 which shows the mean D plus and minus two semi-interquartile ranges (SIQR) plotted against the

Foreign Language Proficiency Interviews 107

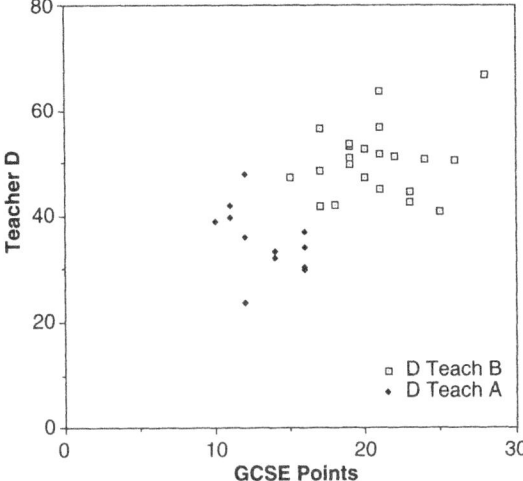

Figure 6.1 Scatterplot of D values for each teacher against students' GCSE points

students placed in ascending order of their GCSE points. From the students' order, it can be seen that all but one student in Teacher B's class were of higher ability than those of Teacher A. Immediately, it can be seen that the upper bound (median plus 2 × SIQR) for Teacher A virtually coincides with the lower bound (median minus 2 × SIQR) for Teacher B. Within each group, the values of D form no particular pattern with respect to students' order, but the two bands formed by the median plus or minus two semi-interquartile ranges of D for each teacher hardly overlap. Only four of Teacher B's Ds fall

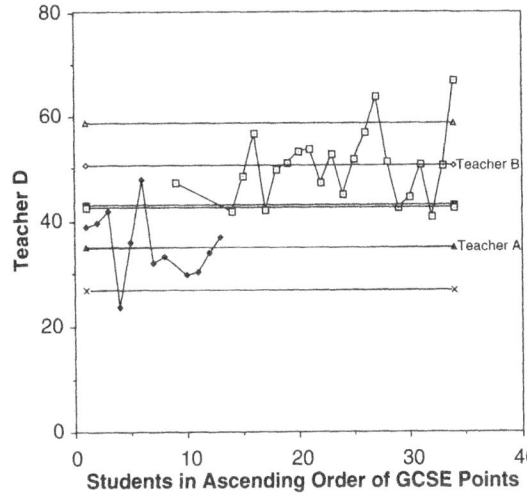

Figure 6.2 D for each teacher against students in ascending order of GCSE points, showing median D and the interval plus and minus 2 × semi-interquartile range for each teacher

within the range for Teacher A, and only one of Teacher A's Ds fall within the range of Teacher B. Therefore, although in terms of lexical diversity the teachers are not accommodating to individuals, each teacher is pitching the general level and range of the diversity of their vocabulary to the collective proficiency of his or her own teaching group.

Conclusion

With regard to the first aim of the investigation, the findings reported above provide evidence of the validity of mathematically modelling the relationship between TTR and token size to assess vocabulary diversity in a new context, that of the foreign language classroom and foreign language oral assessment. As predicted for the student measures, D correlated with another measure of vocabulary diversity, MSTTR-30, rather than with measures of general language proficiency. As expected, there was no correlation between D and overall TTR, and D was significantly correlated with the number of *different* words as opposed to the total number of words. Contrary to predictions, however, D was not related to the ratings of 24 experienced teachers of Range of Vocabulary, but it seems likely that teachers are simply unable to assess lexical diversity independently of other factors, particularly when attempting to do so impressionistically from audio-taped recordings. The idea that such procedures are particularly prone to halo effects is supported by the extremely strong inter-correlations (all over 0.90) among the six factors they rated, and by the failure of Range of Vocabulary to correlate with MSTTR-30, an objective measure of lexical diversity obtained directly from the transcripts.

The second aim of this research was to apply *vocd* and D to a practical research problem in a new context, namely to investigate whether variation in teachers' vocabulary diversity was itself a form of accommodation to the linguistic proficiency of individual students. At first sight this seemed to be the case – there was a significant correlation between the Ds of the teachers and a wide range of language measures for the students, in fact 12 out of the 14 variables studied. Closer investigation, however, showed that this overall effect was not replicated for either teacher when their data were analysed separately. It had been brought about by a significant difference in the ability of each class that corresponded with a significant difference in the average D for each teacher. There was little overlap between the Ds of the teacher of each class. What appeared to be happening was that, while the language of each teacher was not finely tuned to the ability of the individual students, they were pitching their language at an approximate level that was appropriate to the ability of the class as a whole. Whether this general adjustment is in direct response to the input and interaction during the interviews themselves, or to previous perceptions and expectations based on knowledge of the groups derived from teaching them in class, can only be addressed through a parallel study using interviewers who had no previous acquaintance with the candidates. That is a question for future research.

It will be recalled, however, that there was far more variation in the D values for the students than for the teachers. There appears to be a tendency therefore, in the context of a public examination conducted by non-native speakers, for each teacher to provide an approximately standard level of language across all the students he or she is testing. This may well reflect teachers' concerns that public examinations should be reliable and fair and may contribute to greater reliability of the oral examination through standardisation of testing conditions. This and the apparent over-accommodation by both teachers, does, however, introduce the very threats to validity identified by Ross and Berwick (1992), the first of which is the absence of appropriate accommodation. The evidence here is that, although accommodation to individual students may well be absent at a finely tuned level, there is a general adjustment to match the student's level of language, but this adjustment is kept within relatively narrow limits (see Figure 6.2). Clearly, such general adjustment is appropriate, for without it students with low to average ability would find it more difficult to display even the proficiency they have. For these students, therefore, the validity of the test may survive the demand of reliability that the teacher-examiner behaves in a broadly similar way for each candidate. It is more questionable whether or not validity survives the second threat referred to by Ross and Berwick (1992), namely that of inappropriate accommodation which fails to stretch students. Given that lexical diversity is higher on average for candidates than for interviewers, and noting from Figure 6.2 that for six of the top seven candidates the teacher D is at, or well below, the median for the more able group, the evidence on the relative degree of accommodation is that beyond the general adjustment to the ability of the class as a whole, there is no systematic increase in teacher Ds as the candidates' ability rises.

7
A New Measure of Inflectional Diversity and its Application to English and Spanish Data Sets[1]

It will be recalled that in earlier chapters we compared different versions of D that systematically varied the definition of a word type. In Chapter 4 we analysed transcripts from the 38 children in the 32-month directory of the New England Corpus (Snow, 1989; Dale et al., 1989) in the CHILDES database. We compared D calculated from inflected forms ('go', 'goes', 'going' as three types) with D calculated from stems ('go', 'goes', 'going' as one type). Clearly, inflected forms will always give higher values on any lexical diversity measure, provided that subjects are actually using inflectional morphology, and the difference between these two versions of D proved to be highly reliable in the New England data even though the two measures were correlated at a level approaching unity.

In Chapter 5 we added a third analysis based on lemmas, or root forms in the analysis of Gordon Wells's (1985) Bristol transcripts. Here, not only do 'go' and 'goes' count as the same word type, but also 'went'. As would be expected, this measure produces the lowest values of all for D. Intercorrelations for the three versions in the Bristol data were so consistently high for data pooled across ages, for each age separately, and for individual children that further investigation of lexical diversity was conducted using only one version, namely stem forms. It was noted, however, that, although there were no differences at 18 months, between the ages of 21 months and five years there was a steady widening of the gap between the three versions and that this difference became statistically more reliable after 21 months. It can be assumed that this phenomenon reflects developing usage of morphology, and, in as far as the differences between inflected forms and the other two versions are the result of the application of a wider repertoire of inflections to a wider range of stems, could form the basis of a new way of assessing children's morphological development.

Below, we investigate this interpretation by subtracting the D values for stem and root forms (lemmas) from the values obtained for inflected forms to obtain a measure that we refer to as Inflectional Diversity (ID) (Richards and Malvern, 2004). We do so initially with the New England and Bristol data sets in order to see whether ID is correlated with other language measures at various ages. Finally, we compare these results with ID values for children acquiring Spanish, a language whose inflectional morphology is considerably richer than English.

Inflectional diversity in the New England Corpus

As reported in Richards and Malvern (2004), for each child we subtracted the D-score for stem forms from the score for inflected forms to obtain the measure of inflectional diversity (ID) proposed above. The values we obtained for ID varied considerably, ranging from zero to 27.97 with a mean of 6.79 and a standard deviation of 5.03. The validity of our interpretation of this measure was tested through correlations with MLU, and the mean number of inflections per utterance. The latter was calculated from the total number of *tokens* of inflections used by the child and divided by the total number of child utterances. As a token–token ratio this provides an index of frequency of usage which, while it may indicate productivity, is less likely to do so than a measure based on *types*, like ID. Because the children in the 32-month directory of the New England Corpus actually vary in age from 27–33 months, correlation with age was also possible (see also Chapter 4). All three results were highly significant, with particularly strong relationships between D and the two other language measures. As one might expect, the correlation with age ($rho = 0.405$; $N = 38$; $p < 0.01$) was considerably lower than with the indices that tap into grammar, and the correlation with inflections/utterance ($rho = 0.846$; $N = 38$; $p < 0.001$), the measure that is most dependent on use of inflectional morphology, was stronger than the correlation with MLU ($rho = 0.733$; $N = 38$; $p < 0.001$).

Inflectional diversity in the Bristol Corpus

Figure 7.1 reviews the developmental trends in the Bristol data from 18 months to 42 months and at five years for the three versions of D as identified in Chapter 5. The widening gap over time is clearly discernible.

Here we will omit the data from five years and concentrate on the period from 18 to 42 months as the period most relevant to the development of inflections. To obtain the ID scores, D for both root forms and stem forms for each child were subtracted from the D for inflected forms. The two sets of ID scores are plotted in Figure 7.2, which confirms the impression that the gap between the three versions of D widens over time. However, it also suggests that ID for roots (D for inflected forms minus D for root forms) sustains the developmental trend for longer than ID for stems where there is a tailing off at 36 months followed by a fall.

In order to test whether ID is a valid measure of *language* development, and, specifically, a measure of the use of inflections, we ran correlations between

112 *Lexical Diversity and Language Development*

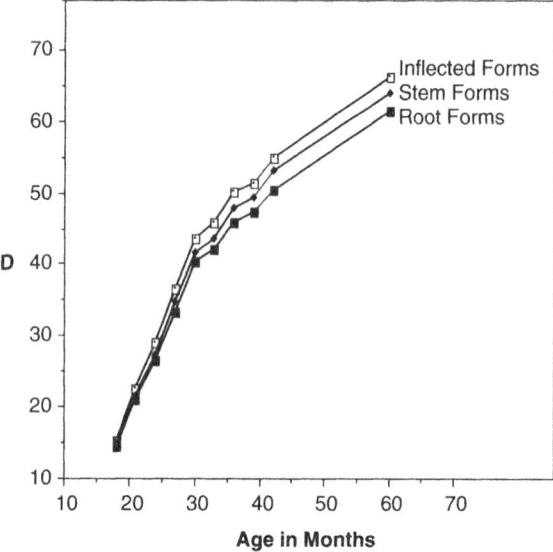

Figure 7.1 Mean D for inflected forms, stem forms, and root forms against age

one version of ID (inflected forms minus stem forms) with other measures of language development: the Bristol Scale Score, Wells's MLUS (mean length of structured utterances) based on morphemes (Wells, 1985), and the mean number of inflections per utterance. We chose ID for stems rather than ID for roots for this analysis because of questions over the productivity of irregular forms and how they are processed (Pinker, 1999). Using stems was the more conservative approach as its developmental trend is less pronounced than that of roots. In line with the results from the New England Corpus we expected that the highest correlations would be between ID and the mean number of morphemes per utterance since the latter is another measure of the production of inflections, but based on token frequency rather than types. Results of the correlational analysis are shown in Table 7.1.

As one can see from the table, these expectations were confirmed by the data: the highest correlations were between ID and the mean number of

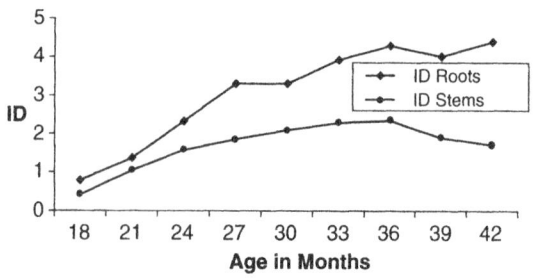

Figure 7.2 The difference between D for inflected forms and D for stems and roots plotted against age

Table 7.1 Correlations between ID stems and other measures of language development

Age in Months	Bristol Scale Score	MLUS	Inflections per Utterance
18	0.001	−0.106	0.400
21	0.494*	0.449*	0.775**
24	0.614**	0.602**	0.693**
27	0.316*	0.532**	0.687**
30	0.703**	0.623**	0.706**
33	0.098	0.166	0.374*
36	−0.060	−0.033	0.288
39	0.095	0.331*	0.583**
42	0.155	0.371*	0.494**

*$p < 0.05$; **$p < 0.01$

morphemes per utterance, these being statistically significant at seven out of nine age points and showing particularly strong relationships between 21 and 30 months, exactly the ages at which we would expect individual differences in the development of inflectional morphology. We also found significant correlations between ID stems and MLUS in six out of nine cases, again with the strongest effects being between 21 and 30 months. Correlations with the Bristol Scale Score were usually lower and less likely to be significant. However, it must be remembered that the level attained on this latter measure is established from a combination of the child's scores on pragmatics, semantics, and grammar. It therefore has a much broader focus than ID and the other language measures and it is not surprising that the correlations between it and ID were lower. From Table 7.1, it can also be observed that there were no significant results at 18 months. Inflections at this age were rare and, as noted in Chapter 5, differences between the three versions of D were not reliable until 21 months. In addition, correlations may have been attenuated at 33 and 36 months by a more restricted range of scores as there are lower standard deviations for ID at these ages. Similarly, weaker but nevertheless statistically significant correlations between ID and MLUS at 39 and 42 months appear to reflect lower standard deviations for MLUS at the older age points. ID, therefore, seems to be at its most effective as a measure of morphology during the period of its strongest developmental trend between 20 and 30 months.

The Spanish data

A further way to test the new measure was to apply it to a language with a richer inflectional system than English. Spanish has an extremely rich inflectional system, particularly in relation to verbs (Durán, 2000, p. 36; Zagona,

2002, pp. 14–15). For subject-verb agreement, Spanish verbs have six different endings depending on the person and number of the subject: first person singular (cant*o* – I sing), second person singular (cant*as* – you sing), third person singular (cant*a* – she/he/it sings), first person plural (cant*amos* – we sing), second person plural (cant*áis* – you all sing), third person plural (cant*an* – they sing). In addition, Spanish verbs also inflect for tense, aspect, and mood. To give a detailed and precise description of these goes beyond the scope of this chapter, but it must be understood that each tense, aspect, and mood has its own set of inflections. So agreement of the verb 'cantar' (to sing) presented above is the present tense, indicative mood. Other endings represent other tenses, aspects, and moods. For example, 'cant*ara*, cant*aras*, cant*ara*, cant*áramos*, cant*arais*, and cant*aran*' (I would sing, you would sing, she/he/it would sing, we would sing, you plural would sing, and they would sing) are the past tense and imperfect aspect of the subjunctive mood. It is easy to see how this results in a much larger number of possible verbal endings in Spanish than in English (for which the only options are ø (no ending), -s for third person singular in the present tense, -ed for past tense and past participle, and -ing for the progressive).

Our prediction was that once children began using inflections, Spanish-speaking children at all comparable ages would obtain higher ID scores than the English children and that differences would increase with age and greater productivity. In order to test this, we used longitudinal data from five Spanish-speaking children whose transcripts were available from the CHILDES database. The children were Juan, from the Linaza Corpus, María, from the López Ornat Corpus (López Ornat, 1994), Koki, from the Montes Corpus (Montes, 1987, 1992), Eduard from the Serra/Sole Corpus, and Emilio from the Vila Corpus (see MacWhinney 2000b, pp. 350–9 for full details). Recordings were selected to correspond as closely as possible to the ages of the Bristol children, that is to say at three-monthly intervals from 18 months to 42 months, and transcripts of ages not sampled in the Bristol project were excluded from the analysis. This is, of course, only a very small Spanish sample, and because the data from each Spanish-speaking child were collected by different researchers and the children came from different parts of the Spanish-speaking world, it might be argued that they are not comparable with the Bristol Corpus. Nevertheless, our purpose was to study the effects of the richness of the inflectional system on ID scores regardless of context or dialect. Whatever effects these might have had on the vocabulary produced and its diversity, the range of morphological options remained considerably higher than for English.

The same methodology for editing and coding the Spanish transcripts was followed as for the Bristol data (see Chapter 5): spelling inconsistencies and phonetic variants of the same word were standardised; exclude files for non-words were compiled; homographs were coded as different words; self-repetition of words and phrases was excluded; and, finally, the boundaries for inflectional morphemes were marked.

First of all, the transcripts of the Spanish-speaking children were run through *vocd* to obtain the same three sets of vocabulary diversity scores that were calculated for the Bristol data. Figure 7.3 shows the development of these over time. As with the Bristol children, the three versions of D show a rising developmental trend where the highest curve is for inflected forms followed by D for stems and finally D for roots. We can see in Figure 7.3 even more clearly than for the Bristol data (Figure 7.1) that the gap between D for inflected forms and the other two versions widens steadily over time.

Before further examination of this widening gap, it is worth superimposing the curves created by the three versions of D for the Spanish-speaking children on the curves representing the English data in order to compare the mean D values for each language. This can be seen in Figure 7.4. With due consideration for the reservations expressed above about the small sample

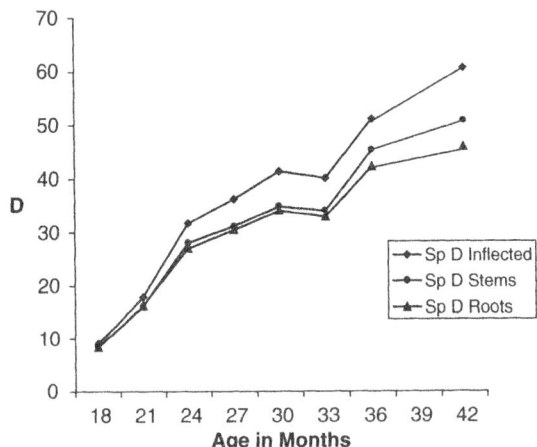

Figure 7.3 The development of three versions of D for five Spanish-speaking children

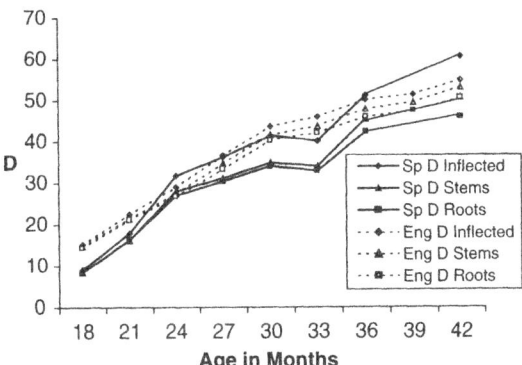

Figure 7.4 The development of three versions of D in English- and Spanish-speaking children

size and the disparate nature of the sampling it is nevertheless interesting that the three curves representing D for the Spanish-speaking children were comparable to those for the Bristol children. In interpreting this apparent similarity in lexical diversity between two different languages it must be borne in mind that *because* of the greater range of inflectional options in Spanish, one would actually expect higher lexical diversity for the Ds derived from inflected forms. On the other hand, the variation in the situational contexts in which the Bristol children were recorded could contribute to higher Ds. Possibly, in this comparison these two effects cancel each other out. It is important to remember, however, that comparing lexical measures between different languages is fraught with difficulties (Berman and Verhoeven, 2002; Strömquist et al., 2002) and may well have suspect validity even when the languages are closely related.

Figure 7.5 now plots the ID values calculated from the difference between D for inflected forms and D for stems (ID stems) and between D for inflected forms and D for roots (ID roots). These clarify the impression gained from the widening gaps between the D values in Figures 7.3 and 7.4 for the Spanish children and confirm that the ID values for the Spanish children are substantially, and consistently, higher than those of the English speakers even where their D values were similar or even lower (cf. Figures 7.4 and 7.5). The developmental trend for Spanish is noticeably more pronounced than for English. These results provide further evidence that is consistent with ID being a valid measure of morphological development.

Conclusion

The validity of ID as a developmental measure is supported by the results from three sets of data. For the 38 children aged 27 to 33 months in the New England Corpus and the 32 children aged 18 to 42 months in the Bristol Corpus we have shown that ID based on word stems shows developmental

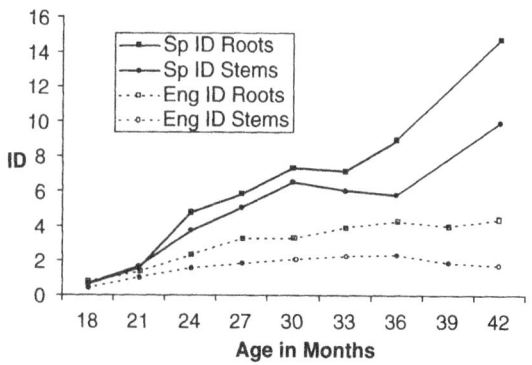

Figure 7.5 Trends in inflectional diversity (ID) in the Bristol and Spanish children

trends related to age and correlates well with other language measures, particularly MLUS and the mean number of inflections per utterance. The findings from the Bristol Corpus suggest that it may be at its most effective for discriminating between English-speaking children from the ages of 21 to 30 months. This is the period of the strongest correlations with other measures and the most consistent upward trend for ID stems, although, as was seen in Figure 7.2, the trend for ID roots was sustained rather longer until 36 months. As far as the Spanish data were concerned, it was to be expected that ID scores would be higher than for English-speaking children. Nevertheless, these were both substantially higher and continued to show a pronounced upward trend even after both ID measures for the Bristol data had reached a plateau. This suggests that ID may be particularly useful with languages with a rich inflectional morphology.

As we have frequently argued, the interpretation of analyses of lexical diversity will always depend to a large extent on the researcher's definition of what counts as a word token and what counts as a different word, and investigators, quite rightly, usually take great pains to make it clear how their corpus was lemmatised. In this chapter we have shown that by systematically varying the definition of a word type and investigating the difference that it makes we are able to assess inflectional morphology at a crucial stage in children's development. Nevertheless, one crucial question remains, and that concerns the extent to which ID is actually measuring *productivity* when it might be possible for a child to achieve a high ID score through the non-repetitive usage of non-productive inflected forms stored as single lexical items. While such an interpretation cannot be entirely ruled out, it is important to consider the implications of how ID is calculated. For each individual, the difference between a measure of lexical diversity that treats the full, inflected form as a type, and a measure that is based on the lemma or stem lies in the extent to which a diversity of inflections is applied to a diversity of content words. ID can therefore be seen as a form of what Stokes and Fletcher (2000) call 'collocational diversity'. In a discussion of the productivity of constructions involving verbs and aspect markers in Cantonese, Stokes and Fletcher point out that groups of speakers could have equal diversity on both these categories, but differ in the productivity with which they combine them to form constructions (Stokes and Fletcher, 2000, pp. 528–9). Indeed, their own data from groups of Cantonese-speaking children with and without SLI attest to this phenomenon. In the case of ID a child's score can be raised both by the application of a single inflection to more word stems or of a number of different inflections to a single lemma or stem. It is for this reason that, at least in early first language as opposed to later second language acquisition where learning unanalysed forms may be more of a factor, it is likely that ID scores are a measure of *productivity* rather than just the variety of *usage*.

Part III

Different Word Categories and their Diversity: Type–Type versus Type–Token

8
Comparing the Diversity of Lexical Categories: the Type–Type Ratio and Related Measures

The aim of this chapter is to provide an empirical demonstration of the sensitivity of type–type ratios to sample size and to outline and demonstrate a solution derived from the mathematical modelling procedures described in earlier chapters. However, because researchers working in language development and education are probably less aware of the problems related to sample size for type–type ratios than they are for type–token ratios, and because of the significance for theory and practice of recent research that has used such measures, we will begin with an extensive review of the issues. This will encompass analyses of rare words or lexical sophistication, studies of vocabulary composition and early lexical style, and of the 'noun bias' issue.

Type–type ratios

As noted in earlier chapters, linguists frequently need to focus on the diversity of a single lexical category, for example the range of verbs used by children with specific language impairment (Jones and Conti-Ramsden, 1997). In addition, however, they may need to relate the diversity of one kind of linguistic unit to that of another, as in the cross-linguistic study of noun bias in children's early vocabularies (Gentner, 1982). This may be achieved simply by calculating a TTR for nouns, verbs or any other category and comparing them. Provided that the TTRs are calculated from a common baseline of tokens for all subjects and for each word class such comparisons are perfectly valid. On the other hand, measures are often used that are based entirely on types, such as the ratio of noun types to verb types. Unlike the type–*token* ratio where, in theory, the number of tokens can increase infinitely, the type–*type* ratio contains a sample from a closed set in both the numerator and the denominator. It will be shown below that this property causes such measures to have complex relationships with sample size and that in the field of child language this is a problem that is usually ignored.

The categories of linguistic unit involved in such comparisons are generally form classes, but we will also consider measures that focus on the relative rarity of words used by speakers or writers where these are expressed as a proportion of total word types. It is also worth noting that measures based on units other than words also exist, and an example from the child language field is Irwin's (1946) use of the consonant–vowel ratio. In a sample of 95 children ranging in age from one month to 30 months, Irwin investigated developmental trends in consonant–vowel ratios calculated from both types and tokens. Both increased over time, the latter in a linear fashion while the curve based on types was more complex with a decelerating rate of progress as the children grew older.

Ratios of different word classes have frequently been used in studies of literary style. Scholfield (1995) comments that verb–noun ratios occur in stylistics as a measure of the continuum between speaking and writing, and in an investigation into the properties of the verb–adjective type–type ratio, Köhler and Galle (1993, p. 46) claim that such measures can serve to describe, classify, and compare texts on the basis of 'style, genre, language ... authorship determination and many more'. But like TTRs, such ratios are a function of sample size. Using Franz Kafka's 'Das Schloß' Köhler and Galle show a steep non-linear fall in the verb–adjective ratio followed by a more gradual rise as the number of tokens increases, which illustrates the complexity of the relationships referred to above.

Ménard (1983) explored noun–verb and adjective–noun type–type ratios in six twentieth-century French literary texts and found them to be positively and strongly correlated with vocabulary diversity (as measured by the number of word types contained in segments of text of a standard length). He concluded that lexically rich texts contain a wider range of nouns and adjectives. A further, less conventional, set of measures consisting of the proportion of types to types was investigated by Ménard. These concern the use of monosemic versus polysemic words. Ménard proposed that greater precision in the use of words led to greater conciseness and that this would be achieved through the words that had the smallest range of possible meanings. Lexically rich texts ought, therefore, to contain a higher proportion of monosemic words. This prediction was tested by developing four measures of polysemy as defined by the number of dictionary definitions for each word contained in the texts. The first measure is mean polysemy: the number of different meanings divided by the number of word types. The second is monosemic rate, or the proportion of types that have only one meaning, and the third is oligosemic rate, or the proportion of types that have only one or two meanings. The fourth measure, which is not a type–type ratio, consists of the total number of meaning tokens divided by word tokens.

As would be predicted, the measures of polysemy were negatively correlated with lexical diversity while correlations for monosemy were positive. Nevertheless, effects were weak, and some analyses were impaired by the disproportionate contribution of some common word types that had an extremely high number of dictionary meanings. The verb 'faire' ('to do/make') had 40 entries, for example. Ménard was forced to conclude that these measures were not good indicators of lexical richness, but what is of particular interest here is their relationship with sample size. Both measures of monosemy increased with more tokens, with a corresponding decrease in mean polysemy. By contrast, and as would be expected, the polysemic measure derived entirely from tokens showed no such relationship.

As far as child language is concerned, we observed above that research into children with SLI has focused on the diversity of individual lexical classes. In at least one case, this has extended into a number of type–type measures. In a study of Cantonese-speaking children with and without SLI, Stokes and Fletcher (2000) used a standard number of tokens across subjects from which to calculate 'proportional diversity' (the proportion of types that belong to certain word classes – nouns, verbs, and other open-class words) and the ratio between open-class and closed-class types. Nevertheless, such measures are the exception in work on SLI. Comparisons between the diversity of linguistic categories in spontaneous speech have, however, been particularly important in three areas of language development research which we will consider in turn in the following sections. In the first of these, we will conduct a particularly extensive examination of the measurement of rare word usage. This is an area of considerable topical interest in second language assessment and, in first language research, as an index of the richness of the linguistic environment in the home and at school that is a powerful predictor of later ability in language and literacy. The other two areas are closely interrelated, and comprise the composition of the early lexicon and individual differences in early lexical style, and cross-linguistic investigations into the universality of the noun bias.

Rare words

Diversity versus sophistication

In Chapter 1 we noted that 'lexical sophistication', as reflected in the proportion of rare words, was one of Read's (2000) four dimensions of lexical richness in second language writing. Meara and Bell (2001), also working in second language, claim that it is necessary to supplement measures of lexical variation that are based entirely on numbers of types and tokens with information about the *quality* of vocabulary being used. They point out that the three sentences 'The man saw the woman', 'The bishop observed the actress', and 'The magistrate sentenced the burglar' all have the same type–token ratio while quite clearly demonstrating different levels of sophistication of lexical choice (p. 6). The appropriate use of low frequency words is interpreted variously as demonstrating greater precision of expression (Read, 2000), concreteness and specificity (Hyltenstam, 1988), a mastery of difficult words, especially in the context of second language learners (Vermeer,

2000), as the use of '"abstract", "literary", "semantically complex"' vocabulary (Weizman and Snow, 2001, p. 266), or as enabling us 'to make some fairly strong inferences about the total lexical resources that are available to the writer' (Meara and Bell, 2001, p. 7). Nevertheless, it would be a mistake to take Meara and Bell's sample sentences as evidence that diversity and rarity are entirely independent factors. To some extent, the two are bound to be interrelated because, over a longer stretch of language, diversity can only increase by the inclusion of additional different words, and the more these increase, the more any additional word types will tend to be rare. And just as we may be able to make assumptions about total lexical resources from rare words, so Sichel's (1986) type–token characteristic is related to total active vocabulary (see Chapter 3).

The extent of the relationship between diversity and rarity is borne out by Ménard's (1983) analysis of French literary texts – the correlations between the number of *different* words and the proportion of *rare* words in texts standardised at a length of 500 words were 0.73 and 0.74, with corresponding negative correlations with the proportion of high frequency words. The proportion of words that are rare is therefore a function of the number of different words, which in turn is a function of the number of tokens. Nevertheless, Ménard argues that a measure of rarity offers a useful stylistic index over and above diversity, as indicated by texts with the same number of word types that still differ on rarity. Interestingly, this conclusion is borne out in the child language field in a study by Hayes and Ahrens (1988) who investigated age-related changes in child-directed speech to 17 children aged from three hours to 12 years. They found that even though there were the expected increases over time in adult MLU and TTR based on a standard 1000 tokens, there was no corresponding increase in the number of low frequency words in the same 1000 tokens. The broadening of vocabulary usage was therefore accomplished by adding words from a similar frequency range.

The connection between rare words and greater *precision* is echoed by Biber's (1988) 'lexical specificity' measures. In his analysis of speech and writing across 23 genres in the Lancaster-Oslo-Bergen and the London-Lund Corpora, Biber treated both the type–token ratio (calculated from the first 400 words of each text) and word length (measured by the mean number of orthographic letters) as reflecting the usage of words with more specific meanings (Biber, 1988, pp. 238–9). Here, word length can be seen as a proxy measure for rarity by appeal to Zipf's Law that shorter words are more frequent and more general in meaning (Zipf, 1949). According to Biber (1988), the correlation between TTR and word length was 0.365, confirming some overlap in what they are measuring, but being sufficiently weak to support Meara and Bell's (2001) and Ménard's (1983) arguments that a rarity measure provides valuable supplementary information. It is easy to imagine genres in which there is a high degree of dissociation between rarity and diversity. As Biber points out, 'non-technical informational discourse has a markedly higher lexical variety than abstract technical discourse' (Biber, 1988, p. 112). If this is because of the repetition of terms with exact technical meanings, one would expect it to be accompanied by a higher incidence of low frequency words.

We will return to the relationships between diversity, rarity, and word length in Chapter 9 in an analysis of children's writing. In the meantime we will devote the following sections to examining ways in which rarity has been assessed in samples of speech and writing, and for what purposes, and consider the problems associated with its measurement.

Intrinsic versus extrinsic measurement of rarity

Meara and Bell (2001) make a useful distinction between intrinsic and extrinsic measures of lexical variety. Intrinsic measures are those, such as TTR and its transformations, that rely exclusively on information contained within the language sample. Extrinsic measures, on the other hand, relate the contents to external criteria such as frequency data. Rarity measures can be either intrinsic or extrinsic, although the former are less commonly used in studies of child language and education.

An intrinsic rarity measure would be one that draws on words that occur only rarely in the text itself, such as the number of types that are *hapax legomena* or *hapax dislegomena* (words which appear only once or twice respectively in a text). Together with lexical diversity and repetition, hapax legomena, in particular, has been seen as an indication of vocabulary richness in literary texts that can assist with the attribution of authorship or to estimate the chronology of a single author's works. Smith and Kelly (2002) have argued recently, however, that the variability between the works of a single author make all such measures less appropriate for author attribution. Sichel (1986) has investigated the relationship between both hapax legomena and hapax dislegomena and token size and has developed equations for them that have been tested on the writings of Macaulay and Dickens. The number of hapax legomena has a curvilinear relationship with the number of tokens, approaching zero after an initial rise. The fall results from the fact that words used once are likely to be repeated eventually. It is more common in linguistic research, however, to express the rarely occurring words as a proportion of the number of types – in other words, a type–type ratio. In this case, the proportion of hapax legomena falls with increasing sample size. According to Sichel, this relationship, which begins with a value of one with the first token, 'is a monotonically decreasing function in N .... Falling first rapidly then less and less rapidly' (Sichel, 1986, p. 53). By contrast, the proportion of hapax dislegomena rises up to 1000 tokens, remains constant between 1000 and 400,000 tokens, and then declines (Sichel, 1986, p. 55).

As noted above, intrinsic measures of rarity are seldom used in education and language development. Nevertheless, one example of a study that does so is an investigation by Hesse and Hesse (1987) into the vocabulary of German children of primary school age. These authors use hapax legomena as a percentage of types (like Sichel they find a tendency to obtain lower values for larger samples). Even though such cases are isolated, however, the potential value of intrinsic measures is illustrated by recent investigations into aphasia (Holmes and Singh, 1996) and Alzheimer's disease (Bucks et al., 2000). Using semi-structured interviews, Bucks and colleagues compared eight subjects with probable Dementia of Alzheimer's Type (DAT) with 16 healthy older controls. Approximately 1000 words were transcribed for each subject and eight quantitative measures were produced that were chosen as likely predictors of group membership. Given the known difficulties of lexical access compared to relatively intact abilities with grammar in Alzheimer's disease (see also Pinker, 1999), three of the measures focused on lexical richness. Two of these were lexical diversity measures and the third was the proportion of types that were hapax legomena. Variation in sample size was controlled using Honoré's statistic (Honoré, 1979). Lexical richness showed significant differences between the groups in all three cases and in a discriminant function analysis made an important contribution to predictions of group membership. In this case the lexical diversity measures were better predictors than the rarity measure. By contrast, Holmes and Singh (1996) used the same set of variables in a comparison of interviews with 100 aphasic patients with 30 normal controls. Again, all three indices of lexical richness showed significant differences between the groups, but here the rarity measure was almost equal to the diversity measures in predictive power.

Having shown the potential usefulness of intrinsic rarity measures, but noted that they, too, can be a function of sample size, we now turn our attention to Meara and Bell's (2001) category of *extrinsic* measures where rare, difficult or advanced words are defined through reference to external criteria. Some examples of such criteria are:

- the million-word corpus of Swedish newspaper text used by Hyltenstam (1988) to identify words used by second language learners that were not among the 7000 most frequent Swedish words;
- word frequencies in the British National Corpus (Leech, Rayson and Wilson, 2001) used by Afitskaya (2002) to identify 'basic' (the 1000 most frequent words) and 'advanced' vocabulary in the spoken narratives of adult learners of English as a foreign language;
- the American Heritage Dictionary list of English types (Carroll, Davies and Richman, 1971) derived from a five million word corpus of children's publications used by Hayes and Ahrens (1988) to study the development of word choice in child-directed speech to children from birth to 12 years;
- the Chall and Dale (1995) list of 3000 words judged by teachers to be known to most fourth graders – this was used by the 'Home-school study of

language and literacy development' (Dickinson and Tabors, 2001) to assess the richness of the linguistic environment at home and at pre-school;
- an official French Ministry of Education list of the 1522 words pupils are supposed to know by the time they reach the lycée, used by Arnaud (1984);
- a list of the 2000 basic words for German as a foreign language used by Daller, van Hout and Treffers-Daller (2003) in a study of language dominance in Turkish-German bilinguals;
- judgements of seven teachers of Turkish as a foreign language on vocabulary produced in picture stories (also used by Daller et al., 2003);
- a list of second language words that should have been taught by a certain school year in Sweden used by Linnarud (1983);
- in a group of second language learners, words that are exclusive to one writer (Linnarud, 1983, p. 250).

This last criterion results in a measure of what Moira Linnarud calls 'lexical originality' or 'lexical individuality' (Read, 2000) that is calculated for each participant as the percentage of words in their compositions that are not used by any other participant in the group.

The validity of such external reference points will depend on the purpose of the assessment and will depend on factors such as level of proficiency, or whether the focus is on first, second or classroom-based foreign language learning. Relative word frequencies in corpus data from native speakers may not be reflected in the content of educational programmes and text books – at school, the second author of this book learnt German from a two-volume textbook (Anderson, 1949) that notoriously taught the 'difficult' words for pollination (*Bestäubung*), sorcerer (*Hexenmeister*), conservatory (*Gewächshaus*) and seven-league boots (*Siebenmeilenstiefel*), but never got round to introducing more useful, high frequency, 'easy' words like knife, fork, and spoon (*Messer, Gabel, Löffel*). For many whose foreign language learning is confined to the classroom, and particularly those at lower levels of proficiency, the notion of difficulty may be more related to content of the syllabus and to the quality and frequency of engagement with it than to frequencies of usage by native speakers.

Extrinsic rarity measures in bilingual and second language research

The use of extrinsic measures has been most obvious in second language research, and in most cases they are the equivalent of Ménard's (1983) rarity measure, that is to say, the proportion of types that are rare. In commonly cited studies they have been applied to comparisons of English speaking and writing ability in Swedish 17-year-olds with native speakers of the same age (Linnarud, 1983; Hyltenstam, 1988), or to determine the validity of a vocabulary test taken by French university students by analysing samples of their writing (Arnaud, 1984). Interestingly, Arnaud found that scores on the test correlated significantly with lexical diversity (r = 0.39) but not with rarity. The correlation between diversity and rarity was significant but weak (r = 0.27). A noteworthy application of an extrinsic rarity measure is a recent study by Batia Laufer (Laufer, 2003) in which she uses a measure of lexical diversity (TTR) and the percentage of infrequent vocabulary to investigate the influence of acquiring Hebrew as an L2 on the L1 of Russian immigrants to Israel. Results show that the percentage of rare words (but not TTR) used by the respondents in an L1 Russian writing task decreases significantly with length of residence.

Not all extrinsic measures used by researchers are a type–type ratio. A recent innovation is the use of 'Advanced TTR' and 'Advanced Guiraud' by Daller and colleagues (2003). These authors applied measures of lexical richness to oral picture descriptions in order to investigate language dominance in two groups of Turkish adults who were bilingual in Turkish and German. One group was still resident in Germany, while the other had returned to Turkey. Two conventional measures of lexical richness were employed: TTR and Guiraud's index or root TTR (Guiraud, 1960; see Chapter 2) and two measures involving 'advanced' vocabulary identified by word lists for German and the judgements of teachers for Turkish (see above). These measures are Advanced TTR (advanced types/tokens) and Advanced Guiraud (advanced types/tokens), and the authors regard their advantage as combining the characteristics of rarity and type–token measures (Daller et al., 2003). Indeed, the results suggest strongly that the advanced versions are far more effective at discriminating between the groups on their proficiency in both German and Turkish than the basic diversity measures, giving further credence to the value of lexical richness indices that go beyond simple type and token counts.

Laufer and Nation's lexical frequency profile

The greatest impact on this kind of measurement in the second language field has perhaps been made by Laufer and Nation. These authors reject conventional measures of vocabulary richness in favour of their lexical frequency profile (LFP) (Laufer and Nation, 1995). The LFP divides the vocabulary in a text into four frequency bands: (1) the 1000 most frequent words; (2) the second 1000 most frequent words; (3) academic words contained in the University Word List; and (4) the lowest frequency words – those not contained in lists 1–3. These frequency criteria are based on Nation's work on vocabulary lists (Nation, 1984, 1996), and the profile consists of the proportion of word types that belong in each band. Laufer and Nation argue for the superiority of this approach over the calculation of lexical diversity from types and tokens: 'The LFP will discriminate between subjects who use frequent and less frequent vocabulary, not just between those who can or cannot vary their possibly limited vocabulary' (Laufer and Nation, 1995, p. 313). They also claim that the profile taps 'how vocabulary size is reflected in use' (p. 307).

The authors validate the procedure on discursive essays written by a group of 22 university students who are learners of English as a foreign language. They show that it does indeed discriminate between levels of proficiency, remains stable across different pieces of writing by the same students, and that the proportions of the lowest frequency words and academic vocabulary are strongly correlated with a test of vocabulary production (coefficients range from 0.6 to 0.8). It should be noted that the results from the four frequency bands can be reduced to a single rarity measure by simply taking the proportion of word types that are not included in the first 2000. Although the LFP was devised for English as a second language, and is particularly appropriate for the writing of intermediate learners, it has also been applied more widely. Meara, Lightbown and Halter (1997), for example, used it to assess the richness of the lexical environment in intensive communicative ESL classrooms in Quebec by profiling the language of ten teachers, and LFP has also been applied to the analysis of technical English in comparison with popular and quality journalism (Milton and Hales, 1997).

Early child language and 'The home-school study of language and literacy development' of Dickinson, Snow and Tabors

We have already referred above to Hayes and Ahrens's (1988) study of rare words in the language addressed to children. Their results suggest that, unlike lexical diversity, rare word usage is not finely tuned to children's age. On the other hand, it should be borne in mind that with such a small sample of children (17) over such a wide age range (birth to 12 years), this study would have lacked the sensitivity to pick up more subtle, stage-related aspects of fine tuning. However, irrespective of this result, it may well be the case that some children are consistently exposed to a wider range of low frequency words than others, or that some activities such as book-reading are associated with a richer and rarer vocabulary (Crain-Thoresen et al., 2001). Rare words tend to be longer and more complex. Exposure to words with more complex morphology may be particularly valuable in the development of certain aspects of language such as an understanding of derivational morphology which in turn bootstraps the acquisition of rarer and more complex lexical items (Anglin, 1993). Additionally, in English-speaking contexts, a linguistic environment rich in rare words, including many with classical rather than germanic roots may be particularly useful in preparing the child for the language of schooling and literacy.

Some of these assumptions are given empirical support by the 'Home-school study of language and literacy development' (Snow, Tabors and Dickinson, 2001). This longitudinal research, which has now been running for over 14 years, focused initially on 83 children of ethnically diverse low-income families living in the Boston area and relates the richness of the language environment at home and pre-school to later outcomes in language and literacy. Home visits were conducted at ages three, four, and five years and further data were collected at pre-school at the age of four, and in kindergarten and the fourth and seventh grades. Even though the sample had reduced to 74 in kindergarten and 57 by the fourth grade, attrition is non-biased in relation to racial background, maternal education, and family income (Snow, 2001). The richness of the language environment at home and pre-school was measured by exposure to rare words (in addition to extended discourse by mothers and teachers), which was found to be an important predictor of later achievement. As noted above, rare words were defined as those not contained in the Chall and Dale (1995) list of 3000 words judged by teachers to be known to most fourth graders. The method of measuring the incidence of rare words in the home ('rare word density') and at school ('exposure to rare words') was usually the proportion of vocabulary in a transcript that was rare, in other words a type–type ratio. The raw number of word types and token–token ratios are also reported for some analyses (Dickinson, 2001a). The mean number of rare words occurring in different school activities (Cote, 2001) was also addressed, but there was no standardisation of the number of tokens across mothers or teachers, or across the contexts compared (e.g., mealtimes versus toy play).

The home-school project's findings in relation to rare words have such theoretical significance for early language and literacy development, with clear implications for practitioners, that it is worth looking at the results in more detail. In a relatively early analysis, Beals and Tabors (1995) compared the use of rare vocabulary by mothers and children during the home visits at ages three and four across four situations: book-reading, toy play, mealtimes, and a report of a recent event. The *percentage* of low frequency word types used by mothers in each context varied considerably, with the mealtimes providing many rare words and elicited reports relatively few. In book-reading the determining factor was the kind of book. The *number* of rare types used by children and mothers in the four contexts were, in seven cases, significantly and positively correlated with children's scores on the Peabody Picture Vocabulary Test – Revised (PPVT; Dunn and Dunn, 1981) at five years, although for the mothers this was only true for the elicited reports and toy play at the age-three visit. The importance of *mealtime* conversations was followed up by Beals (1997) who analysed 1631 conversational exchanges involving rare word usage by family members in 160 transcripts from the children at ages three, four, and five. This time, exchanges were coded for their informativeness, that is to say whether they provided support for learning the rare word in question, either through semantic support, the physical context, social context or prior knowledge. Approximately two-thirds of exchanges provided acquisitional guidance, usually through semantic support. Correlations between the frequency of informative uses at each age and children's PPVT scores at five and seven years were highly significant. Tabors, Beals and Weizman (2001) extended the analysis of informativeness across the additional conversational contexts of book-reading and toy play. Mothers' rare word density in book-reading at three years, during mealtimes at five years and during toy play at all three ages predicted kindergarten PPVT scores; rare word density of all speakers other than the child itself did so for mealtimes at ages three and five. Weizman and Snow (2001) also focused on rare word density and the informativeness of usage in the home visit at five years as predictors of later vocabulary development. In order to have greater confidence in a causal interpretation, these authors controlled for maternal education, nonverbal IQ of the child, and quantity of child talk. Density of exposure to rare words was found to explain as much as 50 per cent of the variance in second grade PPVT scores.

To reduce the number of variables, Tabors, Roach and Snow (2001) produced composite variables for rare words, extended discourse, and home support for literacy. For rare words the composite consisted of the sum of the standard scores for rare word density from the mealtime and toy play contexts at each age. This composite score significantly predicted emergent literacy and receptive vocabulary, but not narrative production in kindergarten assessments at age five after controlling for demographic and other linguistic factors. Rare word density in the home remains as a significant predictor of kindergarten receptive vocabulary in the final statistical model that includes all the home and pre-school environment composites (Tabors, Snow and Dickinson, 2001).

Several analyses focused on children's exposure to rare words in the pre-school. Cote (2001) compared the language sophistication across activities and found that the mean number of rare words produced by both teachers and children was highest during circle time. Dickinson (2001a) found that the children's language and literacy levels in the kindergarten were predicted by several pre-school rare word variables, depending on age and classroom activity. For teachers and children these included variables based on proportions and raw numbers and both types and tokens. Finally, Dickinson (2001b) assessed the overall impact of their pre-school experience on their language and literacy development in kindergarten. The percentage of teachers' rare words produced in free play predicted later emergent literacy, receptive vocabulary, and ability with formal definitions. Rare words at mealtimes predicted receptive vocabulary and formal definitions, and the composite measure of exposure to rare words across three pre-school contexts predicted emergent literacy, formal definitions, and receptive vocabulary.

The relationship between rarity measures and sample size

Longer language samples naturally tend to contain more rare words but not all researchers have controlled for this. Crain-Thoreson and colleagues (2001) concluded that rare words occurred more frequently during book-reading than in toy play or 'remembering a family outing'. However, this result could simply arise from the fact that parents produced both more utterances and longer utterances in this context, substantially increasing the number of word tokens. Others have resorted to proportional measures in an attempt to compensate (e.g. Beals and Tabors, 1995; Weizman and Snow, 2001; chapters in Dickinson and Tabors, 2001). Nevertheless, it is clear that any proportional rarity measure based on *types* will still be sensitive to sample size, although this is unlikely to be the case for any measure that has *tokens* in both the numerator and denominator. For example, one measure that was effectively used by Afitskaya (2002) was the proportion of tokens that were 'advanced', or the ratio of 'advanced' to 'basic' tokens to discriminate between the spoken narratives of intermediate and advanced learners of English as a foreign language. Nevertheless, analyses that depend on token counts can be distorted by highly frequent usage of a small number of rare or advanced words, and may give a less valid picture of lexical richness than those that focus on the range of vocabulary.

The sensitivity of type–type rarity measures to sample size is well attested for the proportion of words that are hapax legomena and hapax dislegomena (Sichel, 1986) and is borne out by Ménard (1983) for the relationship between the number of types and the proportion of words that are rare on an extrinsic criterion. Beals and Tabors (1995) found a similar relationship in their study of pre-schoolers' exposure to vocabulary but since this is based on the correlation across mothers, it cannot necessarily be interpreted as a sample size effect – it may simply mean that the same kind of person that uses a wide range of vocabulary also uses rare words. Meara and Bell claim that Laufer and Nation's LFP is 'very sensitive to text length' and that 'this makes it difficult to compare LFP scores from different sources' (Meara and Bell, 2001, p. 9). Such a relationship would hardly be surprising – as a text gets longer, common vocabulary, and some rare words, will already have been sampled and the only way to add to the total of types will be to add increasingly rare items. As suggested above, if the number of types is a function of the number of tokens and the number of rare words is a function of the number of types, then the number and proportion of rare words will increase with the number of tokens.

This phenomenon makes comparisons between groups, individuals, activities or contexts that use data from different sample sizes problematic. For example, Laufer's (2003) study of the effects of immigration to Israel on L1 Russian (see above) did not control the number of tokens for the analysis of low frequency Russian vocabulary, so the apparent fall in the percentage of rare words used by subjects with longer residence in Israel could also be accounted for by the fact that the length of their compositions also fell significantly. Interestingly, a fall in TTRs, which *were* calculated from a standard 200 words, was not significant. The results from studies that make such comparisons are, at best, difficult to interpret and, at worst, invalid, although in some cases, for instance the home-school study (Dickinson and Tabors, 2001 and related publications), there is a convergence of evidence from a wide range of analyses, for example types versus tokens, and of other variables that lend support to the robustness of the findings. The question arises, therefore, as to how the size of language sample can best be controlled. The Advanced TTR (advanced types/tokens) proposed by Daller and colleagues (2003) will have the same disadvantage as TTR: it will fall with increasing sample size, and the Advanced Guiraud (advanced types/tokens) will be no more able to control for variation in sample size than the original index (see Chapter 2). Laufer and Nation (1995) were obviously aware of the sample size problems and based their LFP analysis on the first 300 words of the learners' compositions, but unfortunately different users employ different standard lengths – Meara and colleagues (1997) standardise at 500 words, and Milton and Hales (1997) at 1000 – making comparisons between the values obtained from different studies impossible.

Meara and Bell (2001) voice additional criticisms of the LFP. It is said to be unstable on texts of less than 200 words, and to have unsatisfactory measurement properties. This is because less than 10 per cent of words tend to fall into the two frequency bands for the rarer words. The quantity of data on which comparisons are based is therefore relatively small, leading to restricted ranges and poor discrimination between texts. This is likely to be particularly problematic with beginners or learners with a low level of proficiency. Meara and Bell's solution is their P_Lex software. This first of all divides all words in a text into two categories, 'easy' or 'hard', and it does so on the basis of Nation's (1984) words lists: all words in Nation's first 1000 (plus all numbers, proper nouns, and 'geographical derivatives') are treated as 'easy' by Meara and Bell's procedure. The software then divides the text into segments of ten word tokens and counts the number of hard words in each segment, and a frequency profile is then produced of the number of segments that contain zero hard words, one hard word, two hard words, and so on. Because of the rarity of hard words, most segments contain zero or few of them, and the result is a heavily left-skewed distribution of the type that can be closely fitted by a Poisson curve. Such curves can be described by a formula containing the parameter lambda whose value determines the exact shape of the curve, and which can be taken as a measure of the density of hard words. Greater detail, including the formula, is supplied in Meara and Bell's technical Appendix (Meara and Bell, 2001, pp. 18–19), but the authors claim that the procedure is: (a) particularly appropriate for texts as short as 120 words produced by low-level learners; (b) discriminates well between levels of proficiency in the essays of students learning English as a foreign language; (c) is stable across two different discursive essays produced by the same students on different occasions; and (d) is not discernibly related to sample size beyond 120 words. One reservation about P_Lex would be that within the ten-word segments it counts rare tokens rather than types (Paul Meara, personal communication). This means that lambda values could be boosted by the repetition of a rare word inside a segment.

When researchers are aware of it, the problem of sensitivity to sample size can usually be handled by standardising the number of tokens, or, preferably, by using P_Lex. Another possibility is to use the rationale behind the mean segmental type–token ratio discussed in Chapter 2 and evaluated in Chapter 6. In research into classical literature, this has recently been applied by Smith and Kelly (2002) to estimate the dates of the tragedies of Euripedes and the comedies of Aristophenes and Terence. These authors divided the parts of the plays that were the focus of analysis into 300-word segments and calculated the average number of hapax legomena (as well as the average number of types and the average Yules's K) across segments. This could be developed further by using an extrinsic criterion to produce a mean segmental rare word density.

These solutions, including P_Lex, seem perfectly valid if the aim is simply to discriminate between levels of proficiency or text difficulty (although one might legitimately ask why it is necessary to compute the mean for Yule's K rather than TTR or simply the average number of different words when variation in sample size is already controlled for by the standard segments). On the other hand, since diversity and rarity *are* correlated (Ménard, 1983; Beals and Tabors, 1995), it could be argued that these methods of controlling the number of tokens confound lexical diversity and rarity. Other kinds of research that require a more diagnostic approach, such as studies of language impairment and delay, or of educational progress, might benefit from a method that disentangled these two dimensions of lexical richness. One way of doing this would be to have two complementary measures – a measure of overall diversity such as D and an index of rarity that controlled, not for the overall number of tokens, but for the number of word types in the whole sample, thus measuring rarity over and above diversity. Using *vocd* to model the ratio of rare types to rare tokens against the number of rare tokens also has potential as an index of the diversity of rare words and is something that needs to be explored in future research.

Vocabulary composition and early lexical style

Type–type measures have been used in both first and second language research to investigate the relationship between the acquisition of different word classes or to assess their relative dominance. For second language, Broeder, Extra and van Hout (1993) made claims for the relative importance of verbs, as opposed to nouns, in the spontaneous acquisition of Dutch by adults on the basis of correlations between overall lexical richness (as measured by theoretical vocabulary and Guiraud's index) and proportional type–type indices – while there was no relationship between the proportion of word types that were nouns, the relationship with verbs was positive and significant.

In first language, much of the focus has been on the open versus closed class distinction, but the emphasis here is on comparing the range of word types as a diagnostic of *style* of language development. This should not be confused with the use of the *token*-based lexical density (Ure, 1971) in other areas of applied linguistics. Lexical density is usually calculated as the percentage of tokens that are lexical/content words, but sometimes includes a higher weighting for low frequency words (Halliday, 1985). Lexical density was originally used as a way of quantifying differences between different registers, particularly speech and writing and is commonly used in second language research (see e.g. O'Loughlin, 1995). According to Read (2000) lexical density can be regarded as tapping the degree of concentration of ideas and information.

An example of the corresponding type–type measure in first language, can be found in research by Augst (1987) who collected the entire sample of tenyear-old German children's writing across a whole academic year and for each child calculated the proportion of types that were content words. However, in the investigation of individual differences in early spoken language, such measures are usually more theoretically motivated. From the late 1970s to the early 1990s there was a series of studies into distinctive 'routes', 'styles', and 'strategies' of language acquisition (see Richards, 1990, pp. 10–14) that built on Nelson's (1973) referential-expressive, Bloom, Lightbown and Hood's (1975) nominal-pronominal, and Peters's (1983) analytic-holistic dichotomies. Measures such as noun–pronoun ratios (e.g. Della Corte, Benedict and Klein, 1983) and the percentage of vocabulary that was accounted for by general nominals (Nelson, 1973; Bates et al., 1988) became important variables in the identification of children with a more referential, nominal, and analytic style, and Nelson's (1973) criterion of a vocabulary consisting of 50 percent of general nominals needed to classify a child as 'referential' was adopted in subsequent research into the one-word stage. In a longitudinal study of individual differences in language development in 32 middle-class children, Elizabeth Bates and her colleagues used seven measures of lexical style in spontaneous speech at two age points: 20 months and 28 months. These were:

Open Class Style = (noun types + lexical verb types + adjective types) / all different morpheme types.
Closed Class Style = closed class morpheme types / all morpheme types.
Adjective Density = open class adjectives / content words.
Verb Density = open class verb types / (open class verbs + nouns + adjective types).
Noun Density = common nouns / content words.
Referential Style = common noun types / all types.

Apart from adjective density and noun density where the information is not provided, all these are explicitly stated to be type–type measures (see Bates et al., 1988, pp. 97–8, 150).

The effect of sample size

We have already noted at the beginning of this chapter that evidence from literary studies shows that type–type measures are not independent of the number of word tokens. Köhler and Galle (1993) found this to be true of the verb–adjective ratio, and Ménard's (1983) measures of monosemy and polysemy, and noun–verb and adjective–noun ratios were all a function of text length. Consistent with these findings is Augst's (1987) observation that in German children's written texts the number of content words as a percentage of all word types increased with sample size. This result is mirrored by an investigation by Richards and Malvern (1997) into Bates and her colleagues' (1988) style measures. For one child at 26 months they plotted cumulative open-class style and closed-class style values against the number of tokens between zero and 300 tokens. After some degree of fluctuation up to 100 tokens, there was a consistent and very clear rise in the open-class values accompanied by a corresponding fall in closed-class values as the number of words increased. The importance of this finding is that unless there are controls for variation in the size of spontaneous speech samples, results are likely to be compromised. This is because:

> ... children who provide larger speech samples and therefore more types, very often the linguistically more advanced children, will have a built-in bias towards a more open-class, referential or 'nouny' style. Conversely, samples from children who talk less will be biased towards a more closed-class, 'expressive', or 'pronominal' interpretation.
> (Richards and Malvern, 1997, pp. 66–7)

It must be stressed that the measurement problem alluded to here applies only to *spontaneous speech* samples, and that these are not the only means of assessing early vocabulary composition. Much early research relied on parental (usually maternal) diary studies and, more recently, checklists have been filled in by parents, in most cases a version of the MacArthur Communicative Development Inventories (MCDI) (Fenson et al., 1993). The relative suitability of these three approaches has been subjected to close scrutiny. In an article titled 'How referential are referential children', Pine (1992) compared cumulative maternal diary data with 60-minute home recordings for eight children when their vocabulary size was 50 words and 100 words. The proportion of types that were common nouns was calculated for each method of data collection, and at each stage of development the results were compared. Results showed a higher percentage of noun types from diaries than from spontaneous speech, but the two measures correlated significantly at 50 words ($r = 0.66$) and strongly at 100 words ($r = 0.89$). Pine's conclusion was that the maternal reports were oversensitive to referential items and therefore tended to overestimate the proportion of common nouns. These findings were followed up by Pine, Lieven and Rowland (1996) using a similar approach to compare observational data with a version of the MCDI adapted for British English. They pointed out that in recent research into early vocabulary composition these two methods had produced conflicting results. This time their analyses included the percentage of vocabulary that consisted of frozen phrases as well as common nouns. Correlations between the proportional vocabulary scores obtained from the two approaches again proved to be statistically significant at each stage, but percentages for common nouns were higher using the checklist than for spontaneous speech, while the percentage of frozen phrases was lower. This time, rather than attribute these findings *solely* to a referential bias in maternal reporting (whether by checklist or diary), the authors point out that both methods have inherent biases and recommend more comprehensive data from both sources.

The disadvantage of spontaneous speech is that it is less comprehensive than maternal reports and tends to favour certain contexts and activities that suit audio recording. It is therefore less reliable. In addition, observations may fail to sample lower frequency items of vocabulary. Pine and colleagues also note that checklists are designed to capture individual differences between children, for example differences in vocabulary size, rather than to estimate the proportional make-up of the vocabulary itself. Their comments are undoubtedly true – low frequency vocabulary items may often be highly salient and more likely to be reported in diaries than contained in checklists or captured in speech samples; checklists are standardised instruments that do not allow for the idiosyncrasies of individual children; the proportions of words belonging to different classes and, crucially, *the opportunities offered to parents to select them* will not accurately reflect the constitution of children's vocabulary if it varies from the norm offered by the instrument.

In addition, the point above about the relative frequency of lexical items leads us to the issue of sample size in relation to spontaneous speech data, something that Pine and colleagues (1996) briefly acknowledge as a problem (p. 583) but do not expand on. Suppose, for example, a child had a large repertoire of common nouns, many of which were used relatively infrequently, and a small repertoire of other words, many of which were interactive words, proper nouns, onomatopoeic words, and other words such as pronouns (based on the Pine et al. coding scheme), many of which had a high frequency of usage. A short transcript from this child is likely to be dominated by the high frequency word types. However, in a longer transcript most of these would already have been sampled and could make no further contribution to the total number of types. Common nouns with a lower frequency of usage, on the other hand, will now have greater opportunity to be added to the type count. This accords exactly with the evidence above that larger samples tend to produce more 'nouny' or referential-looking children and gives another possible explanation for the discrepancies in referential style indices between maternal reporting through diary or checklist and observational data, namely that the recordings were too short or too context bound. Pine and colleagues (1996) suggest that the true proportion of nouns contained in children's vocabularies may lie somewhere between the values obtained for checklists and transcripts (pp. 585–6). We would argue, however, that the truth of this statement will depend on the size of language sample obtained from the child.

At first sight, there seems to be a simple, common-sense solution: standardise the number of word tokens across transcripts. Certainly this is a step forward, in as far as it increases the validity of comparisons between children and between stages of vocabulary development for the same children. Unfortunately, however, we have no way of knowing the optimum sample size that would accurately reflect the composition of children's vocabulary, or even the extent to which different sample sizes would be appropriate at different stages.

The 'noun bias' issue

A particular application of the kind of measure discussed above lies in cross-linguistic research into the relative status of nouns, verbs, and other predicate terms in early vocabulary development. The impetus is Gentner's (1982) Natural Partitions hypothesis which engaged with the supposedly universal predominance of nouns in early vocabularies. This was explained by cognitive-perceptual predispositions to distinguish between concrete objects and other kinds of concept that themselves underlie the *linguistic* distinction between nouns and predicate terms. A combination of such a pre-existing structure with the relative conceptual simplicity of the noun category leads, according to Gentner, to the prediction 'that terms denoting objects and entities will be acquired first across languages and that these terms will be nominals' (Gentner, 1982, p. 304). Gentner finds support for the latter statement in data from 16 children distributed across six languages (Mandarin, Japanese, Kaluli, German, English, and Turkish): the proportion of early vocabulary accounted for by nominals ranged from 50 per cent for a Kaluli child to 85 per cent for an English-speaking child.

The Natural Partitions hypothesis contrasts with a Linguistic Relativity or language-specific position that disputes the idea of a natural order, and accounts for variation within and between languages through features of child-directed speech and contextual-situational factors. Indeed, research during the last decade has called into question the dominance of words for objects, particularly for non-Indo-European languages. Studies of Korean (Choi and Gopnik, 1995; Gopnik and Choi, 1995; Kim, McGregor and Thompson, 2000) show that children as young as 1;3 use verbs productively, and with inflections, to encode activity and that verbs and nouns are equally dominant at the one-word stage. Korean children acquire significantly more verbs than children learning English. Tardif, Shatz and Naigles (1997) found that Mandarin-speaking children tended to favour nouns less than those acquiring English and Italian. Findings from Tzotzil (de León, 2001) suggest that verbs outnumber nouns in the early lexicon and have clearer reference than nouns. The universality of a strong noun bias has also been disputed on the basis of data from German (Kauschke and Hofmeister, 2002) and English (Nelson, Hampson and Kessler Shaw, 1993).

The fundamental questioning of a universal pattern has led to a number of foci for recent research. First is the systematic, empirical study of input (as opposed to theoretical discussions of typological features of different languages) to establish whether the statistical patterns of children's vocabulary composition are reflected in the language they hear, and to test theory-driven questions about factors such as the salience of different word classes, their relative morphological complexity as measured by the degree of variation in their morphological forms (Tardif et al., 1997), and the role of pragmatic features in influencing children's vocabulary usage and acquisition. Thus Goldfield (1993) finds evidence supporting the salience of nouns in child-directed speech in English while for Turkish (Küntay and Slobin, 2001) and Italian (Camaioni and Longobardi, 2001) verbs are claimed to be more salient. A second research focus is the importance of the context in which data are collected, as noun dominance in a book-reading context can turn into verb dominance during toy play (e.g., Tardif, Gelman and Xu, 1999, for English and Mandarin; Ogura, 2002, for Japanese). Third, because of possible biases introduced by the method of data collection discussed in the previous section, an additional concern is the extent to which spontaneous speech favours the sampling of verbs and checklists favour nouns (Tardif, 2001; Tardif et al., 1999).

It can be seen from the above just how far the methodology of cross-linguistic research into early vocabulary has progressed. Gentner's (1982) study was a straightforward report of the first words children learn and the proportion of nominals in their early vocabulary based on a mixture of retrospective reports by parents, journals or diaries, and transcripts. Studies making speech recordings are now carefully controlled with the intention of allowing systematic, valid, and reliable comparisons of the relative importance of different word classes (usually nouns versus verbs), between languages (for example English versus Mandarin), contexts (toy play versus book-reading), between input and the language of the child, between spontaneous speech and checklist, and different ages (Bassano, 2000; Kauschke and Hofmeister, 2002; Ogura, 2002). In addition, researchers may investigate subcategories of nouns and verbs (Bassano, 2000) or systematically examine the effect of variation in the set of words defined as nouns or verbs (Goldfield, 1993).

Although some studies report analyses of tokens, these are mainly for purposes of comparison with the main thrust: the number or proportion of word types that belong to a certain class, or the diversity of words within a word class. The measures that serve as dependent variables for mother or child include the following:

1. Raw number of noun types and raw number of verb types (Tardif et al., 1997).
2. Noun type–token ratio and verb type–token ratio (Bassano, 2000; Camaioni and Longobardi, 2001).
3. Noun *token–type* ratio and verb *token–type* ratio (Goldfield, 1993; Küntay and Slobin, 2001).
4. Noun types per utterance and verb types per utterance (Ogura, 2002) or per 100 or 200 utterances (Choi and Gopnik, 1995; Kim et al., 2000).
5. Types belonging to each word class as a proportion of all word types (Kauschke and Hofmeister, 2002).
6. The ratio of verb types to noun types (Küntay and Slobin, 2001).
7. Noun types as a proportion of noun types plus verb types (N/N + V) (Tardif et al., 1999; Ogura, 2002).

Readers will be aware that the first four of these measures suffer from the same problems related to variation in sample size that were discussed in Chapter 2. Measure 1 is the equivalent of total number of words (TNW), but for separate word classes. Numbers 2 and 3 are TTR and its reciprocal, and these respectively decrease and increase with the token count. Number 4 is analogous to TTR because utterances are an open set, and samples with more utterances, and/or longer utterances will also have more words. This measure is, for nouns only and verbs only, the equivalent of Yoder, Davies and Bishop's (1994) 'prorated number of lexically free words' (p. 275), that is to say, the range of productive vocabulary in 100 utterances, whose sensitivity to sample size is demonstrated in Richards and Malvern (1997). By contrast, the last three measures are type–*type* measures of the kind discussed in this chapter and are equally likely to be a function of sample size, although the nature of this relationship is less well understood in the language development literature than the type–token indices. If variation in sample size is an issue, then clearly any comparison between groups of speakers or any of the other contrasts referred to above should ideally control for the sample size in each level of the variable under scrutiny.

In spite of this, methodological discussion in the 'noun bias' literature has tended to focus on the method of data collection, controls for context, and definition of nouns and verbs rather than the statistical properties of the measures themselves. Tardif and colleagues (1997) control sample size in their comparisons of word types by entering the number of tokens as a covariate in analyses of covariance, but this is an exception and, of course, it is a statistical method that assumes linear relationships rather than the curvilinear patterns we observe with vocabulary. On the other hand, if authors supply full information about the mean token counts that each comparison is based on, then results are often more easily interpretable. In some cases, the means are almost equivalent and results may be acceptable at their face value, although the means may conceal considerable 'noise' in the data in the form of within-group variation in token count. In others, scrutiny of these data may make findings appear less secure. For example, high noun TTRs and low verb TTRs may go hand in hand with a lower number of noun tokens than verb tokens (for example Camaioni and Longobardi, 2001, p. 778) so it is difficult to tell whether there is really more repetition for verbs or whether this result is an artefact of the respective token counts. Unfortunately, published reports do not always give information about numbers of tokens.

An interesting parallel to the 'noun bias' literature lies in the field of specific language impairment (SLI). Here, investigations into the extent to which children with SLI have low verb diversity and a high frequency usage of a small number of general, all-purpose (GAP) verbs compared with age-matched and language-matched controls have produced conflicting results. The failure to calculate verb diversity measures from a common baseline of tokens in many of these studies have made their results extremely difficult to interpret (Richards and Malvern, 1997) and in some cases (Hansson, 1996; Watkins et al., 1993) may even cause real differences to be underestimated (see also Richards and Malvern, 1996). Some earlier findings of significant differences between children developing normally and with SLI (e.g. Watkins et al., 1993) have more recently been called into question. Here, too, the issue of data collection by recording spontaneous speech or through checklists has been discussed (Hick, Joseph, Conti-Ramsden and Serratrice, 2002). As a result, the research methodology, and measurement issues in particular, have been subjected to scrutiny (see Thordardottir and Ellis Weismer, 2001, for an excellent critical review, including a section on measuring verb diversity on pp. 222–6). Recent empirical research on SLI and GAP verbs (Thordardottir and Ellis Weismer, 2001) and on SLI in Cantonese-speaking children (Stokes and Fletcher, 2000) have failed to find group differences on verb diversity. Importantly, these later investigations, unlike much earlier research, have based comparisons on a standard overall token size. Thordardottir and Ellis Weismer (2001) used 315 tokens for analyses of overall lexical diversity, and 80 verb tokens for verb diversity. Stokes and Fletcher (2000) used the first 117 words in their transcripts for all between-group comparisons of raw number of types belonging to each word class. In addition, they employed 'proportional diversity' type–type ratios to compare the proportion of all types accounted for by different word classes.

Clearly, the approach to standardisation of sample size differs between these studies. There is not just the issue of whether measures have been calculated from a standard number of tokens overall (as in Stokes and Fletcher, 2000), but, for raw numbers of different words, TTRs, *and* type–type variables, whether it is more appropriate that they should be derived from a

142 Lexical Diversity and Language Development

standard number of tokens within each word class (as in Thordardottir and Ellis Weismer, 2001). Otherwise, it can be argued that within that standard size of sample one can obtain more verb types through a higher number of verb tokens, for example. The resolution to this problem lies in the precise nature of the research questions and whether comparisons are made between subjects or within subjects, for example whether noun diversity is greater than verb diversity over the whole population sample.

Nouns versus verbs: the effect of sample size

We have already discussed evidence in the section on vocabulary composition and early lexical style that spontaneous speech variables consisting of the proportion of different words belonging to a certain class can be a function of sample size. We now turn our attention to two kinds of measure exemplified by items 6 and 7 in the list above, of which the first is a true ratio and the second a proportional measure. These are the ratio of verbs to nouns (and nouns to verbs) and nouns as a proportion of nouns plus verbs. For each we will provide an investigation of sample size effects.

An empirical demonstration

To investigate the effects of sample size we needed transcripts that were as long as possible to guarantee high frequencies of each word class. They also needed to have a reliable grammatical coding tier (the '%mor' tier in CHAT) that could be processed by the CLAN software (MacWhinney, 2000a). Both criteria were fulfilled by the Manchester Corpus (Theakston, Lieven, Pine and Rowland, 2001) in the CHILDES database (MacWhinney, 2000b) and we chose the first and last transcripts in this corpus for the child known as Anne, at the ages of 1;10.7 and 2;9.10 respectively. An extract from Anne's first transcript that illustrates the %mor tier is provided in Appendix IV.

In the younger transcript there are 254 child word tokens coded for their syntactic category on the %mor tier. The analyses reported here use the first 250 tokens. Of these, there are 40 different nouns and 14 different verbs. The noun category included all lexical items coded as 'n' on the %mor tier and included proper nouns. Verbs were those coded as 'v' but excluded auxiliaries and copulas. For both categories different word *roots*, rather than the full, inflected forms, were treated as different types. Figure 8.1 shows how these unfold as the sample size increases by plotting the number of word types in each class against the number of tokens at intervals of ten tokens. These curves therefore represent *cumulative* totals as one reads through the transcript in sequence from beginning to end. It can be seen that the number of verb types increases at a slower rate than the number of noun types and reaches a plateau at about 190 tokens. After this point Anne continues to use verbs, but she is repeating types that have previously been sampled. New noun types, on the other hand, are still being sampled. From these conspicuously diverging

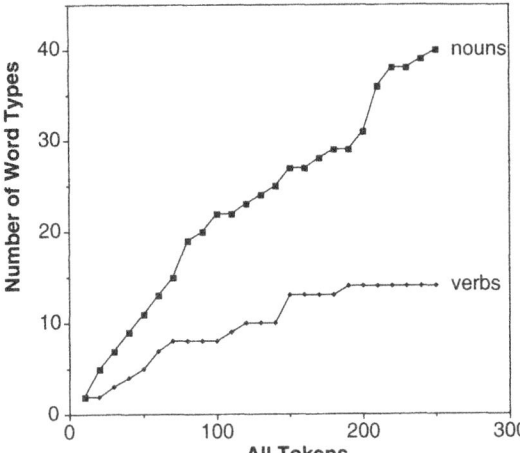

Figure 8.1 Cumulative noun and verb types plotted against number of words for Anne at 1;10.7

plots it is clear that ratios and proportions with nouns in the numerator will increase, while those with verbs in the numerator will decrease. Indeed, when these measures are calculated at each point on the graph, the Spearman rank order correlation for cumulative Verbs/Nouns, Nouns/Verbs and Nouns/(Nouns + Verbs) with the number of tokens is 0.428 in all three cases (-0.428 for Verbs/Nouns; $p < 0.05$; $N = 25$).

Cumulative analyses have the disadvantage that they can be distorted by local clustering of word types at various points in the transcript. A clearer indication of the true relationship with sample size can be obtained by averaging the number of verb and noun types across segments of the transcript that increase in size in increments of a constant number of tokens, and calculating the ratios and proportions from these. Thus, for this transcript of 254 child tokens, we were able to average across 25 segments of 10 tokens, 12 segments of 20 tokens, 8 segments of 30 tokens and so on, until we reached a segment size of 120 tokens, after which only one segment was available. The resulting plots for our three measures are shown in Figure 8.2. Because the scale on the y-axis is the same for all three measures, only the effect for Nouns/Verbs can be seen clearly. By appropriately changing the scale for each plot, however, the close relationship between the three plots and the sensitivity of all three measures to sample size can be observed. This is shown in Figures 8.2a to 8.2c. The rank order correlations between the measures and the token count are again the same for all three measures and are, indeed, stronger than for the cumulative versions ($rho = 0.538$; $p < 0.005$; $N = 25$). As would be expected, the correlation is negative for Verbs/Nouns and positive for the other two measures.

In order to judge the extent to which these relationships might be sustained in a longer transcript we then carried out the same procedures with

144 *Lexical Diversity and Language Development*

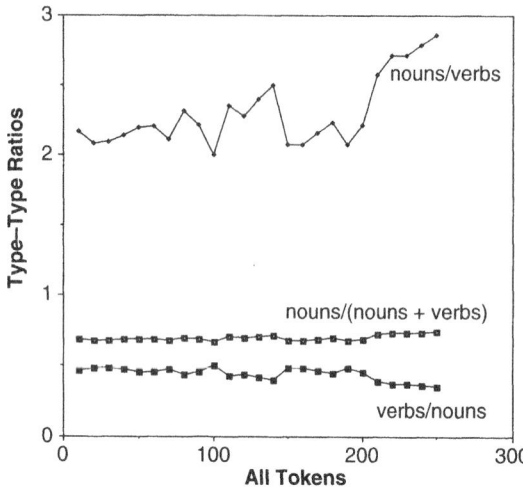

Figure 8.2 Averaged type–type measures plotted against number of words for Anne at 1;10.7

Anne's final transcript at the age of 2;9.10. This contained 1314 child tokens, and 236 types. Analyses were limited to the first 1310 words spoken by Anne. Of the word *types* there were 59 nouns and 40 verbs. At first sight, this appears to be a more rigorous test of sample size effects because the number of verb types and noun types are much closer than at 1;10.7 where there were nearly three times as many nouns as verbs. On the other hand, Anne says more than four times the number of words at the older age, which ought to allow more reliable identification of trends.

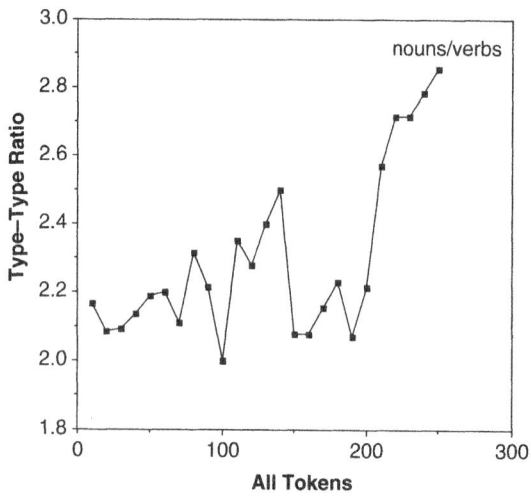

Figure 8.2a Averaged noun types/verb types plotted against number of words for Anne at 1;10.7

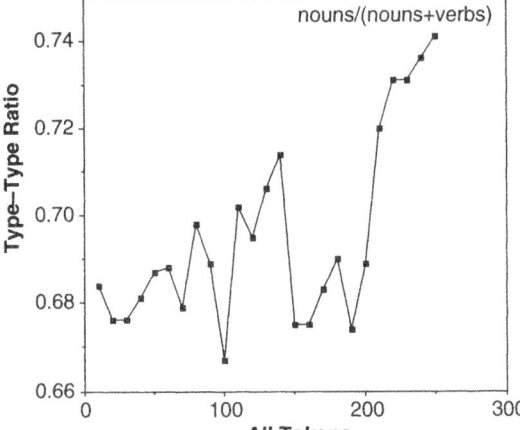

Figure 8.2b Averaged noun types/(noun types + verb types) plotted against number of words for Anne at 1;10.7

Cumulative noun and verb types are plotted at ten-token intervals against the number of tokens in Figure 8.3. This time, there is an initial surge of verbs that becomes less steep once high frequency types have been sampled. The advantage for verb types continues up to 390 tokens when noun dominance establishes itself and is consolidated in the widening gap between the two plots as the transcript progresses. This is reflected in the rank order correlations between cumulative Verbs/Nouns, Nouns/Verbs, and Nouns/(Nouns + Verbs) that are considerably stronger for this longer transcript than for the previous one ($rho = 0.895$; $p < 0.001$; $N = 131$). The cumulative analysis was then supplemented by the averaging process described above,

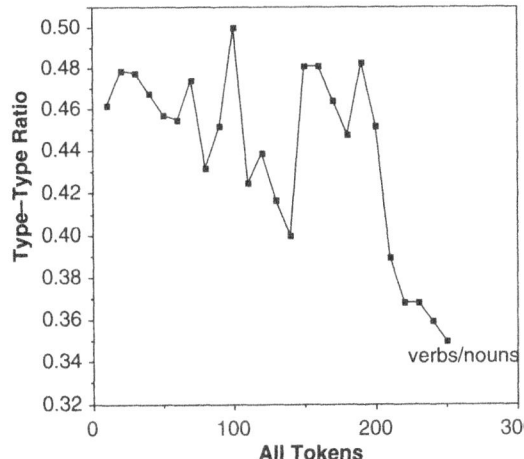

Figure 8.2c Averaged verb types/noun types plotted against number of words for Anne at 1;10.7

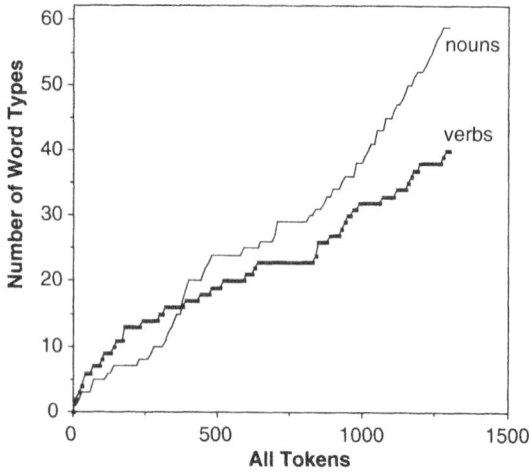

Figure 8.3 Cumulative noun and verb types plotted against number of words for Anne at 2;9.10

and the resulting plots are shown in Figure 8.4. Again, it can be seen clearly that the ratio of the mean number of Verbs to Nouns across segments falls, while its reciprocal, Nouns to Verbs, and Nouns/(Nouns + Verbs) rise. The rank order correlations with sample size are large ($rho = 0.857$; $p < 0.001$; $N = 131$) although not as large as for the cumulative analysis. The crossover between the plots for nouns and verbs in Figure 8.3 and the Verb–Noun and

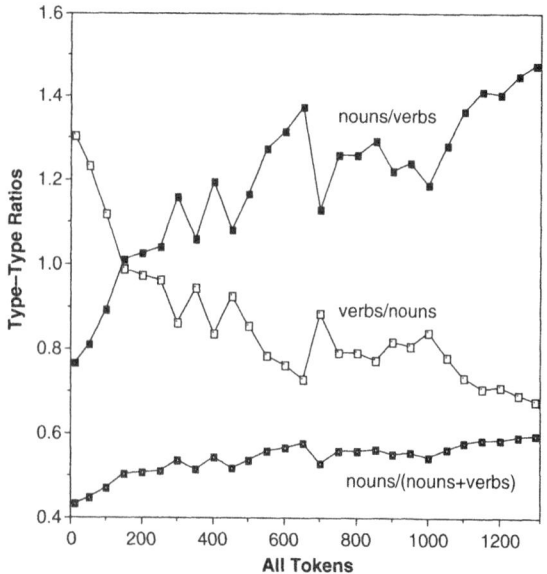

Figure 8.4 Averaged type–type measures plotted against number of words for Anne at 2;9.10

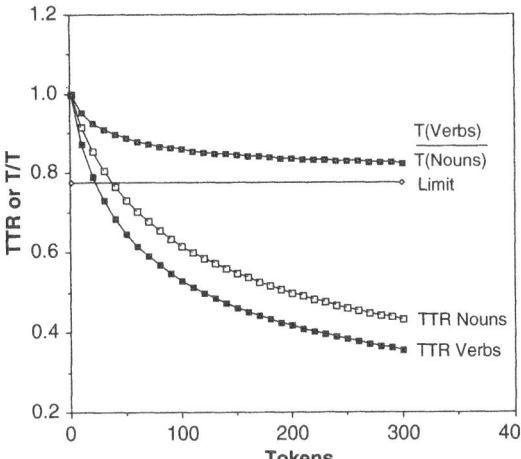

Figure 8.5 Type–type ratio (verbs to nouns), derived from dividing TTR verbs by TTR nouns, plotted against tokens

Noun–Verb ratios in Figure 8.4 demonstrate not just how and why these measures are related to sample size, but also how, for the same child at the same age, a short language sample could appear to show verb dominance while a longer language sample could appear to show noun dominance.

A proposed solution to the sample size problem

Comparing results from different transcripts would be impossible without some sort of standardisation of the size of the language samples. There is a further complication with type–type ratios, however, in that at any one point in the transcript the token counts of verbs and of nouns will differ and so their type counts will be derived from different bases of tokens. This partly accounts for the fluctuations in the general trend of the graphs above and makes comparison among researchers even more difficult, as standardising the overall size of language sample for calculating a type–type ratio does not guarantee that internal sub-samples for each class are also standardised.

These problems can be addressed by first noticing that a type–type ratio can be derived by dividing the TTR of one class by the TTR of the other, provided they are both calculated over the same token size (N) so that the Ns cancel. This can be done for all values of N by dividing the TTR against token curve for one class by the curve for the other class. The outcome, as shown in Figure 8.5 (above) would be the type–type curve against tokens that approaches a particular limiting value the larger and larger N becomes.

The TTR against token curve for each class is approximated by our mathematical model (see Chapter 3), however, so this can be shown analytically as in Figure 8.6. The result is a remarkable simplification. A type–type ratio attempts to measure the relative diversity of two word classes but its value alters with sample size. For a particular transcript, it approaches a limiting value, however,

Let T_i be the number of types of word class i in N_i tokens.
Consider type-type ratio T_1/T_2

$$\frac{T_1}{T_2} = \frac{T_1/N_1}{T_2/N_2} \text{ for } N_1 = N_2 (=N)$$

i.e. $\frac{T_1}{T_2} = \frac{T_1/N}{T_2/N} = \frac{TTR_1}{TTR_2}$

where TTR is the type-token ratio as a function of N.
Recall that in our mathematical model

$$TTR = \frac{D}{N}\left[\left(1 + 2\frac{N}{D}\right)^{1/2} - 1\right]$$

hence

$$\frac{T_1}{T_2} = \frac{\frac{D_1}{N}\left[\left(1 + 2\frac{N}{D_1}\right)^{1/2} - 1\right]}{\frac{D_2}{N}\left[\left(1 + 2\frac{N}{D_2}\right)^{1/2} - 1\right]}$$

For large N, the 1s are negligible and

$$\frac{T_1}{T_2} \rightarrow \frac{\frac{D_1}{N}\left(2\frac{N}{D_1}\right)^{1/2}}{\frac{D_2}{N}\left(2\frac{N}{D_2}\right)^{1/2}}$$

Cancelling and rearranging,

$$\text{Limit} \frac{T_1}{T_2} = \frac{D_1}{D_2}\left(\frac{D_2}{D_1}\right)^{1/2} = \sqrt{\frac{D_1}{D_2}}$$

which gives the Limiting Relative Diversity (LRD).
The example in Figure 8.5 is for $D_{verbs} = 30$ and $D_{nouns} = 50$
and the Limiting Relative Diversity of verbs to nouns is

$$LRD = \sqrt{\frac{D_1}{D_2}} = \sqrt{\frac{D_{verbs}}{D_{nouns}}} = \sqrt{\frac{30}{50}} = 0.7746$$

Figure 8.6 Mathematical note on type–type ratios

which depends on the *relative* diversity of the two classes but is not a function of sample size. Moreover, the value for this limit can be derived theoretically from the Ds for the two word classes calculated separately, and, as demonstrated in Figure 8.6, is the square root of (D1/D2). We have called this the Limiting Relative Diversity (LRD) and suggest it is a better measure for comparison of transcripts of differing sizes than their overall type–type ratios.

Programming for limiting relative diversity (LRD)

An LRD subroutine was developed in the *vocd* software, selected by a new (+ g) switch on the main command line. This gives access to the analyses for separate word classes and the user enters instructions in two separate command lines, one for each word class or combination of word classes, to be compared. The software carries out the mathematical modelling procedure for each command line separately, providing a D value for each word class. In calculating the square root of the ratio of the D values, the word class entered into the first command line will be the numerator, and the second word class will be the denominator. The following is an example of the sequence of commands required to produce verb–noun ratios in the analyses of the Manchester Corpus described below:

vocd +t"*CHI" +t"%mor" –t"*" +g filename [limits the analysis to the child's speech on the **%mor** tier and invokes the LRD subroutine]

+s"v|*" +s"*–%%" [selects verbs for the numerator and removes inflections]

+s"n|*" +s"*–%%" [selects nouns for the denominator and removes inflections].

An example of *vocd*'s output from this procedure is contained in Appendix VII.

LRD for Anne and her mother

In order to test the new procedure and to see whether maternal and child Verb/Noun diversity was related in their interactions across ages, we obtained Verb/Noun LRD for Anne and her mother over 11 recordings made at approximately one-monthly intervals between the ages of 1;11.4 and 2;9.10. One feature of the mathematical model is that it requires 50 tokens from each word class to calculate reliable D values, and as Anne produced less than this at 1;10.7, her earliest transcript had to be omitted.

As is evident from Figure 8.7, values for both mother and child show a predominantly higher diversity for nouns, with a mean of 0.839 for Anne ($SD = 0.153$) and 0.751 for her mother ($SD = 0.130$). Nevertheless, values do vary considerably from recording to recording – Anne's range is from 0.615 to 1.222 and contains two values of greater than one, indicating greater verb diversity. Her mother's scores range from 0.514 to 0.966 which is significantly lower than Anne on a Wilcoxon signed ranks test ($Z = 2.40; p < 0.05$; $N = 11$). There is no discernible developmental trend but the plots of LRD (Verbs/Nouns) in Figure 8.7 are very closely matched between mother and child ($rho = 0.727; p < 0.05; N = 11$). These results suggest that LRD is sensitive to relationships between relative verb and noun diversity and factors such as the situational context and activities (Tardif et al., 1999; Ogura, 2002), as well as to topics and reciprocal influences in the interaction.

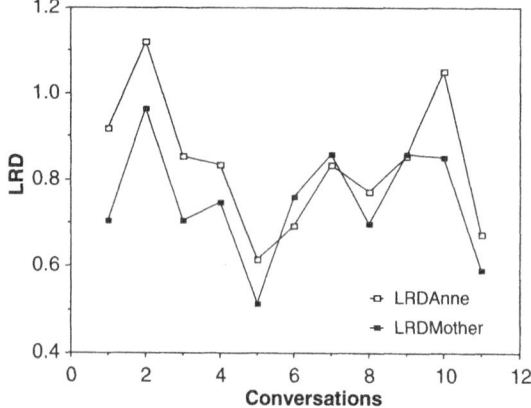

Figure 8.7 Verb/noun LRD for Anne and her mother over 11 conversations between 1;11.04 and 2;9.10

Conclusion

In this chapter we have shown that the sensitivity of type–type ratios to sample size that had previously been identified by researchers working on literary texts can be problematic when applied to the assessment of early language development and the language addressed to the child. We have demonstrated this by reference to previous research, and empirically from the data of one child.

The study of early vocabulary composition and usage, specific language impairment, and the acquisition and deployment of low frequency vocabulary are areas that have highly significant implications for theory, practice, and education. Our review has highlighted the extent to which both the method of data collection and, in the case of spontaneous speech samples, the size of the language sample and the distribution of types and tokens within it can influence measurements and the overall interpretability of results. It is possible that some children appear to have a more sophisticated vocabulary simply because they produce more speech. It is also likely that the degree of comparability between checklists or diaries and analyses of spontaneous speech will depend on the size of the speech sample. In addition, we have demonstrated empirically that the relationship between type–type measures and the number of tokens in the sample is far from being a trivial matter. The correlations between the two are statistically significant and, in some cases, very high, and we have shown how, for the same child at the same point in time, a smaller or larger sample can determine whether he or she will be diagnosed as verb or noun dominant.

The empirical demonstration of the effect of the number of words on type–type measures also illustrates exactly *how* this comes about, that is to say, it is the result of the relative size of each closed set of words and the frequency distribution of each closed set within the language sample. Anne's transcript at 1;10.7 contained 40 different nouns and 14 different verbs. We saw from Figure 8.1 that as we progressed through her utterances, there was a steady increase, continuing to the very end of the transcript in the new nouns that were added to the set of noun types. We assume that these were being drawn from a much larger pool that could be accessed and deployed appropriately as the situation demanded. Verbs, by contrast, added types at a slower rate from the beginning and the rate became slower until there was no further increase at all. At this point verb usage consisted of the repetition of types that had already been sampled. It was the widening gap between the rate of increase of verb and noun types that brought about the positive relationship between Nouns/Verbs and Nouns/(Nouns + Verbs) and the number of tokens and the negative relationship for Verbs/Nouns that was illustrated in Figure 8.2.

Regarding how to control variation in sample size when focusing on individual classes of words, we pointed out two contrasting approaches. The first was simply to standardise the overall number of tokens, and the second was to standardise the number of tokens in each word class. The first approach is given support by Chotlos (1944):

> *The type–token ratio for nouns, verbs, adjectives and adverbs.* This measure is not equivalent to ... [TTRs from standard-sized segments] ... since the number of tokens on which the number of types is based is not equal from individual to individual. Usually type–token ratios are not directly comparable unless they are based on the same number of tokens for each individual, but in this instance, it is felt that distributions of type–token ratios derived from a varying number of tokens can be justifiably used because the total number of tokens is the same in all the manuscripts.
>
> (Chotlos, 1944, pp. 85–6)

This conclusion does not seem unreasonable if the aim is to compare the diversity of one particular word class across individuals, although the values obtained cannot be interpreted purely in terms of the diversity of that word class, as they will be influenced by the token frequencies of all the other word classes. If, however, comparisons are to be made within individuals across word classes, or in a single type–type measure that combines more than one word class, then the comparative diversity, range or repetitiveness can be validly assessed only if the number of tokens is controlled both within and between word classes.

Our view is that this is exactly the kind of control that is achieved by the LRD procedure through modelling TTR against increasing token count for each word class separately. Initial analyses suggest that the procedure, as implemented in *vocd* produces interpretable results with values that are sensitive to the kinds of variation in situational context that influence the relative dominance of usage of nouns and verbs.

9
Lexical Diversity and Lexical Sophistication in First Language Writing

The research reported in this chapter has several aims. First, we wished to extend the exploration of vocabulary richness, particularly lexical diversity to the medium of writing. It was important to assess the extent to which vocabulary diversity as measured by D, and word rarity continued to be valid developmental measures in older children producing samples of writing. That is to say, do these measures continue to improve in line with increasing age and developing proficiency in the written modality? In respect of D, Ruth Berman's project 'Developing literacy in different contexts and in different languages' (Berman, 2000) that we referred to in Chapter 1, has already applied D to both the speech and writing of children in three age groups (9–10, 12–13, 16–17) and adults across two genres in seven languages. Results show main effects for age, language, and genre but not for modality, that is to say, speech versus writing (Berman and Verhoeven, 2002). In an analysis that focused exclusively on the results for Swedish, on the other hand, differences were found between modalities at all four ages, and an overall effect of age on writing (Strömqvist et al., 2002). However, differences between individual age groups at the older and younger ages were not significant. This study gives further support to D as a developmental measure, but it is not possible to scrutinise the results for writing within a single language. In addition, there is no single independent measure of the quality of the writing produced that can be used for validation purposes, and this is one of the strengths of the research to be described in this chapter.

Second, the previous chapter provided an extensive discussion of word rarity or difficulty as a measure of lexical richness. In this chapter, we extend that discussion by describing a study that allowed us to compare rarity and lexical diversity directly and to explore the complex inter-relationships between these and other indicators of text quality. These include word length and spelling as additional word-level variables that reflect further aspects of vocabulary richness.

Third, we wished to investigate whether quantitative methods could successfully predict writing quality. Specifically, we studied the extent to which a variety of quantitative variables could predict the grades that a team of professional markers had assigned to a collection of narrative compositions written by over 900 schoolchildren in three different age groups. Finally, we aimed to compare the relative contribution of diversity, rarity, and other variables to the quality of the written narratives.

The design of our study had a precursor in the work of Page (1994). Since the mid-1960s, Page has been working on a computerised system of assessment known as Project Essay Grade (PEG). The basic model underlying the system has remained unchanged over the last 36 years. The PEG system involves analysing a graded subset of compositions in terms of a variety of quantitative variables. A regression analysis is performed in order to measure the relative contribution of each variable to the assigned grades. The resulting regression equation then functions as a model for assigning grades to the remaining compositions. Given that our approach was very similar, our study can also be seen as making a contribution to computerised assessment theory.

We are aware that computer-based surface feature quantification is a controversial topic in the assessment of writing (see Weigle, 2002) and many teachers and other educationalists are suspicious of this approach. Scepticism often springs from the view that ignoring meaning results in an unacceptable loss of information. While this view is contestable on theoretical grounds, we addressed concerns about surface feature quantification as a purely empirical question by measuring the proportion of variance in composition grades that is attributable to quantitative variables. The amount of variance accountable in this way would thus provide a numerical indication of the value of the approach.

Overview of the study

The study is based on a cross-sectional sample of nearly one thousand narrative compositions written by English schoolchildren at ages 7, 11, and 14 years (corresponding to Key Stages 1, 2, and 3 in the English school system). The compositions had been graded into eight levels of writing attainment in accordance with the National Curriculum guidelines for English. We analysed each script in terms of six quantitative variables and then carried out a series of statistical analyses.

The aim of the first analysis was to enable us to look at the relationship between each quantitative text variable and age and the quality of writing. First, we carried out two-way analyses of variance with age, as represented by Key Stage, and National Curriculum Writing Level as independent variables and each text variable as the dependent variable. This allowed us to detect any significant differences between Key Stages and Levels. These were then explored further through correlational analyses between Level and the text variables and inter-correlations among the text variables themselves.

The aim of the second analysis was to assess the extent to which the students' essay grades could be predicted by the six quantitative measures. We achieved this by carrying out a regression analysis with National Curriculum Level as the dependent variable, the independent variables being Key Stage and the six text variables: spelling, word length, word rarity, lexical diversity, t-unit length, and text length. Finally, we repeated the regression analysis separately for each Key Stage.

Method

The data

The student compositions for the study were made available to us by the University of Cambridge Local Examinations Syndicate (UCLES), an international examining body that had collected the sample for its own research purposes. As the age of the sample ranged from seven to 14 and straddled primary (elementary) and secondary schooling, homogeneity had been preserved by sampling from secondary schools and their feeder primary schools. No systematic attempt was made to determine the language background of students, so it is likely that there were some pupils with English as a second language in the sample.

UCLES collected the data by asking teachers to administer a task to their pupils during an English lesson. The task was the same for all age groups. The pupils were asked to write a narrative composition within one hour which began with the words: '*The gate was always locked but on that day someone had left it open ...*'. When the hour was up, the compositions were handed in to the teachers, who then forwarded them to the examining body. The scripts were marked by a team of trained markers, who were experienced in the teaching of English. Each script was marked by at least two markers and given a numerical score between one and eight. The scores correspond to the eight Levels of writing ability defined in the English National Curriculum (Qualifications and Curriculum Authority, 2001). These guidelines provide level descriptors defined in terms of punctuation, spelling, range and appropriateness of vocabulary, cohesion, coherence, thematic development, and overall textual organisation. Where the markers assigned different scores to the same script, the mean of the scores was taken and rounded up. If the scores differed widely, then the final score was negotiated between the markers.

It is important to note that the markers had no access to information about the age, sex, language background or ability level of each writer. It is, of course, possible that handwriting quality may have influenced markers, either by allowing them to infer age or in some other way predisposing them to leniency or strictness (see Chase, 1968; Markham, 1976). There is, in fact, some evidence that handwriting had an effect on the grades. In a follow-up study, the examinations syndicate investigated the effect of using typed versus handwritten scripts. They found that markers tended to be less generous with the typed scripts, which they reportedly expected to display a higher standard of language than handwritten ones. However, this was a general effect over the entire sample and it did not appear that handwriting quality had a significant differential effect on marks.

The examining body also word-processed the scripts into machine-readable form, taking care to preserve the original text as much as possible, even to the extent of reproducing the drawings that some of the younger writers had thoughtfully provided to illustrate their stories! It was the availability of the scripts in machine-readable format that made it possible for us to carry out the computer-based analyses reported here.

The quantitative text variables

We now turn to a discussion of the variables that were employed. We begin by making a distinction between what we wanted to measure and how we actually measured it. According to Page (1994), markers assign scores on the basis of certain qualitative or intrinsic variables of interest such as fluency, punctuation, grammar, and so on. Such variables often cannot be analysed directly by computer software. It is, however, possible to identify surface feature approximations or correlates of these intrinsic variables, which do yield to direct quantification. Page refers to the intrinsic variables as 'trins' and the approximate variables as 'proxes'.

Though Page does not make this point, the distinction between trins and proxes actually provides a theoretical justification for the quantitative approach. The justification is based on the following observation. Language is a code based on systematic correspondences between meanings and forms. Linguistic forms and meanings are therefore isomorphic, a fact underscored by the observation that written language comprehension takes place through the analysis of linguistic form. In that case, it should come as no surprise that purely formal analyses yield significant information about text quality.

In the following paragraphs, we describe some correspondences between the qualitative features of text quality (trins) that we were interested in and their formal correlates (proxes) which we analysed directly. The relationship between trins and proxes is often not one-to-one. Sometimes proxes are closely related to other proxes and often the same proxy corresponds to a number of different trins and vice versa.

T-unit length

The National Curriculum guidelines for assessment identify the deployment of progressively complex syntactic forms as a sign of growing maturity in the use of written language. It is difficult, however, to study syntactic complexity directly without resorting to the use of syntactic parsers. At present, these tools are error-prone and require considerable post-editing, especially in the case of children's language. For early speech, mean length of utterance (Brown, 1973) is treated as a measure of complexity and mean clause length has been used for both speech and writing (for example, Berman and Verhoeven, 2002). We chose to use a proxy devised by Hunt (1965) – the t-unit. Hunt defined the t-unit as a main clause plus all its dependent clauses. By counting the number of words in a t-unit, he obtained a useful approximation of syntactic complexity.

The approximation is limited in that it does not discriminate between clauses with deep or shallow levels of syntactic embedding (see Sampson, 2001, for the importance of this distinction). Nevertheless, Hunt (1965) found a positive correlation between t-unit length and age. A number of subsequent studies confirmed the status of the t-unit as a valid developmental measure (O'Donnell, Griffin and Norris, 1967; Loban, 1976). We can therefore expect t-unit length to vary with Writing Level and Key Stage.

Text length

The quantity of language produced in a set time period is frequently treated as a proxy measure for the fluency of speech or writing. In the same way that in early spoken language development the number of words spoken by children is strongly related to age and linguistic complexity, several studies show that the quality of written text correlates highly with text length (Nold and Freedman, 1977; Stewart and Grobe, 1979; Breland and Jones, 1984; Carlson, Bridgeman, Camp and Waanders, 1985; Reid, 1986, 1990; Connor, 1990; Ferris, 1994; Page, 1994; Frase, Faletti, Ginther and Grant, 1999; Grant and Ginther, 2000). There are a number of possible reasons for this correlation.

First, and particularly when there is a wide age range, it is likely that text quality is correlated with aspects of writing skill that just happen to be strongly correlated with manual writing skill through the mediation of age. A second possibility is that short texts provide insufficient opportunities for writers to display the range of skills necessary for them to be awarded higher grades. Third, it may be that writing quality is directly related to the complexity of narrative structure, of which text length itself is a function. Finally, it could be the case that the scorers themselves are more impressed by students who write more, at least up to a certain threshold (Page, 1994, p. 8). Whatever the case may be, text length appears to be a powerful correlate of writing quality (bearing in mind, of course, that this relationship may well be genre-specific). In our data we would therefore expect text length to display significant variation in terms of Key Stage and Level.

Spelling

The National Curriculum guidelines identify spelling as a developmental measure. Spelling is a surface feature in its own right so there is no need to find a proxy for it. There are at least two reasons to expect spelling to vary with Key Stage and Level.

First, researchers into this area often perceive clear stages in the development of spelling ability. For instance, Gentry (1982) identified five stages of spelling development in English: pre-phonemic (in which a child may represent a whole word by one letter or has memorised the spellings of a set of words); semi-phonemic (in which the child has learned some correct phonetic–orthographic mappings); phonemic (in which each sound in a word is represented by a letter); transitional (in which the child displays an awareness that there is not necessarily a one-to-one mapping between phonemes and graphemes but has yet to master all the mappings), and, finally, correct or standard spelling.

Second, spelling proficiency appears to be related to the amount of exposure to written language. Spencer (1999) models behaviour in English in terms of the frequency of phoneme–grapheme mappings. If this model is accurate, then we would expect spelling ability to vary with the amount of reading. That amount, in turn, is likely to be linked to age and interest in reading. Given that exposure is an important variable in language development (see the discussion of rare words in the last chapter), we can also expect spelling ability to be related to other measures of written language ability.

We may also note that spelling is a salient feature of text because spelling errors stand out clearly, in contrast to more subtle indicators of writing quality, such as lexical diversity or even word rarity, which are manifested in a more diffuse fashion. This means that, potentially, spelling can exert a strong influence on markers and there is strong anecdotal evidence that spelling is a powerful source of halo effects in written language.

Word length

The National Curriculum guidelines treat vocabulary usage as an indicator of development in written language ability. The quality of vocabulary can be broken down or related to lexical features such as rarity, diversity, morphological complexity, lexical density, and lexical specificity. These variables all appear to correlate with one surface feature – word length. This surface feature is a well-established stylistic measure that has long been used in authorship attribution (see Mendenhall, 1987; Holmes, 1994). In the developmental context, a number of studies relate word length to writing quality (Reid, 1986; Reppen, 1994; Frase et al., 1999; Grant and Ginther, 2000). There are a number of reasons for correspondences between word length and aspects of vocabulary usage.

First, and as noted in the previous chapter, word length is related to word rarity. According to Zipf (1932, 1935) the length of a word is inversely related to its frequency, with frequently used words being more likely to be shorter and rare words longer. As shown in the previous chapter, rare words are closely associated with various aspects of language development.

It is therefore possible that word length is linked with written language development at least partly through the mediation of word rarity.

Anglin (1993) carried out a study which suggests that vocabulary growth during the school years is largely due to the development of derivational morphology. Given that morphologically complex words are likely to be longer than morphologically simpler words, it is possible that word length may also be related to language development through the mediation of morphology. A third mediating factor is lexical diversity. It is reasonable to suppose that individuals displaying greater lexical diversity also display a greater diversity of word lengths, with the presence of longer words increasing the mean word length score. However, the relationship between word length and lexical diversity is likely to be a complex one, given that, up to a certain point, one can display diversity using exclusively short or exclusively long words.

A fourth possible mediating factor is lexical density – the ratio of content words to function words (see review in Read, 2000). Studies have shown that conversational language contains a lower proportion of content words than written language, possibly because written language tends to be more informative than conversational language. In the developmental context, once the majority of closed class items have been acquired, it could be that less mature writers use a more oral rather than written style, resulting in a lower lexical density when compared to more mature writers. Since, on average, function words are shorter than content words, this will also impact on mean word length.

Finally, it is possible that word length is related to written language development through the mediation of lexical specificity (see Biber, 1988). It has been said that high frequency words, which tend to be short according to Zipf's law, are more polysemous that low frequency words, which tend to be longer. If that is the case, then it may be that high quality writing that has a rich vocabulary displays longer words out of a concern with greater precision of meaning.

There are, therefore, at least five possible reasons why we would predict that word length should vary with Key Stage and Level in the writing of schoolchildren across the age range under investigation.

Word rarity

Because the importance of word rarity to language development was discussed extensively in the last chapter, this section will concentrate on the problems associated with operationalising word rarity as a research variable.

First, word rarity is an inherently relative concept. A word may be rare in one domain of discourse and common in another. For instance, one measure of rarity is to classify the 2000 most frequent words as common and the rest as rare. According to this approach, a word like 'hall' must be classified as rare, given that it does not belong to the set of the 2000 most frequent words in English. However, 'hall' is very common in a school context, for example 'assembly hall' or 'dining hall'. This kind of anomaly arises because word frequencies are calculated on the basis of large corpora that encompass many domains of discourse. As a result, patterns of usage specific to particular domains are distorted. It is not easy to address this problem because each individual language speaker may belong to a unique combination of speech communities so that some words that are rare to one speaker will be common to another.

The second problem relates to the existence of homographs – words with the same form but different meaning. The problem here arises when two homographs straddle the common/rare word divide. For example, a word like 'can' can denote a modal auxiliary, which is a common usage or it can denote a container, which is a less common usage. Another example of this arises when derivational processes assign the same word to different lexical categories. Hence, we have 'can' as a noun or 'can' as a verb, as in 'to can fruit'. A word and its derivative might, in principle, also straddle the common/rare word divide. This problem can be solved by analysing each word in context in order to determine the sense in which it is being used. However, this is an arduous and time-consuming task, especially with a large corpus, as every potential homograph must be examined.

A third and closely related problem has to do with derived and inflected forms of the same root. There are cases where the singular and plural forms of the same word straddle the common/rare word divide. It is tempting to solve this problem by assigning all forms of a word the same classification. For instance, Laufer and Nation (1995) classify whole word families as common or as rare. However, this procedure assumes a degree of morphological knowledge on the part of the speaker/writer which may not be warranted in a developmental context.

The foregoing considerations indicate that separating rare words from common words is not an easy task. Any cut-off point based on word frequency is likely to be arbitrary. That said, however, the fact remains that defining the first 2000 most frequent words as common words does make it possible to discriminate objectively between writing samples of differing quality (see Laufer and Nation, 1995; Meara and Bell, 2001). In our analysis we decided to settle on the 2000-word threshold, notwithstanding the problems associated with it, because it has been shown to work in a developmental context. The use of this criterion does involve, given the foregoing, a degree of counter-intuition at times. For instance, we treat 'always' as rare, simply because it does not appear among the 2000 most frequent words in English. Nevertheless, for the sake of objectivity we have not deviated from the word frequency information in identifying 'rare' words.

As if the problems involved in defining word rarity were not enough, there are also problems in measuring it. These were discussed in the previous chapter and will not be repeated here. Rather than use the popular Laufer and Nation (1995) lexical frequency profile, which has been shown to be sensitive to text length, we decided to use Meara and Bell's (2001) P_Lex software that outputs the measure, *lambda*, as an index of rare word usage. As described in the previous chapter, this measure is based on modelling the frequency distribution of rare words across ten-word segments of text by a Poisson curve. The parameter in the Poisson formula, called lambda, comprises a numerical measure of rare word usage, with higher values of lambda denoting greater degrees of rarity. However, one disadvantage could be that P_Lex operates on the probability of sampling tokens of rare words rather than types. This means that it might be possible for a text to be assigned a high lambda value on the basis of a few rare words which occur frequently. We will return to this issue later in the chapter.

Lexical diversity

The case for lexical diversity as a developmental measure has already been made in earlier chapters. This section will therefore focus on the relationships one might expect to find between lexical diversity and the other word-level variables – rarity, spelling, and word length. All four lexical variables are well-established developmental measures and, as indices that are related to various dimensions of vocabulary richness, we would expect them to be inter-correlated. However, tensions may exist between them which attenuate these relationships.

One possible tension between diversity and rarity has already been touched on above – it is possible that a high lambda score may be achieved by repeating a small number of rare words, in which case a low diversity score will be achieved. This possibility, of course, arises from our choice of the measuring instrument, but it is probable that the relationship between rarity and diversity, just like the relationship between word length and diversity, is a highly complex one. It might therefore be the case that high diversity scores can be achieved on the basis of a diverse common-word vocabulary or that, as noted in the previous chapter, there are genres in which there is frequent repetition of low frequency technical vocabulary (Biber, 1988). The study therefore sought to determine if these possibilities are manifested in the corpus.

Tensions might also exist between diversity or rarity and spelling. It is possible that some pupils might achieve high scores in spelling by 'playing safe' and restricting their vocabulary to just those words that they can spell confidently, in which case they would run the risk of achieving low diversity or rarity scores. Conversely, more adventurous pupils might risk low spelling scores by deploying words whose spelling they have not yet mastered. Such pupils would, however, stand to gain high diversity scores. The extent to which the top-down pressures of current educational assessments in the UK and other school systems can have adverse backwash effects in the form of inhibiting such behaviour is something that deserves further investigation.

Coding schemes and analytical procedures

The corpus was analysed using both standard and purpose-written software. For some variables, a considerable amount of manual coding was needed and for some analyses, punctuation had to be stripped from each text in order for CLAN software to operate properly. The prompt sentence was also removed from all essays prior to analysis.

Word and text length

A word was defined as a string of alphabetic characters enclosed by spaces. Hyphenated words were treated as one word. Word lengths were calculated on the basis of the actual words in the script even if there were spelling errors. A specially written computer program[1] counted the total number of letters in the text and divided it by the number of words to obtain a mean word length. Text length was obtained as the total number of words in the text.

T-unit length

Each text was segmented into t-units. Co-ordinated clauses were treated as separate t-units in order to prevent inordinately high t-unit lengths being assigned to scripts in which an entire narrative might consist of a single sentence made up of co-ordinated clauses. This is a well-known feature of immature writing. The first clause in reported speech was treated as subordinate to the reporting clause. Subsequent main clauses plus their subordinate clauses in reported speech were treated as separate t-units. Incomplete syntactic fragments were coded as errors and omitted from the analysis. A purpose-written computer program then counted the total number of words in valid t-units and divided it by the total number of t-units to obtain a mean t-unit length.

Spelling

Spelling was measured as the percentage of correctly spelt words in a text. A word was considered to be a misspelling if it deviated from the spelling conventions taught in British schools (American English forms were therefore treated as misspellings). Mis-segmented words, for example, 'alot' instead of 'a lot' or 'some where' instead of 'somewhere') were also treated as errors. A correctly spelt homophone in an inappropriate context was treated as a spelling error (for instance, 'they went *their*' instead of '*there*'). Indecipherable words were ignored. In a few cases, writers deliberately used incorrect orthographic forms, for instance, to indicate dialect. Such forms were ignored in the analysis. Spelling errors were transcribed and coded using the CHAT replacement facility on the main tier (e.g. '... freind [: friend] ...').

A specially written computer program then counted all the correct forms and expressed the count as a percentage of the total number of words in the text (leaving out the excluded words from that total).

Word rarity

Word rarity was calculated using Meara's P_Lex program (Meara and Bell, 2001). A new lexicon was constructed for the analysis, derived from the words in the corpus. Words were then coded as common if they were a member of the set of the 2000 most frequent words in English. Otherwise they were deemed to be rare. The 2000 most frequent words in English were determined on the basis of the P_Lex lexicon, which is derived from lists compiled by Paul Nation (Nation, 1984).

Lexical diversity

Lexical diversity was calculated using the *vocd* program. As part of the suite of CLAN programs, *vocd* automatically replaced the incorrect spellings with correct spellings on the basis of the coding described above, so the analysis was carried out on correctly spelt words only. This is important because without taking this precaution the existence of incorrectly spelt forms would have inflated the type counts of poor spellers if they were inconsistent in the way they spelt the same word. A batch file was used to process all 918 scripts using a single command. A purpose-written program then extracted D values from the *vocd* output and formatted them into a spreadsheet.

Results

Four kinds of statistical analysis were carried out: (a) descriptive statistics; (b) a (3) Key Stage x (7) Level analysis of variance (ANOVA) was carried out on each of the text variables; (c) inter-correlations between all text variables and Level; and (d) a regression analysis, in which Level was the dependent variable and age and the six text variables were the independent variables. We will begin by looking at trends of each text variable in turn in relation to Level and Key Stage.

Trends in the text level variables

T-unit length

Figure 9.1 shows mean t-unit lengths for each Key Stage by Level and Table 9.1 provides more detailed descriptive statistics. This and the tables that follow also indicate which levels were attained, and by how many children at each age (see, for example, Table 9.1). As hinted by the graph, there is a main effect of Key Stage ($F(2,902) = 15.355; p < 0.001$) and *post hoc* Scheffé tests show that the differences between individual Key Stages are significant at $p < 0.001$. There is also a main effect of Level ($F(6,902) = 3.644; p < 0.001$). A *post hoc* analysis shows that there is no significant difference between Levels 1 and 2. Otherwise, Levels 1, 2, and 3 differ significantly from each other and from each of the other Levels. Further, there is no significant

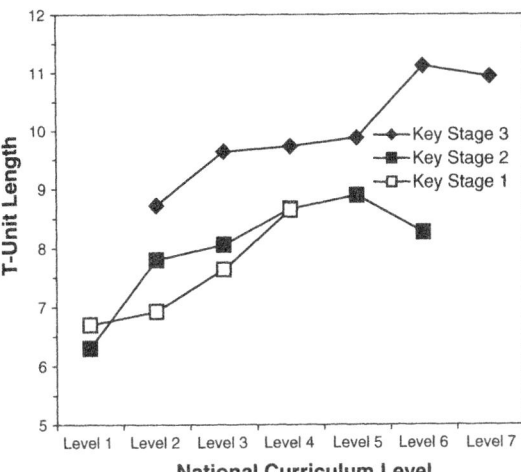

Figure 9.1 T-unit length plotted against Level at three ages

difference between Levels 4 and 5, Levels 5 and 7, and Levels 6 and 7, but all other differences are significant. Effect sizes are similar for each factor with Key Stage having a slightly higher partial Eta^2 value of 0.033 compared to 0.024 for Level.

Table 9.1 Descriptive statistics for t-unit length

Key Stage	Level	Mean	SD	n
1	1	6.70	1.99	47
	2	6.92	1.58	204
	3	7.64	1.41	54
	4	8.65	1.69	6
	Mean	7.05	1.66	311
2	1	6.30	0.98	4
	2	7.81	2.64	74
	3	8.06	1.54	118
	4	8.67	1.42	138
	5	8.89	1.30	46
	6	8.27	1.80	3
	Mean	8.31	1.79	383
3	2	8.72	1.70	5
	3	9.64	2.11	34
	4	9.73	1.98	55
	5	9.88	1.43	59
	6	11.12	2.52	56
	7	10.94	1.92	15
	Mean	10.16	2.10	224

Text length

Figure 9.2 shows mean text length by Key Stage and Level, with more detailed descriptive statistics provided in Table 9.2.

The analysis of variance shows a significant main effect for Level ($F(6,902) = 18.316$; $p < 0.001$), and Scheffé tests show that all the differences between Levels are significant at the $p < 0.001$ level, except for the differences between Levels 1 and 2 ($p > 0.05$) and Levels 6 and 7 ($p > 0.05$). Key Stage also has a significant effect ($F(2,902) = 19.628$; $p < 0.001$). *Post hoc* tests show that all differences between Key Stages are significant at the $p < 0.001$ level. As is suggested by Figure 9.2, there is a larger effect size for Level with an Eta^2 value of 0.109 compared with Key Stage ($Eta^2 = 0.042$).

Spelling

The mean percentage of correctly spelt words is plotted against Level at each Key Stage in Figure 9.3. More precise details are provided in Table 9.3. These data show a ceiling effect in the development of spelling ability as the pupils who reach the highest levels approach 100 per cent. There is also a suggestion that, at the higher levels, as scores approach the ceiling, the earlier separation of the plots for the different ages disappears and Key Stage 2 means are as high or even very slightly higher than Key Stage 3 means.

The ANOVA shows effects for both Level and Key Stage. Level has a significant main effect ($F(6,902) = 20.315$; $p < 0.001$) and *post hoc* tests show that differences between Levels 1, 2, and 3, and each of the other Levels are significant, but that there are no differences between Levels 4, 5, 6, and 7. There is also a main effect for Key Stage ($F(2,902) = 5.09$; $p < 0.01$) and Scheffé tests

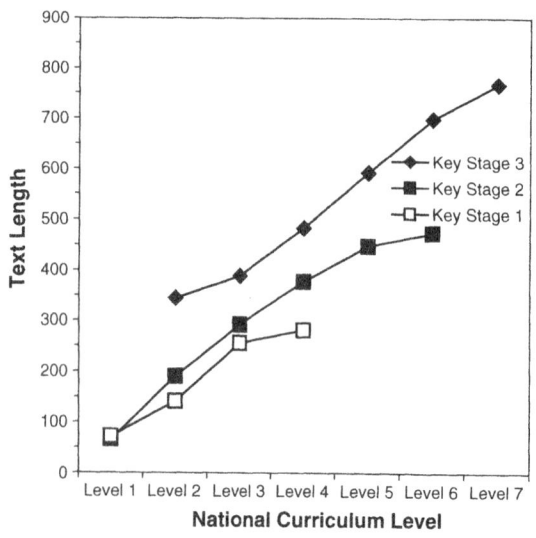

Figure 9.2 Text length plotted against Level at three ages

First Language Written Narratives 165

Table 9.2 Descriptive statistics for text length

Key Stage	Level	Mean	SD	n
1	1	72	36	47
	2	142	90	204
	3	256	154	54
	4	281	149	6
	Mean	154	115	311
2	1	66	22	4
	2	190	83	74
	3	291	115	118
	4	377	129	138
	5	448	235	46
	6	474	174	3
	Mean	321	160	383
3	2	344	158	5
	3	389	186	34
	4	484	170	55
	5	592	178	59
	6	698	387	56
	7	767	194	15
	Mean	567	274	224

show that all differences between Key Stages are significant at $p < 0.001$. Again, effect sizes are larger for Level ($Eta^2 = 0.119$) than for Key Stage ($Eta^2 = 0.011$).

Word length

Figure 9.4 shows the trends in the development of word length. It can be seen that from Levels 2 to 5, Key Stage 2 displays slightly higher means

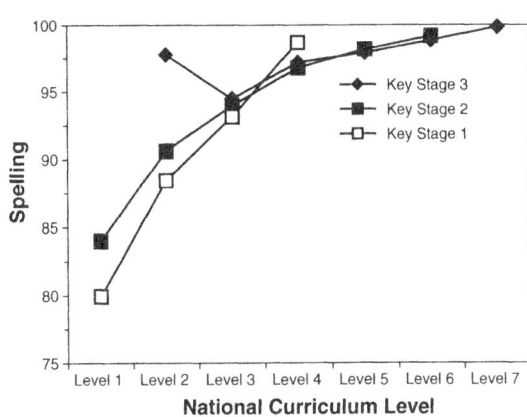

Figure 9.3 Spelling plotted against Level at three ages

Table 9.3 Descriptive statistics for spelling

Key Stage	Level	Mean	SD	n
1	1	79.93	8.07	47
	2	88.44	6.60	204
	3	93.15	3.62	54
	4	98.69	0.79	6
	Mean	88.17	7.57	311
2	1	84.00	5.05	4
	2	90.61	5.68	74
	3	93.97	3.49	118
	4	96.76	1.87	138
	5	98.18	1.60	46
	6	99.18	0.66	3
	Mean	94.77	4.40	383
3	2	97.77	0.62	5
	3	94.46	3.30	34
	4	97.18	1.66	55
	5	97.91	1.43	59
	6	98.86	1.10	56
	7	99.86	0.19	15
	Mean	97.57	2.33	224

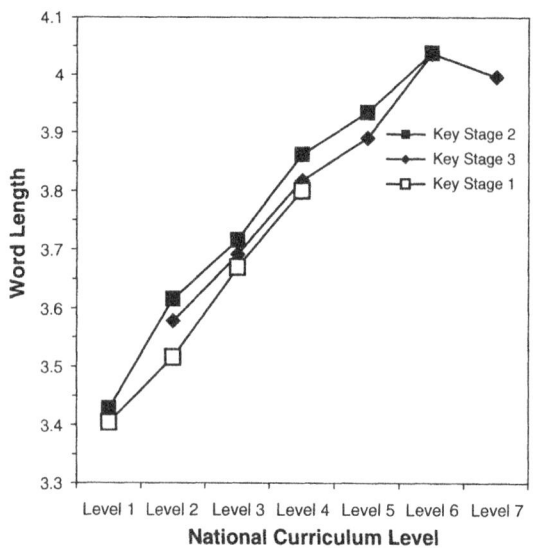

Figure 9.4 Mean word length plotted against Level at three ages

than Key Stage 3. However, it must be remembered that level-by-level differences do not reflect overall, average age differences in the text variables – it simply means that children who receive the same grades have different scores on the text variable at different ages. As can be seen from Table 9.4, the overall Key Stage 3 mean for word length is higher than the Key Stage 2 mean.

The analysis of variance shows a main effect of Level ($F(6,902) = 15.374$; $p < 0.001$; $Eta^2 = 0.93$), and Scheffé tests show that Levels 1, 2 and 3 differ significantly both from each other and from the other Levels at $p < 0.001$. Levels 5, 6, and 7, on the other hand, do not differ significantly from each other, although Level 4 differs significantly from Level 6 at the $p < 0.001$ level. There was no effect of Key Stage ($F(2,902) = 1.253$; $p > 0.05$).

Word rarity

Mean word rarity as represented by lambda values are plotted in Figure 9.5 (see Table 9.5 for descriptive statistics). It is notable, as with spelling and word length, that Key Stage 2 appears to display slightly higher level-by-level means than Key Stage 3. Again, however, it is important to point out that the overall Key Stage 3 mean is higher than the Key Stage 2 mean, as shown by Table 9.5.

As with word length, there is no significant main effect of Key Stage, ($F(2,902) = 0.680$; $p > 0.05$). There is, however, a main effect of Level

Table 9.4 Descriptive statistics for word length

Key Stage	Level	Mean	SD	n
1	1	3.40	0.34	47
	2	3.52	0.25	204
	3	3.67	0.22	54
	4	3.80	0.10	6
	Mean	3.53	0.27	311
2	1	3.43	0.29	4
	2	3.62	0.23	74
	3	3.72	0.20	118
	4	3.86	0.19	138
	5	3.93	0.16	46
	6	4.04	0.24	3
	Mean	3.78	0.23	383
3	2	3.58	0.22	5
	3	3.69	0.16	34
	4	3.82	0.15	55
	5	3.89	0.13	59
	6	4.04	0.14	56
	7	4.00	0.11	15
	Mean	3.88	0.19	224

168 *Lexical Diversity and Language Development*

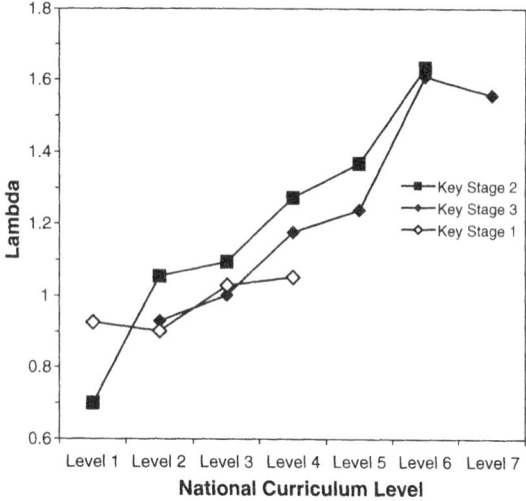

Figure 9.5 Word rarity plotted against Level at three ages

($F(6,902) = 7.751$; $p < 0.001$; $Eta^2 = 0.049$). A *post hoc* analysis shows that there are no significant differences between each of Levels 1, 2, and 3, and no differences between Levels 4, 5, 6, and 7 or between Level 4 and 5. All other differences are significant.

Table 9.5 Descriptive statistics for word rarity

Key Stage	Level	Mean	SD	n
1	1	0.93	0.50	47
	2	0.90	0.42	204
	3	1.03	0.39	54
	4	1.05	0.24	6
	Mean	0.93	0.42	311
2	1	0.70	0.57	4
	2	1.05	0.44	74
	3	1.10	0.40	118
	4	1.27	0.34	138
	5	1.37	0.31	46
	6	1.63	0.19	3
	Mean	1.18	0.40	383
3	2	0.93	0.27	5
	3	1.00	0.40	34
	4	1.18	0.30	55
	5	1.24	0.30	59
	6	1.61	0.43	56
	7	1.56	0.32	15
	Mean	1.29	0.41	224

Lexical diversity

Figure 9.6 shows D values by Level and Key Stage, with more detailed descriptives provided by Table 9.6. As with spelling, word length, and rarity, that is to say the other word-level variables, Key Stage 2 displays slightly higher level-by-level means than Key Stage 3. There is a much larger difference at Level 6, but,

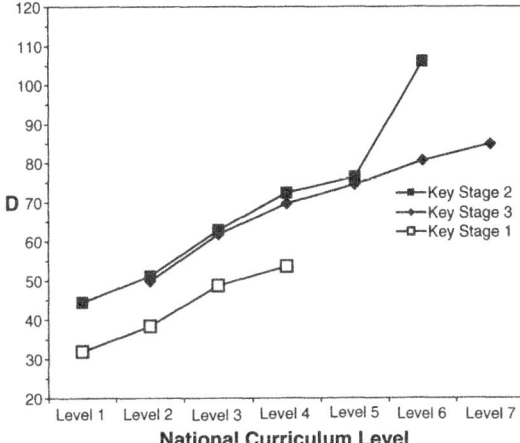

Figure 9.6 Lexical diversity plotted against Level at three ages

Table 9.6 Descriptive statistics for lexical diversity

Key Stage	Level	Mean	SD	n
1	1	31.93	10.48	47
	2	38.37	14.47	204
	3	48.70	15.19	54
	4	53.59	18.10	6
	Mean	39.48	15.04	311
2	1	44.42	14.89	4
	2	51.11	16.75	74
	3	62.89	16.21	118
	4	72.41	18.13	138
	5	76.40	18.26	46
	6	106.05	32.80	3
	Mean	65.81	19.74	383
3	2	49.81	5.35	5
	3	61.82	16.16	34
	4	69.67	13.03	55
	5	74.49	12.75	59
	6	80.60	15.69	56
	7	84.81	12.38	15
	Mean	73.05	15.85	224

as shown by Table 9.6, this is unreliable because only three children attained this Level at Key Stage 2. Again, the overall Key Stage 3 mean is higher than the Key Stage 2 mean.

There are significant main effects of both Level and Key Stage. For Key Stage $F(2,902) = 18.269$, $p < 0.001$, and *post hoc* tests show that the difference between each Key Stage is significant at $p < 0.001$. For Level, $F(6,902) = 16.335$, $p < 0.001$. Scheffé tests show that the difference between Levels 1 and 2 is not significant. Neither are the differences between Level 4 and Levels 5 and 7, and between Levels 5, 6, and 7. All other differences are significant at $p < 0.001$. Once again, Level has a larger effect size ($Eta^2 = 0.980$) than Key Stage ($Eta^2 = 0.039$).

Inter-correlations

Inter-correlations among the quantitative variables and Level are displayed in Table 9.7. All correlations are statistically highly significant ($p < 0.001$) but vary in magnitude from the weak (correlations of lambda with text length and spelling) to a strong correlation between text length and Level. It is notable that text length is the strongest predictor of Level, but all the other quantitative text variables are at least moderately strong predictors.

Table 9.7 Inter-correlations between text variables and Level

	1	2	3	4	5	6	7
1 Word length	–						
2 Text length	0.434	–					
3 Spelling	0.481	0.474	–				
4 Lambda	0.566	0.267	0.246	–			
5 D	0.678	0.574	0.477	0.423	–		
6 T-unit length	0.493	0.479	0.341	0.316	0.386	–	
7 Level	0.628	0.721	0.666	0.436	0.664	0.529	–

*All correlations are significant at the $p < 0.001$ level

Regression analysis

A regression analysis was carried out with Level as the dependent variable and Key Stage, text length, t-unit length, spelling, word length, rarity, and diversity as the independent variables. Given that Key Stage is an ordinal variable with only three possible values, we recoded it as two separate dummy variables, KS (A) and KS (B) (see Munro, 2001, p. 258). In this first model, all the independent variables were entered simultaneously. The results, which are presented in Table 9.8, show that all variables are significant predictors and confirm the importance of text length. In total, 76 per cent of the variance in Level scores is explained.

Table 9.8 Regression analysis predicting Level

	Unstandardised Coefficients		Standardised Coefficients	
	B	Std Error	Beta	*p*<
(Constant)	−6.194	0.499		0.001
KS (A)	0.231	0.068	0.081	0.001
KS (B)	0.809	0.093	0.248	0.001
Text length	0.002	0.000	0.284	0.001
Spelling	0.057	0.004	0.268	0.001
Word length	0.603	0.135	0.118	0.001
Diversity	0.008	0.002	0.119	0.001
Rarity	0.315	0.064	0.098	0.001
T-unit length	0.033	0.013	0.051	0.016
R^2			0.760	

In order to assess further the relative contribution of each variable to Level, we then carried out a regression analysis for each text variable separately while controlling for age. These results are shown in Table 9.9 which shows that text length accounted for the greatest proportion of variance, closely followed by spelling. Word length and lexical diversity also explain a substantial proportion of additional variance, while the effects of rare words and length of t-unit, although highly significant, are less powerful.

Discussion

The study reported in this chapter sought to observe trends in the development of lexical diversity, word rarity, and other quantitative text-level variables during the school years and to measure the variance in grades for narrative essays that can be accounted for through the quantification of

Table 9.9 Contribution of each variable to Level

Model	Variable	R^2	R^2 Change
1 ***	Key Stage	0.535	
2 ***	Key Stage + text length	0.642	0.107
3 ***	Key Stage + spelling	0.635	0.100
4 ***	Key Stage + word length	0.629	0.096
5 ***	Key Stage + D	0.621	0.086
6 ***	Key Stage + lambda	0.579	0.044
7 ***	Key Stage + t-unit length	0.561	0.026
8 ***	Key Stage + all variables	0.760	0.225

*** Model is significant at the $p < 0.001$ level

features of text. It also attempted to explore inter-relationships between the word-level variables. Overall, the results confirm previous research which shows continuous development during the school years (see Perera, 1984). The ANOVAs show that there are main effects of all the text variables with Level and main effects with Key Stage for all variables except word length and rare words. In all cases except t-unit length, effect sizes are larger for Level than for Key Stage. The only variable for which there appeared to be ceiling effects was spelling.

Differences by Key Stage and Level

The interrelationships between each variable and Level and Key Stage are interesting and complex. While we would naturally expect scores on the quantitative variables to increase with age and developing maturity, if our variables were a perfect reflection of the qualities that the markers were sensitive to when assigning the essays to Level, then the plots for the three Key Stages in Figures 9.1 to 9.6 ought to be represented as a single continuous line rather than separate parallel lines. That is to say, the mean scores for children at a certain Level should be the same, regardless of age. However, this is not always the case, something that is particularly apparent from text length, where the three plots are clearly differentiated. In this case, the interpretation is that in attaining a given Level older children write more. The effect for t-unit length is similar, though less clearly differentiated between Key Stages 1 and 2. The relationships with the word-level variables are more complicated, however. For spelling, age effects similar to those for text length disappear beyond the lower Levels. For word length, rarity, and lexical diversity there is less differentiation between Key Stages. All three of these show Levels where younger children obtain higher scores, although these differences are usually small and word length shows three almost continuous linear plots. Lexical diversity is particularly interesting because, while Key Stages 2 and 3 for the most part show parallel, overlapping plots, children at Key Stage 1 clearly obtain lower scores to obtain the same Level.

Predicting National Curriculum Levels

The results of the regression analysis show that a combination of Key Stage and the quantitative language variables account for 76 per cent of the variance in grades. An analysis that omitted Key Stage found that the text features accounted for 74 per cent, but even when Key Stage is controlled, an additional 22.5 per cent of the variance is explained by the text variables. This result is encouraging, given that we entered only six variables. There are studies that consider more than 60 variables, for example Biber (1988), so there is a possibility that at least some of the remaining variance in our study could be explained by quantifying other factors that contribute to National Curriculum assessments such as punctuation or cohesive markers or another dimension of vocabulary richness such as lexical density (e.g. Strömqvist et al., 2002). The results suggest that quantification of surface features does provide useful information about text quality. As argued earlier, this is only to be expected given that text meanings are encoded in surface text features, but, as noted above, it is a concept that, in our experience, many educationalists find uncomfortable.

Of the textual variables, the regression analysis indicates that text length is the strongest predictor of Level when age is controlled. According to Page (1994), markers cease to pay attention to text length after a certain length has been achieved and therefore advocates using the fourth root of text length rather than raw text Length. We did not follow this procedure in the analysis reported above, but the transformation does indeed appear to have the desired effect. It raises the magnitude of our zero order correlation between text length and Level from 0.721 to 0.773 and there is a slight increase in the amount of variance explained in the regression to 77 per cent.

Spelling is the next strongest predictor of Level, accounting for only slightly less additional variance than text length. As discussed earlier, spelling errors are highly salient and the number of spelling errors in a text has been reported to be a source of halo effects in assessment. Next is word length, followed by diversity, then lambda. T-unit length is a relatively weak predictor. The word-level variables, especially word length, rarity, and lexical diversity are of particular interest, but before further discussing this we will re-examine the correlations between them. For convenience, we reproduce an abridged version of the table presented earlier (Table 9.10).

It is notable that spelling has the strongest correlation with Level. This is consistent with the regression analysis, which shows that spelling comes second after text length as the strongest predictor when age is controlled. However, it is also notable that the correlations between spelling and the other word-level variables tend generally to be slightly lower than the other inter-correlations in the matrix. A possible reason for this is that, in some cases, there may be tensions between performing well on the other variables and performing well on spelling in ways suggested below.

In the case of word length, it is plausible to suppose that the longer words provide greater opportunities for making spelling errors than shorter words. Therefore we can infer that, on average, spelling is better for short words and deteriorates progressively with increasing word length. Pupils also run a similar risk in using high diversity. Clearly, using a wider variety of words increases the chances of using words whose correct spelling has not yet been mastered. By contrast, spelling scores are likely to be higher if pupils avoid risks and confine themselves to a more restricted range of words, which of course, leads to lower diversity scores.

Spelling has the weakest correlation of all with word rarity. There are two possible reasons for this, both of which may apply simultaneously. First, rare words tend to be longer words, so rare words may stand a greater chance of being misspelled on account of their length. Second, as mentioned in the introduction, spelling behaviour can be modelled in terms of the frequency of phoneme–grapheme mappings (Spencer, 1999). Rare words, by virtue of being rare, have fewer opportunities to display their phoneme–grapheme mappings and, according to Spencer's model, may stand a greater chance of being misspelled.

In this volume we have taken the view that lexical diversity and rarity are two distinct, but overlapping dimensions. We would therefore expect the correlation between them to be at an intermediate level, and this is exactly what we find in Table 9.10. What is perhaps surprising, however, is that the correlation between them is weaker than that between either of them and word length. In fact, and even more surprisingly, word length has a higher correlation with diversity than it does with rarity. This is counter-intuitive because the relationship between diversity and word length ought to be weaker than that between rarity and word length, for the following reasons.

In the case of rarity we would predict a strong relationship with word length because Zipf's law states that there is an inverse relationship between word length and frequency. High word length scores should therefore be accompanied by high rarity scores. For lexical diversity, on the other hand, it is possible to display a diverse vocabulary using high frequency, short words up to a certain point, after which higher scores can only be obtained by adding rarer word types. A significant positive correlation between diversity and word length would therefore be predicted but it ought to be weaker than between rarity and word length.

A possible reason for this anomaly may lie in the way that we measured word rarity. The lambda measure, as it is implemented in the P_Lex program, depends on the number of rare word tokens rather than on rare word types. This means that it is possible to achieve a high rarity score on the basis of a few rare words that are repeated frequently. We tested this hypothesis by replacing all the rare words in one script by the same rare word. We then obtained lambda values both for the original and for the transformed text. The value was the same.[2]

This outcome for lambda has two possible implications. First, it is possible for the same script to be assigned a very high rarity score and a very low diversity score, and we have identified several writers in the sample who are

Table 9.10 Inter-correlations among word-level variables

	1	2	3	4	5
1 Spelling	–				
2 Word length	0.481	–			
3 D	0.477	0.678	–		
4 Lambda	0.246	0.566	0.423	–	
5 Level	0.666	0.628	0.664	0.436	–

at opposite ends of the spectrum on these two variables. This can be at least partially explained by the repetitive use of a small range of rare words. Second, if some high scores for rarity are achieved on the basis of a few rare words, then these scores may not be a true reflection of students' writing ability, thus weakening all correlations with other variables that measure the quality of writing, including word length. It is worth noting that lambda has the weakest zero order correlation with Level. It may therefore be the case that a problem with the lambda measure is responsible for the unexpected inter-relationships between rarity, diversity, and word length.

Nevertheless, there is another issue to consider. In separate regression analyses for each Key Stage (see Tables 9.11a–9.11c) that controlled for text

Table 9.11a Regression analysis for Key Stage 1

Model	R^2	R^2 Change
1 Text length + t-unit length	0.242	
2 Text length + t-unit length + spelling	0.449	0.207
3 Text length + t-unit length + word length	0.285	0.043
4 Text length + t-unit length + D	0.260	0.018
5 Text length + t-unit length + lambda	0.246	0.005

All models are significant at the $p < 0.001$ level

Table 9.11b Regression analysis for Key Stage 2

Model	R^2	R^2 Change
1 Text length + t-unit length	0.309	
2 Text length + t-unit length + spelling	0.511	0.202
3 Text length + t-unit length + word length	0.446	0.137
4 Text length + t-unit length + D	0.387	0.082
5 Text length + t-unit length + lambda	0.365	0.056

All models are significant at the $p < 0.001$ level

Table 9.11c Regression analysis for Key Stage 3

Model	R^2	R^2 Change
1 Text length + t-unit length	0.232	
2 Text length + t-unit length + spelling	0.428	0.196
3 Text length + t-unit length + word length	0.509	0.277
4 Text length + t-unit length + D	0.344	0.112
5 Text length + t-unit length + lambda	0.402	0.170

All models are significant at the $p < 0.001$ level

length and t-unit length, we found that rarity was a much stronger predictor of Level at Key Stage 3 compared to the other age groups. Together with the results of the *post hoc* tests for differences between Levels this finding indicates that rarity, as measured in our investigation, discriminates more effectively between scripts at the top Levels of writing ability.

The separate analyses show that text length and spelling are the strongest predictors at Key Stage 1 (note that t-unit length accounts for such a small amount of variance at all Key Stages that the R^2 in the tables can be taken to represent text length). The rest of the word-level variables account for little additional variance. However, this pattern changes, and the word-level variables begin to account for progressively more variance with increasing age. The change is particularly dramatic in the case of word length, but rarity, which accounts for only 0.005 of the additional variance at Key Stage 1, and 0.056 at Key Stage 2, accounts for 0.17 at Key Stage 3. By contrast, spelling is quite stable across the three Key Stages probably reflecting the fact that spelling errors are highly salient to markers at all ages.

In relation to the original aims of this study, we have shown that our quantitative text variables are valid measures of the quality of narrative writing in children between the ages of seven and 14 and that these, together with age are capable of predicting a substantial proportion of the variance in National Curriculum Level. The relations between these variables are complex, particularly between the two measures of lexical richness – rarity and diversity – and between these and word length, but all the variables are sensitive to writing quality and show almost continuous development across Levels. Although we believe that more research is needed into the measurement of rarity, the results underscore our earlier observation that vocabulary richness cannot be indexed by a single measure and further suggest that different measures may be more appropriate for different levels of sophistication in language use. As far as lexical diversity is concerned, it is clear that, in addition to the encouraging results obtained from speech corpora and Berman's cross-linguistic research (Berman, 2000; Berman and Verhoeven, 2002), D can be applied effectively as a developmental measure of writing in English that discriminates between different ages during the school years and shows a continuous trend across Levels.

Part IV
Conclusion

10
Overview and Conclusions

Flawed measures and confused results

At the beginning of this book, we compared the search for a single, all-embracing, measure of the quality of vocabulary deployment with 'a quest for the Holy Grail'. As we have shown, even for the attempt to define a valid measure of lexical diversity independent of text length, the journey, like all such quests, has been full of wrong turnings, false dawns, and confusion. That there has been confusion is in no doubt (see, for example, Malvern and Richards, 1997; Richards and Malvern, 1997), and research results have frequently been uninterpretable, or possibly wrong, because the authors are unaware of, or simply ignore, the sensitivity to sample size of simplistic measures, such as NDW, TTR, and related indices.

In previous chapters, we have given a number of examples of the problems of interpretation caused by flawed measures. These are present even in relatively recent research. For instance, in Le Normand and Cohen's (1999) work on verbs in pre-term children, it is clear that those in the control group of full-term children produced more utterances at each age than the pre-term children. The lower number of different verbs in the latter could therefore be attributable to a smaller number of word tokens in their language samples. In the case studies of developmental dysphasia by Ouellet and colleagues (2000), the reader is not given sufficient information to judge whether the child who apparently made rapid progress on NDW between 54 and 60 months only did so because the language sample was larger. Elsewhere, Delaney-Black and colleagues (2000) assigned children to low- and normal-language groups on the basis of a combination of TTR and NDW scores in their prospective study of pre-natal exposure to cocaine. But even though the *mean* number of tokens was similar in each group, there was a considerable amount of variation, raising the likelihood of the misclassification of some children.

Similar problems exist across many linguistic areas, and include the use of NDW to compare parent–child interaction in different contexts

(Crain-Thoresen et al., 2001); TTRs in investigating the credibility of witness statements (Colwell et al., 2002); the percentage of rare words in the language of Russian immigrants to Israel (Laufer, 2003); the use of TTR and NDW for research into stuttering (Onslow et al., 2001); NDW per minute in the language development of children with cochlear implants (Geers et al., 2002).

These things matter. Much of the research based on flawed measures has significant implications for theory, practice, and policy. It is important therefore that the methodological issues of measuring vocabulary richness are understood and that these confusions are cleared up.

A more robust measure

In the first part of this book, we outlined significant steps towards a more complete mathematical model of lexical diversity and developed a more robust method for its measurement. While we make no claim that it is perfect or the end of the story, the evidence is that D is not flawed by being a function of sample size in the way NDW, TTR, and related measures clearly are. As is to be expected, however, D like any measure is subject to error – no measure in human affairs is ever entirely accurate. We stress again the need to consider the context in which language samples are taken. We have seen that topic change and content cohesion will cause local variations in the TTR versus token curve. There are authors or speakers who, while undoubtedly highly skilled language users, will on occasion deliberately lower their lexical diversity for stylistic or rhetorical effect. For these and other reasons, not all language samples follow the ideal curves of the model and the error in D will vary for some samples. None the less, the evidence from the cohorts cited here demonstrates high reliability and a robustness in D as a measure. Its development refutes the previous conclusion of Wimmer and Altmann in their revue article '*On vocabulary richness*':

> If we determine that for a given text Yule's index has the value $K = 153.2$, Guiraud's index $R = 12.4$, Dugast's index $U = 19.5$, what do we learn about the text even if we know the formula? *Practically nothing* [our emphasis]. We do not know whether 153.2 is small or large and even if we have results from other texts, we cannot say whether the given text has a rich vocabulary or a poor one. Even if we have several texts for comparison, the value of the index is not worth more than an ordinal number showing the rank of the text in a group of others.
>
> (Wimmer and Altmann, 1999, p. 2)

This is far too negative a view that grossly underestimates the value of ordinal-level data. There is now an accumulation of evidence, presented in this volume and elsewhere by ourselves and others (Allen, 1998; Richards and Malvern, 1999; Malvern and Richards, 2000b; Berman, 2000; Hoare, 2000/2001; Berman and Verhoeven, 2002; Jarvis, 2002; Owen and Leonard, 2002; Silverman and Ratner, 2002; Strömqvist et al., 2002; Wright et al., 2003), that in a range of different languages and language typologies D effectively measures a *relative* degree of development or maturity in speech and writing in first and second language for both children and adults. Patterns of correlation have shown us that the measure does indeed tell us something useful about the quality of writing, speaking proficiency, and vocabulary deployment of learners. It is also successful in discriminating between different groups of language users such as children with stutters and their normally fluent peers, children with specific language impairment versus children developing normally, adults with fluent and non-fluent aphasia, and different groups of second language learners, as well as between different modalities and genres.

Interpreting the values of D

The various corpora that have been analysed throughout this book give us some indication of the average values of D and the range of scores that can be expected in various populations. In Chapter 5 we supplied this information for the Bristol Corpus. To give these data some perspective and to provide further information about the possible extent of variation in D-scores, we have placed in Figure 10.1 some of the results from the Bristol project together with those from other, contrasting corpora, including the written narratives analysed in Chapter 9.

It shows the means and sub-ranges, from the 10th to the 90th percentiles, of D for the oral data of the Bristol children at six ages and from the writing data at three ages from Chapter 9. For comparison, we have added the spoken data from the 16-year-olds learning French as a foreign language in Chapter 6, and also include data from 32 adults learning English as a second language provided by Peter Skehan's project 'Syntactic and pragmatic modes in task-based foreign language learning' (Foster and Skehan, 1996). These learners, who were aged between 18 and 30, were described as 'pre-intermediate' level and from a variety of L1 backgrounds. They had been recorded in pairs carrying out an oral decision-making task under three experimental conditions. The D-values omit back channels and self-repetition and reformulation (retracing). As a final point of reference, some samples of adult writing are included in the figure – a set of 23 chapters by teachers, educationalists, and academics from a book for parents and educational professionals on language and education, edited by Yamada-Yamamoto and Richards (1999).

As one would expect, the highest scores in Figure 10.1 are provided by the adult writers with a mean of 90.59, a standard deviation of 10.79, and a range of 69.74 to 119.20. It is interesting to compare this mean with Berman

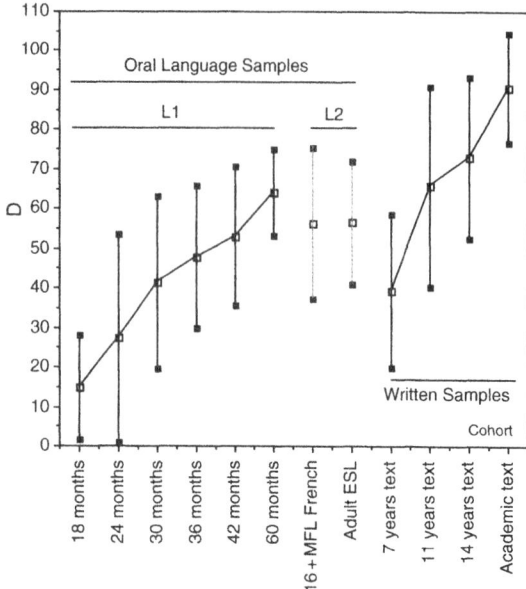

Figure 10.1 Means, 10th and 90th percentiles of D for speech of children from 18 to 60 months, French as a foreign language (aged 16) and ESL (adults); and for writing of children aged 7–11 years and adults

and Verhoeven's (2002) results for writing in the expository genre condition. Although precise values are not quoted, it is possible to obtain an approximate estimate of the mean for adult expository writing for English from their Figure 3d (Berman and Verhoeven, 2002, p. 30). This suggests a value of somewhere between 85 and 90, very close to the mean for the educational book.

The learners of English as a second language have a mean of 56.58 with a standard deviation of 12.10 and a range of 35.78 to 91.99. This is close to the mean for foreign language learners of French, but because of the different language involved we should be wary of interpreting this further. It can be seen that the mean for the learners of English is a little higher than the Bristol children at 42 months and with a similar spread.

As far as the children's narrative writing at three ages is concerned, it is striking how low lexical diversity is in the writing of seven-year-olds at Key Stage 1 (seven years). At this age one might expect children's writing to be a fairly close reflection of their spoken language before they refine their written language and move towards a more adult model of greater complexity and lexical richness than in speech (see, for example, Berman and Verhoeven, 2002). On the other hand, and even though schoolchildren in the UK are introduced to the writing process at an earlier age than in many other countries, this is still an early stage in the mastery of complex phoneme–grapheme relationships, punctuation, and the manual skills required to commit words to paper, all of which puts extra pressure on the child's processing resources compared with the spoken word. Again, it is useful to compare these data with the results from Berman and Verhoeven, this time with the trends for written narratives presented in their Figure 3c (Berman and Verhoeven, 2002, p. 30). Their youngest age group consists of the nine-year-olds who have a mean D of somewhere between 45 and 50, which falls neatly between our seven-year-olds with a mean of 39.48 and our 11-year-olds with a mean of 65.81.

Cross-linguistic comparisons of lexical diversity

One area that is still not fully understood is the cross-linguistic comparison of lexical diversity. It too has been prey to flawed measurement. A recent publication concerning maternal interaction style with late-talking toddlers by Girolametto and colleagues (2002) makes much of the fact that Italian mothers had higher TTRs from 100 utterances than Canadian mothers. This result may, in fact, underestimate the true difference because the Italian mothers also had higher MLUs and therefore would have contributed more word tokens to the TTR. There are, however, deeper issues.

Many authors have pointed out the difficulties of consistently defining a word or comparing diversity scores between languages and have drawn attention to the linguistic or cultural factors that are likely to contribute to differences between languages (for example, Meara, 1978, in relation to English, French, and Spanish; Berman and Verhoeven, 2002, for Dutch, English, French, Hebrew, Icelandic, Spanish, and Swedish; Daller et al., 2003, for Turkish and German; Dewaele and Pavlenko, 2003, for Russian and English). Referring to Ruth Berman's Spencer Foundation study 'Developing literacy in different contexts and in different languages' (Berman, 2000; Berman and Verhoeven, 2002), which used D as the measure for lexical diversity, Strömquist and colleagues (2002) caution that:

> Our findings suggest that lexical measures of diversity, density and [word] length are sensitive to modality and age, but they should be used with care and qualification in cross-linguistic comparisons. Language particulars constitute a powerful corrective to universal tendencies. The universal tendency in our study is the direction of the difference in lexical diversity, density and length between spoken and written discourse within a given language .... The absolute scores, however, can vary substantially for reasons of language typology.
>
> (Strömqvist et al., 2002, p. 60)

Although it may be possible to make valid comparisons by using scores standardised for each language separately, as shown by Daller and colleagues

(2003), direct comparisons of raw values from different languages are beyond our current state of knowledge and require further study.

In conclusion

The preceding chapters have offered potential solutions to the problems of measuring lexical diversity, morphological development, and comparing the diversity of different word classes. We have also presented a considerable amount of evidence that these solutions are practical, flexible, and effective, and in this chapter we have offered data that can assist with the interpretation of the outcomes. In addition to providing typical ranges for differing populations to aid the interpretation of the numerical value of D, Figure 10.1 shows unambiguous and continuous development in lexical diversity in the speech of children acquiring their first language and in writing from the seven-year-old novices through teenage and into expert adulthood. This in itself clears away the major confusion and uncertainty caused by contradictory or uninterpretable results based on previous flawed measures. Language development does include greater diversity in the *deployment* of vocabulary as well as simply an increase in the number of known types.

Moreover, by applying the same methodology to inflected, stem, and root forms we have developed a measure of inflectional diversity that demonstrates a similar development in morphology, which is also not simply the acquisition of more types (of inflections this time) but also a greater range in their deployment to an increasing variety of stem type. The third exploitation of our approach was in comparing the relative use of differing word classes, which yields a further, and mathematically satisfying, measure derived from the Ds for each class. Our approach therefore not only offers a set of measurements that can be applied by researchers and practitioners in the linguistic domains that we have discussed, but also provides a common thread binding together vocabulary diversity, inflectional diversity, and lexical style into a consistent set of theoretical relationships.

Notes

2 Traditional approaches to measuring lexical diversity

1 Log is used to denote the natural logarithm throughout this volume.

4 Early child language 1: the New England Corpus

1 Interestingly, TTR is even more reliable, with a coefficient for half the sample of 0.882. Clearly, however, this is a case of one kind of reliability without overall validity if sample sizes are not standardised. In the split-half analysis, the number of tokens is controlled in the sense that each half will contain equal numbers, or will differ by only one token in the case of a transcript containing an odd number of words.
2 The results in this section have previously been published in Richards and Malvern (2004).

5 Early child language 2: the Bristol Corpus

1 An earlier analysis on a much smaller sub-sample of 19 of the Bristol children (Skehan, 1986) had included variables such as TTR, number of word types (NDW), rare words, decontextualised vocabulary, and psychological verbs. Results for TTR were uninterpretable because it tended to be negatively correlated with the other vocabulary variables.
2 This is borne out by the fact that the rank order correlation between MLU in morphemes and the total number of words in each transcript for the New England children at 30 months was 0.610 ($N = 38$; $p < 0.001$).
3 This view is supported by evidence from Croll's study (unpublished data from Croll, 1995), that the item–total correlation for MLUS was also relatively low at 18 months in spite of a larger sample of children. Interestingly, there is a close match between the relative magnitude of item–total correlations for MLUS and D across the nine recordings (18–42 months) that the two investigations had in common, with a rank order correlation of 0.783 ($p < 0.01$; $N = 9$).

6 Lexical diversity and the investigation of accommodation in foreign language proficiency interviews

1 Parts of this chapter have been reported in Malvern and Richards (2002).
2 We are grateful to Brian MacWhinney for making us aware of this problem.
3 In fact this student's performance on the tape recording was so like that of a native speaker of French that we had to contact the school for assurance that he really was a foreign language learner.
4 See Chapter 9 in this volume for a particularly strong relationship between text length and other proficiency measures in children's writing.

5 In addition, all seven students for whom D could not be calculated were in Teacher A's group. This meant that the degrees of freedom fall to four, making the detection of reliable differences extremely unlikely.

7 A new measure of inflectional diversity and its application to English and Spanish data sets

1 Results from the New England Corpus on inflectional diversity have previously been reported in Richards and Malvern (2004).

9 Lexical diversity and lexical sophistication in first language writing

1 Other than the CLAN software and *vocd*, the programs for obtaining the text variables were written by Ngoni Chipere.
2 Since we carried out these analyses Paul Meara has offered to re-program P_Lex so that it operates on types rather than tokens. This offers a potential solution to the problem.

Glossary of Technical Terms and Acronyms

*Cross-references to other entries are shown in small capitals.

accommodation The adaptation of one's language to become closer to, or more divergent from, that of one's interlocutor. It is commonly used in the sense of *convergent* accommodation, and this may result from the need to communicate more efficiently or to obtain social approval (*see* Thakerar et al., 1982).

adjective density A measure used by Bates et al. (1988, p. 98) consisting of open-class adjectives as a proportion of content words. We assume that it is a type-type ratio, although this is not explicitly stated.

advanced Guiraud A type-token measure used by Daller et al. (2003) for profiling language dominance in groups of Turkish-German bilinguals. It is based on GUIRAUD'S INDEX* in that it has the square root of the number of tokens as the denominator, but the numerator is the number of word types that are 'advanced' (as opposed to basic vocabulary). This measure is unusual because formulae that focus on low frequency or advanced words are usually type-type ratios.

advanced TTR A type-token measure used by Daller et al. (2003) for profiling language dominance in groups of Turkish-German bilinguals. It is based on the TTR in that it has the number of word tokens as the denominator, but the numerator is the number of word types that are 'advanced' (as opposed to basic vocabulary).

AH2 A test of general verbal intelligence (Heim, et al., 1975). AH2 was used in Chapter 5 of this volume to supplement tests of Foreign Language Aptitude.

averaging When plotting the relationship between a measure and the number of tokens in a sample, averaging is an alternative to producing a CUMULATIVE PLOT. Each point on the curve is calculated from the average values for the measure obtained across sub-samples of the transcript for that token size. Sub-samples may either be segments of the transcripts or random samples of tokens (*see* Chapters 3, 4, and 8 in this volume).

back channels Contributions that consist of nothing more than 'yes', 'mm', 'mm hmm', 'uh-huh', and similar utterances and function as feedback to signal continuing interest, attention or understanding, or to give encouragement to one's conversation partner (*see* Duncan and Fiske, 1977; Schegloff, 1982, p. 78). Frequent use of back channels has implications for assessing LEXICAL DIVERSITY and mean length of turn (MLT) (*see* Chapter 6).

bilogarithmic TTR *See* HERDAN'S INDEX

binomial probability Probability based on there being only two possible outcomes to an event, for example either a particular type appears next in a language sample (probability = p) or it does not (probability = q). As one or the other must happen, $p + q = 1$. Repeating the event n times leads to a number of possible outcomes – the type appears $n, n-1, n-2, n-3 \ldots 3, 2, 1$ or 0 times – the probabilities of which are each given by the successive terms of the binomial expansion of $(p + q)^n$.

BLADES The Bristol Language Development Scales (Wells, 1985; Gutfreund, et al., 1989) are a profile of early language development consisting of separate assessments of syntax, semantics, and pragmatics, each divided into ten levels. These are combined into a single ordinal scale. Items included in the scale are derived from an analysis of the sequence of emergence in the 60 younger children in the BRISTOL CORPUS.

Bristol Corpus A collection of transcripts of early child language and the outcome of Gordon Wells's normative study of 128 pre-school children conducted in the City of Bristol in the south-west of England for more than a decade during the 1970s and 1980s (Wells, 1985). A cohort of 60 younger children was recorded in their homes at three-monthly intervals between the ages of 15 months and 42 months, and there were ten recordings of an older cohort from 39 months. The transcripts of 32 of the younger children from 18 months to 42 months are in the CHILDES database, plus five-year transcripts for 15 children. These are contained in the 'Wells' subdirectory of the 'English Data'. Distinguishing features of the Bristol Corpus are the naturalistic recordings made without the presence of an observer, the representative sample of the local population, and the longitudinal design. An analysis of data in the Bristol Corpus is undertaken in Chapter 5.

Bristol Language Development Scales *See* BLADES

Brunet's index A measure of lexical diversity, known as W, that has been used in stylometric analyses of text and is often claimed to be independent of text length. Its calculation is $W = N^{V^{-a}}$, where N is the text length, V is the number of different words, and $-a$ is a scaling constant that is usually set at -0.172 (Tweedie and Baayen, 1998). The richer the vocabulary, the lower the values for W which, according to Holmes and Singh (1996) typically ranges between ten and 20. This measure has recently been applied to the study of DAT (dementure of Alzheimer's type) (Bucks et al., 2000) and to aphasic patients (Holmes and Singh, 1996). It is often claimed to be independent of text length, but actually increases with larger samples.

Carroll's lexical diversity measure *See* CTTR

CDI *See* MCDI

CHAT (Codes for the Human Analysis of Transcripts) The coding and transcription format of the CHILDES project, full details of which are given in MacWhinney (2000a).

check A program in CLAN that assists with the preparation of transcripts in CHAT format by verifying that the file adheres to the required syntax and providing a report of errors.

CHILDES (Child Language Data Exchange System) The CHILDES project, directed by Brian MacWhinney is a collaborative enterprise for researchers into early child language, language impairment, second language, and bilingualism. The project consists of three tools: a system for transcribing and coding language data (CHAT), the CLAN software for analysing transcripts in CHAT format (MacWhinney, 2000a), and a database of transcripts (MacWhinney, 2000b). The CHILDES web site, from which the software and transcripts can be downloaded, is to be found at http://childes.psy.cmu.edu/ (*see also* MacWhinney and Snow, 1990; MacWhinney, 1995a).

CLAN (Computerized Language Analysis) Software for the analysis of language transcripts, one of the three tools of the CHILDES project (MacWhinney, 2000a).

closed-class style A type–type ratio used by Bates et al. (1988), defined as the 'total different closed-class morphemes, including bound morphemes and free-standing function words, divided by the total number of different morpheme types' (p. 150).

Communicative Development Inventories *See* MCDI

contiguity rating *See* CR

corrected TTR *See* CTTR

CR (contiguity rating) One of four measures developed by Mick Perkins and used for investigating repetitiveness in language disorders. CR consists of the 'proportion of stem tokens which ... occur immediately next to a token of the same stem' (Perkins, 1994, p. 330). 'Stem' is used here in the sense of a schema for a sentence or phrase. CR is a token–token ratio and is not a function of sample size. *See also* LTTR, STTR, SVQ.

CTTR (corrected TTR) Also known as Carroll's lexical diversity measure, this is the number of types divided by the square root of twice the number of tokens (Carroll, 1964). It is not a constant (*see* Chapter 2).

cumulative plot A method of investigating the relationship between a measure and the number of tokens in a language sample. Taking the words in the transcript in the sequence in which they occur, the value for the measure is plotted at regular intervals as the number of tokens increases. This method can give a distorted picture of the relationship with sample size because of the clustering of word types at points in the transcript and some researchers prefer AVERAGING values for segments or random samples. Others, however, argue that the cumulative method preserves the original structure of the text.

D A measure of lexical diversity developed by David Malvern and Brian Richards (McKee, et al., 2000). D is a measure based on the parameter $\mathcal{D}$ in the equation that represents TTR × token curves. Higher curves are obtained from language samples with greater diversity. The value of D determines the height of the curve and therefore measures the diversity of vocabulary (*see* Chapter 3).

$\mathcal{D}$ The parameter in Malvern and Richards's version of the small sample (short texts) approximation for the relationship between TTR and tokens derived from Sichel's formulation (*see* Chapter 3).

DAT (dementure of Alzheimer's type) A form of progressive dementia in which communication difficulties are particularly prevalent. These are characterised by word-finding difficulties, impoverished vocabulary, use of inappropriate words, impaired verbal fluency, and problems of comprehension (Blanken et al., 1987; Bucks et al., 2000).

dementure of Alzheimer's type *See* DAT

dN and dV Small increments in N (tokens) or V (types): dV/dN (or V differentiated by N) gives rate of change of V with respect to N, that is the slope of the V against N graph.

Dugast's U *See* UBER INDEX

DW *See* NDW

echolalia A kind of repetition that is a symptom of certain speech disorders, autism, and Alzheimer's disease. In echolalia it is the speech of one's conversational partners that is repeated rather than the speaker's own utterances (*see* Perkins, 1994).

English Picture Vocabulary Test *See* EPVT

EPVT (English Picture Vocabulary Test) A standardised test of receptive vocabulary published by the National Foundation for Educational Research (Brimer and Dunn, 1963).

exclude file A list of words in a text file that need to be excluded from an analysis using VOCD or other CLAN programs.

exposure to rare words A measure of the richness of the linguistic environment at school used in the Home-School Study of Language and Literacy Development by Catherine Snow, David Dickinson and Patton Tabors (Snow et al., 2001). This was usually measured by the proportion of word types in a transcript judged to be rare. It is therefore a type–type ratio. *See also* RARE WORD DENSITY.

extrinsic measures Meara and Bell (2001) define extrinsic measures as those which rely on criteria that are external to the text or transcript being analysed in order to assess the richness of its vocabulary. Such criteria may be word frequency data, educational syllabuses, judgements of teachers, and so on (*cf.* INTRINSIC MEASURES).

foreign language *See* L2

freq A program in CLAN that outputs vocabulary lists and type and token counts. The text-handling features of the VOCD software are modelled on *freq*.

GAP verbs (general all purpose verbs) A limited set of high frequency, often monosyllabic, verbs with semantically general, less specific meanings (e.g. 'make', 'do', 'go'). These have also been described as 'light verbs' (Pinker, 1989). There have been conflicting findings concerning high usage of GAP verbs in children with SLI, but it is now thought that this is a normal phase of development in both children developing normally and those with SLI (Thordardottir and Ellis Weismer, 2001).

GCSE (General Certificate of Secondary Education) A set of public examinations taken by school pupils in England and Wales normally at 16 years, at the end of KEY STAGE 4, which marks the end of compulsory schooling.

General Certificate of Secondary Education *See* GCSE

granularity A qualitative dimension of texts that is reflected in lexical diversity values and entails fine-grained levels of lexical detail. Drawing on unpublished work by Colette Noyou and her colleagues, Dewaele and Pavlenko (2003) explain that high granularity 'entails the presentation of a detailed series of micro-events, while a low degree [of granularity] (reduced partitioning) presents the event from a macro perspective, where the different components are fused as either one single event or a limited number of events' (p. 124).

Guiraud's index *See* RTTR

H *See* HERDAN'S INDEX

hapax dislegomena Word types that occur only twice in text. *See also* HAPAX LEGOMENA, MICHÉA'S M and SICHEL'S S.

hapax legomena Word types that occur only once in a text. The number or proportion of these is often taken as an indication of lexical richness. Both this and HAPAX DISLEGOMENA are a function of sample size (Sichel, 1986). *See also* HAPAX DISLEGOMENA and HONORÉ'S STATISTIC.

harmonic series hypothesis Hypothesis introduced by Condon and developed by Zipf, Carroll, and others, which states that the frequencies of types in a language sample form a harmonic sequence when arranged in order from the most to the least often occurring. The total number of tokens is the sum of the resulting, harmonic series, for example:

$$\frac{N}{10} + \frac{N}{20} + \frac{N}{30} + \cdots \frac{N}{10r} + \cdots$$

It leads to the so-called Zipf's law, 'frequency × rank is a constant' (which fails to fit empirical language data adequately – *see* Chapter 3).

Herdan's index Also known as LogTTR, bilogarithmic TTR, and H. A measure of lexical diversity that divides the log of the number of types by the log of the number of tokens (Herdan, 1960). It is not independent of text length (*see* Chapter 2).

Honoré's statistic This statistic, known as *R* (but also sometimes as *H*), is an index of vocabulary richness that has been used in stylometric analyses of texts. It is based on the principle that texts with richer vocabulary have a higher proportion of words that are HAPAX LEGOMENA. The formula is $R = 100\log(N)/(1-v_1/V)$, where N is the number of words in the text, v_1 is the number of words used only once, and V is the number of different words (Honoré, 1979, quoted in Holmes and Singh, 1996). The richer the vocabulary, the higher the values for R. This measure has recently been applied to the study of DAT (dementure of Alzheimer's type) (Bucks et al., 2000) and aphasic patients (Holmes and Singh, 1996). It is, however, sensitive to sample size, decreasing as N increases (*see* Chapter 3).

ID (inflectional diversity)   A measure developed by Richards and Malvern (2004) as an index of morphological development. It consists of the difference scores between the lexical diversity (D) of INFLECTED FORMS and STEM FORMS. It is therefore sensitive to a combination of the variety of inflections and the variety of stems to which they are applied (*see* Chapter 7).

inflected forms   In this volume, the description of a unit of vocabulary analysis equivalent to the word as written in the transcript. 'Go', 'goes', 'going', and 'went' are therefore treated as four different word types. This unit contrasts with ROOT FORMS and STEM FORMS.

inflectional diversity   *See* ID

inflections per utterance   The mean number of inflections per utterance is calculated from the total number of tokens of inflections used by the child divided by the total number of child utterances (tokens). It directly measures frequency of usage, and may also reflect productivity of inflections, although this will not always be the case. In Chapter 7 of this volume, inflections per utterance is used as a measure of the development of morphology. It is significantly correlated with ID.

intrinsic measures   Meara and Bell (2001) define intrinsic measures of vocabulary richness as those that rely entirely on counting numbers of types and tokens within a single language sample without any reference to criteria of the quality of language from outside the text or transcript. They would therefore include most measures of LEXICAL DIVERSITY, as well as HAPAX LEGOMENA and HAPAX DISLEGOMENA.

inverse Gaussian distribution   A distribution capable of describing populations which are highly skewed near the origin and then have a long tail, chosen by Sichel to describe how words in a subject's active vocabulary are distributed by their probability of occurrence. There are many, many words with a very low probability of occurring in a language sample, and fewer and fewer with relatively higher and higher probability (*see* Chapter 3).

inverse Gaussian-Poisson formulation   Analysis of the relationship between types and tokens in language samples due to Sichel and based on the proportion of types with a given probability of occurrence in a language sample being best described by the 'inverse Gaussian distribution' and their probability of occurring not at all, once, twice, three times, and so on being describable by a mixture of binomials expressed in the exponential form due to Poisson (*see* Chapter 3).

K   *See* YULE'S CHARACTERISTIC, K

k   *See* RUBET'S K

Key Stage (KS)   Compulsory schooling in the public sector in England and Wales is divided into four Key Stages. Pupils are tested at the end of each Key Stage, that is at 7, 11, 14, and 16 years.

L1   The language acquired first, native language or 'mother tongue'.

L2   The second or foreign language. In this volume we adopt the convention of referring to an L2 acquired within the speech community of the target language as a 'second language' and a language formally taught outside the speech community of the target language as a 'foreign language'.

lambda *See* P_LEX
LDV Acronym for lexical diversity used by Jarvis (2002).
lemmatisation The process of editing a corpus so that analyses can access the ROOT FORMS of words.
lexical density Usually refers to the proportion of *tokens* that are content words as opposed to function words (Ure, 1971). A more sophisticated version (Halliday, 1985) gives a higher weighting to low frequency words. As a proportional token/token measure it is not a function of sample size. Occasionally authors (e.g. Carter, 1987) and linguistic dictionaries (e.g. Richards, Platt and Platt, 1982) treat lexical density as being synonymous with TTR.
lexical diversity The range or variety of vocabulary, traditionally conceptualised as the number of different words (word types) used in a text or transcript, or in terms of the relationship between the number of types and the text length measured by the total number of words (tokens) (*see* TTR). There are exceptions, however, as at least one author (Laufer, 2003) defines lexical diversity as a combination of RARE WORD DENSITY or LEXICAL SOPHISTICATION and LEXICAL VARIATION or TTR. Later conceptualisations include the presence or absence of repetition, usually through some interpretation of the frequency distribution of types. We define it as the combination of properties which determine the location of the TTR versus token curve for the language sample between the graphs for the two clear extremes – lowest possible diversity (every token the same type) and highest possible diversity (every token a different type).
lexical frequency profile *See* LFP
lexical individuality *See* LEXICAL ORIGINALITY
lexical originality Also referred to as 'lexical individuality' (Read, 2000). A relatively unusual measure of the LEXICAL SOPHISTICATION of writing, that consists of the percentage of words that are exclusive to one writer in the group of writers being investigated. For each writer the number of 'lexical words that are exclusive by one writer' is divided by the total number of lexical words (Linnarud, 1983, p. 250). It is not clear whether this is implemented as a type–token or a token–token ratio.
lexical richness John Read (2000) treats this as the superordinate term for the effective use of vocabulary in good writing. It consists of four components: lexical variation (LV), LEXICAL SOPHISTICATION, LEXICAL DENSITY, and a low NUMBER OF ERRORS. Although some authors treat lexical richness as being synonymous with LEXICAL DIVERSITY (e.g. Wimmer and Altmann, 1999), and, although Read is dealing with the context of second language writing, we also treat features of written texts and transcripts such as LEXICAL DIVERSITY (as measured by D), use of rare words (LEXICAL SOPHISTICATION), WORD LENGTH, text length, and lack of vocabulary errors as separate but interrelated dimensions of lexical richness (e.g. Chapter 9). Ménard's (1983) 'indice de richesse' is the number of word types that occur in standard text lengths of 500 and 2000 words.
lexical sophistication (LS) One of Read's four components of lexical richness, described as the 'selection of low frequency words that are appropriate to the topic and style of the writing' (Read, 2000, p. 200). In practice, lexical sophistication is often measured purely by reference to word frequency data and ignores the appropriateness of usage. Very often it is simply the proportion of word types that are rare (Linnarud, 1983) and is therefore a type–type ratio. Occasionally, however, the analysis is carried out on tokens – the proportion of all tokens that are rare (e.g. Dickinson, 2001a).

lexical specificity Biber (1988) sees this as a characteristic of formal, academic texts that have greater precision of meaning and a high lexical diversity. He measures it in two ways: the TTR (the number of different words as a percentage of the first 400 words in a text) and the mean WORD LENGTH.

lexical variability quotient See LVQ

lexical variation See LV

LFP (Lexical Frequency Profile) A tool developed by Batia Laufer and Paul Nation (1995) for assessing LEXICAL SOPHISTICATION in learners of English as a second language. Software allocates all the words of a text into four frequency bands by reference to Nation's word lists (Nation, 1984, 1996) and the proportion of word types in each band is profiled. This information can be collapsed into a single measure showing the proportion of rare words (*see* Chapter 8).

limiting relative diversity See LRD

linearisation A method of producing a straight line graph from a curved graph by taking logarithms of the variables. For example, if the graph of *y* against *x* is curved, a straight line might be found for the graph of log *y* against *x*, or log *y* against log *x*, or loglog *y* against loglog *x* and so on (*see* Chapter 2).

LogTTR See HERDAN'S INDEX

LRD (limiting relative diversity) An approach devised by Malvern and Richards to compare the diversity of different word classes. It is intended to overcome the problem of the sensitivity of type–type ratios (e.g. noun types/(noun types + verb types)) to the size of the language sample, and is an extension of their mathematical model for overall diversity. The procedure is implemented in the *vocd* software and the output is the square root of the division of the diversity of one word class by the diversity of the other. See Chapter 8.

LTTR An acronym both for *logarithmic* type–token ratio (i.e. HERDAN'S INDEX) and *lexical* type–token ratio. The lexical type–token ratio is one of four measures developed by Mick Perkins and used for investigating repetitiveness in language disorders. This is the standard TTR but the number of tokens is standardised, with a recommended minimum of 350 tokens (Perkins, 1994). *See also* CR, STTR, SVQ.

LV (lexical variation) One of Read's (2000) four components of LEXICAL RICHNESS and synonymous with LEXICAL DIVERSITY. It is traditionally measured by the TTR (e.g. Linnarud, 1983).

LVQ (lexical variability quotient) A measure considered and rejected by Perkins (1994, pp. 327–8). LVQ assesses 'morphological variability' (i.e. the extent to which individual lexemes are realised in different forms, e.g. go, goes, going, went) for each separate lexeme by dividing the number of different forms by the number of tokens of that lexeme. The mean LVQ can then be calculated across all lexemes. Mathematically, LVQ is therefore a variety of TTR with its accompanying sensitivity to sample size. Perkins rejects this measure because the lack of morphological variation in English means that it gives similar results to TTR. Its potential for morphologically richer languages than English is still open to investigation.

M See MICHÉA'S M and SICHEL'S S

Maas's a^2 An index of lexical diversity (Maas, 1972): $a^2 = (LogN - LogV)/(Log^2 N)$. This is the inverse of the UBER INDEX.

MacArthur Communicative Development Inventories See MCDI

Manchester Corpus A corpus in the CHILDES data base containing the transcripts of 12 children (6 boys and 6 girls) from middle-class families in the Manchester and Nottingham areas collected by Elena Lieven, Julian Pine, Caroline Rowland and

Anna Theakston (Theakston et al., 2001). These are particularly rich data, consisting of two one-hour recordings made in the children's homes at three-weekly intervals between the ages of two and three years. They contain high numbers of child word tokens. Transcripts are MORPHEMICISED on the main speaker tier and the MOR TIER is fully, and reliably, coded (*see* MacWhinney, 2000b, pp. 74–6). Analyses using data from one child in the Manchester Corpus are reported in Chapter 8.

mark–recapture   A solution applied by Marcus, Pinker, Ullman, Hollander, Rosen and Xu to the problem of estimating the proportion of children's vocabulary that consists of regular verbs from spontaneous speech samples. Marcus and colleagues use a technique from demographic research and zoology, whereby word types are treated as the equivalent of different animals of the same species whose population size is to be estimated. When captured (or sampled, in the case of words) the animals are marked (or tagged) and released (sampling with replacement). Further trapping of the same number of animals (resampling) will indicate how many of the species (word types) have already been tagged. From this an estimate of the total population can, in theory, be made. However, the procedure needs to take into consideration that, just as some animals are more shy than others and therefore less easy to catch, so some verbs have lower frequency than others and are less likely to be sampled. Marcus and colleagues overcome this in the same way as bio-statisticians by applying a 'generalized Jackknife estimator' that takes multiple recaptures into account (*see* Marcus et al., 1992, pp. 83–96). *See* SPECIES-AREA PROBLEM for another link between biology and language. *See* Chapter 3.

MCDI   (MacArthur Communicative Development Inventories)   A parental report instrument for assessing early child language, particularly vocabulary, developed by Elizabeth Bates and her colleagues. The MCDI exists in two versions, one for infants and the other for toddlers. The infants' version, which was normed on 673 parents, consists of a vocabulary checklist on which the caregiver indicates both comprehension and production, and a list of gestures. The toddlers' version, which was normed on 1130 parents, consists of a checklist for productive vocabulary and questions about the onset of word combinations and grammatical complexity (Fenson et al., 1993). Derivatives of the MCDI now exist for many different languages, including Arabic, British English, Hebrew, Icelandic, Italian, Japanese, and Spanish.

mean length of utterance   *See* MLU

mean length of structured utterance   *See* MLUS

mean length of turn   *See* MLT

mean polysemy   Two out the of four measures of monosemy and polysemy designed and rejected by Ménard (1983) as indices of LEXICAL RICHNESS after testing them on twentieth-century literary texts. These measures are based on the assumption that concise writing makes greater use of monosemic rather than polysemic words, as measured by the number of dictionary definitions for each word. Mean polysemy for a text is *either*: the total of the different meanings for all the different words divided by the total number of word types, that is to say a type–type ratio, *or* the corresponding token–token ratio. As would be expected, both of these were negatively correlated with lexical diversity, but only weakly so. The former, type–type version, was found to decrease with increasing sample size while the latter, token–token version was unaffected by size of text. One problem is that results tend to be distorted by a few high frequency verbs that can have as many as 40 meanings (*cf.* GAP VERBS). *See also* MONOSEMIC RATE, OLIGOSEMIC RATE.

mean segmental type–token ratio   *See* MSTTR

mean word frequency (MWF) The inverse of TTR. *See* TOKEN–TYPE RATIO

Ménard's rarity measure The proportion of word types in a text that are rare, that is have a low frequency of usage in the language in general. This is a type–type measure. *See* Ménard (1983).

Michéa's M and Sichel's S An apparent constancy in the ratio between the number of types occurring twice (HAPAX DISLEGOMENA) and the total number of types in a text, noticed by Michéa and in its inverse form by Sichel. Sichel's formulation shows the ratio is not constant, but rises with increasing N to a maximum and then falls very slowly giving the appearance of constancy only for a range of N (*see* Chapter 3).

minimal terminable unit *See* T-UNIT

MLAT (Modern Language Aptitude Test) A battery of tests of foreign language learning aptitude devised by Carroll and Sapon (1965) (*see* Chapter 5).

MLT^1 (mean length of turn) A measure of early child language, used in Chapter 6 as an index of foreign language students' ability to participate in conversation. Here, MLT is the average number of utterances in a single speaker's turn in the conversation, but it can also be the mean number of words or morphemes in a turn.

mlt^2 A program in CLAN for calculating mean length of turn (*see* MLT^1), either in words or utterances, from transcripts in CHAT format.

MLU^1 (mean length of utterance) A measure of language development calculated in morphemes by Roger Brown and shown to be a reliable indicator of linguistic progress over time. It is the total number of morphemes divided by the total number of utterances (*see* Brown, 1973 for precise details of calculation). MLU has been successfully applied to many different languages, although there is much debate about how to count morphemes in highly inflected languages. Some researchers prefer to count MLU in words (*see* discussion in Hickey, 1991). *See also* MLUS.

mlu^2 A program in CLAN for calculating mean length of utterance (*see* MLU^1), either in words or morphemes, from transcripts in CHAT format.

MLUS (mean length of structured utterance) A refinement of Brown's (1973) MLU made by Gordon Wells. *Un*structured utterances, defined as 'utterances that have no explicitly mentioned topic' (Wells, 1975, p. 65) are excluded from morpheme counts. One advantage of MLUS is that it avoids scores being depressed by parents' elicitation of single words 'yes' or 'no' responses (*see* Wells, 1985, for an evaluation of MLUS and a comparison with Brown's MLU). MLUS is used in the analyses of the Bristol Corpus described in Chapter 5 of this volume.

Modern Language Aptitude Test *See* MLAT

monosemic rate One of four measures of LEXICAL RICHNESS designed and rejected by Ménard (1983) after applying them to twentieth-century literary texts. These measures are based on the assumption that concise writing makes greater use of monosemic rather than polysemic words, as measured by the number of dictionary definitions for each word. Monosemic rate for a text is the proportion of types that have only one meaning, that is to say a type–type ratio. As would be expected, this measure was positively correlated with lexical diversity, but only weakly so, and was found to increase with increasing sample size. *See also* MEAN POLYSEMY, OLIGOSEMIC RATE.

morphemicisation The preparation and editing of transcripts so that morpheme boundaries are coded and analyses of INFLECTED FORMS of words, STEM FORMS, and ROOT FORMS are possible.

mor tier (%mor tier) A dependent tier in transcripts in the CHAT format of the CHILDES project that contains grammatical coding (*see* MacWhinney, 2000a; Appendix IV in this volume).

MSTTR (mean segmental type–token ratio)   A method of overcoming the sensitivity of TTR to sample size recommended by Johnson (1944). MSTTR is the average TTR for successive segments of text or transcript that contain a standard number of tokens. For MSTTR-100, for example, the text would be divided into segments of 100 tokens. If the total number of words is not a multiple of 100, the final segment is omitted. Advantages and disadvantages of the MSTTR are discussed in Chapter 6.

MWF   *See* MEAN WORD FREQUENCY, TOKEN–TYPE RATIO

N   In equations, the symbol for the number of word tokens. *See also* V.

natural partitions hypothesis   A prediction formulated by Gentner (1982) that children acquiring different languages would first learn words for objects because of cognitive and perceptual predispositions, leading to a predominance of nouns in early vocabulary. This has led to a wealth of cross-linguistic research into the so-called 'noun bias' and the relative status of nouns and verbs in early acquisition (*see* Chapter 8).

NDW (number of different words)   Also referred to as DW (e.g. Miller, 1996b). Information output by SALT and by the FREQ program in CLAN and often used as a measure of LEXICAL DIVERSITY. NDW is often counted from a standard baseline of utterances, usually 50 (Klee, 1992) or '100 complete and intelligible utterances' (Miller, 1991, p. 215). NDW gained credibility because of its ability to discriminate between children with SLI and normally developing children better than four types of TTR measure in a study by Klee (1992). Nevertheless, even when the number of utterances is controlled, NDW is confounded with sample size because of variation in utterance length (i.e. children with a higher MLU produce more word tokens) (*see* Chapter 2).

New England Corpus   A set of transcripts of 52 children contained in the CHILDES database. Recordings were made at three ages: 14 months, 20 months, and between 27 and 32 months. Transcripts are fully morphemicised. Details can be found in Dale et al. (1989), Snow (1989), and MacWhinney (2000b). An analysis of the 27–32 month transcripts is presented in Chapter 4.

noun bias   *See* NATURAL PARTITIONS HYPOTHESIS

noun density   A measure used by Bates et al. (1988, p. 98) consisting of common nouns as a proportion of content words. We assume that this is a type–type ratio, although this is not explicitly stated.

number of errors   A low number of vocabulary errors is one of Read's four dimensions of lexical richness that reflect effective vocabulary use in the writing of second language learners (Read, 2000, pp. 200–1).

oligosemic rate   One of four measures of LEXICAL RICHNESS designed and rejected by Ménard (1983) after testing them on twentieth-century literary texts. These measures are based on the assumption that concise writing makes greater use of monosemic rather than polysemic words, as measured by the number of dictionary definitions for each word. Oligosemic rate for a text is the proportion of types that have only one or two meanings, that is to say a type–type ratio. As would be expected, this measure was positively correlated with lexical diversity, and was found to increase with increasing sample size. *See also* MEAN POLYSEMY, MONOSEMIC RATE.

open-class style   A type–type ratio used by Bates et al. (1988), defined as 'total different open-class nouns, verbs and adjectives divided by the total number of different morpheme types' (p. 150).

Orlov's Z   A parameter, suggested as an index of lexical diversity, in a relationship between V and N derived by Orlov from a generalisation of Zipf's law, which depends on the frequency of the most common word in a text (*see* Chapter 3).

perseveration In this volume perseveration refers to a common form of self-repetition in which words or phrases are repeated, often out of context (see Perkins, 1994).
PLAB (Pimsleur Language Aptitude Battery) A set of tests of aptitude for foreign language learning devised by Pimsleur (1966) (*see* Chapter 5).
P_Lex A procedure and accompanying software developed by Meara and Bell (2001) for assessing the sophistication of vocabulary used by learners of English as a second language. It does so by plotting the proportion of segments of text that contain N difficult (rare) words against the number of difficult (rare) words per segment. The resulting curves are typical of Poisson distributions and can be described using a formula in which the variable, *lambda*, can be adjusted to provide the best fit. Lambda scores have been shown by Meara and Bell to be much less sensitive to sample size than LFP scores. For full details *see* the technical appendix in Meara and Bell (2001, pp. 18–19).
Poisson distribution An exponential form of the binomial distribution formulated by Poisson (*see* Chapter 3).
proportional diversity A term used by Stokes and Fletcher (2000) in a comparison of Cantonese-speaking children with SLI and children developing normally. Proportional diversity is the proportion of word types in spontaneous speech that are accounted for by nouns, verbs, and other open-class words. All calculations are based on a standard sample size: in this case, the first 117 words of all kinds in each transcript.
prorated number of lexically free words A measure developed by Yoder et al. (1994, p. 275) to investigate the impact of 'commenting' versus 'questioning' interaction styles on the language obtained from children during clinical assessments. The measure assesses LEXICAL DIVERSITY by expressing the number of 'lexically free' word types (i.e. those used in at least two different combinations of words) as a percentage of the number of non-imitative utterances. Because this is a variety of type–token ratio, one would predict that larger samples would produce lower scores. In Chapter 2 we refer to such measures as TYPE–UTTERANCE RATIOS (TUV).
rare word density A measure of the richness of the linguistic environment in the home used in the Home-School Study of Language and Literacy Development by Catherine Snow, David Dickinson and Patton Tabors (Snow et al., 2001). This was usually measured by the proportion of word types in a transcript judged to be rare. It is therefore a type–type ratio. See also EXPOSURE TO RARE WORDS.
Reading Corpus A set of French as a foreign language transcripts in CHAT format (*See* MacWhinney, 2000b, pp. 161–4 for details). The data are from 34 16-year-old learners of French as a foreign language and are transcribed and coded from the actual recordings of the 'free conversation' component of their GCSE oral examination by Francine Chambers and Brian Richards. These oral interviews were conducted by their teachers and last about five and a half minutes on average (*see* Chambers and Richards, 1995; Richards and Chambers, 1996). The transcripts are available to other researchers from the TalkBank database (http://talkbank.org/data/SLA) where the 'reading.zip' file should be selected. An analysis of the Reading Corpus is undertaken in Chapter 5 of this volume (*see* Appendix III for a sample transcript). Note that here, Reading (pronounced *Redding*) is the name of the University and town in which the compilers of the corpus work.
referential style A type–type ratio used by Bates et al. (1988), defined as 'the proportion of the child's vocabulary consisting of common nouns' (p. 97).
reliability The internal consistency of measures of lexical richness is usually measured by a split-half coefficient produced by dividing the transcript or text into two

equal halves and correlating the first half with the second half across subjects. Using this procedure, Chotlos (1944) investigated the reliability of TTR and MSTTR in scripts written by subjects aged 8–18 years. The coefficient for TTR was 0.813 for 1000 words and 0.657 for 500 words. However, in the investigation of normal and impaired child language, researchers are often guided by the Hess et al. (1986) study of the reliability of TTR, CTTR, RTTR, HERDAN'S INDEX, and YULE'S K. For standard sized language samples Hess et al. found no advantage for the other indices they studied over TTR in terms of reliability, and recommended that the sample required for a minimum split-half reliability of 0.7 was 350 words. In this volume we investigate the reliability of D by splitting the words of a speaker into odd- and even-numbered words (see Chapter 4 for discussion). We also assess the stability over time of children's vocabulary usage as measured by D using Cronbach's (1951) coefficient alpha (see Chapter 5).

retracing   The term used in the CHAT transcription scheme in the CHILDES project for speakers' self-repetition, and self-repetition with self-correction. These features are coded on the main speaker tier and can be filtered out by VOCD and other CLAN programs, if they are not excluded by default, by using the +r switch in the command line (see Appendix V for an example).

richness   See LEXICAL RICHNESS

root forms   In this volume, the description of a unit of vocabulary analysis equivalent to the lexeme or base form. 'Go', 'goes', 'going', and 'went' are treated as four tokens of a single word type. This unit contrasts with INFLECTED FORMS and STEM FORMS.

root TTR   See RTTR

RTTR (root TTR)   Also known as Guiraud's index ('indice de richesse'), this measure of lexical diversity consists of the number of types divided by the square root of the number of tokens (Guiraud, 1960). It is not independent of text length (see Chapter 2).

Rubet's k   An index of lexical diversity: $k = (LogV)/(LogLogN)$ (Dugast, 1979). It is not independent of text length (see Chapter 2).

S^1 See MICHÉA'S M AND SICHEL'S S

S^2 See SOMERS'S S

SALT (Systematic Analysis of Language Transcripts)   Software used particularly in the study of language impairment developed by Miller and Chapman at the Language Analysis Laboratory, University of Madison-Wisconsin (Miller and Chapman, 1993). For each transcript SALT will output 29 variables in a 'standard measures report' that can be related to norms in a 'reference database' containing data from over 250 normally developing children between the ages of three and 13 years (Miller, 1996a, pp. 314–15). For vocabulary, word lists can be generated and the variables: number of different word roots (excluding mazes), total number of words (excluding mazes), and TTR (Miller, Gillon and Johnston, 2002).

second language   See L2

Sichel's formulation   A solution to the relationship between type count and token count in a language sample developed by Sichel (1986) and also known as the INVERSE GAUSSIAN-POISSON FORMULATION.

SLI (specific language impairment)   Children with SLI experience long-lasting language difficulties that are not associated with hearing difficulties, low non-verbal intelligence or other abnormalities. The features of the linguistic deficits suffered by children with SLI are diverse (Miller, 1996b) but there are often problems with morphology and grammatical structure (see Leonard, 1996, 1998). Many investigations into SLI have used a measure of overall lexical diversity as well as diversity measures for separate word classes, especially nouns and verbs (*See* Thordardottir and Ellis Weismer, 2001, for a discussion of the measurement issues).

Somers's S An index of vocabulary diversity (Somers, 1966): $S = (LogLogV)/(LogLogN)$. It is not independent of text length (*see* Chapter 2). *See also* TULDAVA'S T.

species area problem Brainerd (1982a, 1982b) has pointed out that the problem of the relationship between the number of words in a text and the number of different words is analogous to the species–area problem in biology, that is the relationship between the number of animals in a fixed geographical area and the number of species. Brainerd (1982b) compares the assumptions of models in both domains and provides a critique (*see* Chapter 3).

split-half reliability *See* RELIABILITY

stem forms In this volume, the description of a unit of vocabulary analysis consisting of words stripped of their inflections. 'Go', 'goes', 'going', and 'went' are therefore treated as two word types ('go' and 'went'). This unit contrasts with INFLECTED FORMS and ROOT FORMS.

stem type–token ratio *See* STTR

stem variability quotient *See* SVQ

structured utterances *See* MLUS

STTR (stem type–token ratio) One of four measures developed by Mick Perkins and used for investigating repetitiveness in language disorders. The STTR is based on the analysis of strings of words ('stems') that share 50 per cent–100 per cent of their morphemes with any other string of words. The 'global STTR' for a transcript will be the number of different stems, plus the number of different word strings that occur only once, divided by the total number of word strings (*see* Perkins, 1994, pp. 329–30). The number of word strings is standardised to avoid contamination from variation in sample size (Perkins, personal communication, 29/5/96). *See also* CR, LTTR, SVQ.

SVQ (stem variability quotient) One of four measures developed by Mick Perkins and used for investigating repetitiveness in language disorders. SVQ is based on the analysis of 'stems'. These are defined as strings of words that share 50 per cent–100 per cent of their morphemes with any other string. SVQ is the total number of different stems divided by the total number of strings (Perkins, 1994, p. 330). It is therefore a form of TTR and the total number of strings is standardised to avoid sample size effects (Perkins, personal communication, 29/5/96). *See also* CR, LTTR, STTR.

T *See* TULDAVA'S T

theoretical vocabulary (V') A method that attempts to compare the vocabulary diversity in language samples of different lengths, by predicting analytically the number of types each sample would have were they all to be of the same (reduced) length. The calculation is based on simple binomial probability (*see*, e.g., Ménard, 1983, pp. 107–17). If the Theoretical Vocabulary is divided by the token count of the chosen reduced length, we obtain a type–token ratio (V'/N_{chosen}) which can be described as a 'Theoretical Segmental TTR' as it is the equivalent of a MEAN SEGMENTAL TYPE–TOKEN RATIO (MSTTR), but the type count is calculated analytically instead of by averaging sub-samples of that length. Theoretical Vocabulary, then, has the advantages and disadvantages of MSTTR. For example, it depends on a single value of types for an arbitrary number of tokens (usually determined by the size of the smallest sample), which differs from study to study, thus making cross-research comparisons difficult (*see* Chapter 3).

threshold *See* TTR THRESHOLD

TNW (total number of words) Also referred to as TW (e.g. Miller, 1996b). Information output by SALT and by the FREQ program in CLAN as a measure of speaking rate, fluency, or, in the diagnosis of language impairment, 'rate of message transference problems' (Miller, 1996b, p. 305). TNW correlates highly with age (Miller, 1991).

token–type ratio The reciprocal of the TTR, used for example by Goldfield (1993) to quantify the average number of occurrences of nouns and verbs in maternal speech to one-year-olds. Contrary to the TTR, the token–type ratio increases with increasing sample size. This measure is sometimes referred to as mean word frequency (MWF).

topic bias A form of repetitive language in which the speaker persistently returns to a limited range of topics (see Perkins, 1994).

TTR (type–token ratio) A much used measure of lexical diversity that is the number of different words in a sample of speech or writing divided by the total number of words. As Schofield has pointed out, the type–token ratio is not a true ratio at all, but a 'proportion score', as true ratios are produced from the division of two mutually exclusive categories (Schofield, 1995, p. 167). TTR is often wrongly attributed to Mildred Templin (1957) by reference to her study of 480 children between the ages of 3;0 and 8;0. However, she did no more than observe that in the different groups and ages there was roughly one different word for every two words spoken. It appears to have been Miller (1981) who converted Templin's data on mean numbers of raw types and tokens into TTRs at different ages and this is also the origin of the TTR THRESHOLD of 0.5. In fact, TTR gained prominence in the 1940s in a programme of research described by Johnson (1944) designed to develop quantitative linguistic measures to apply to the speech and writing of a variety of populations, including school children (Chotlos, 1944), university students and schizophrenics (Fairbanks, 1944; Mann, 1944). These early investigations show an awareness of TTR's sensitivity to sample size that is not acknowledged in a lot of later research, and make use of the MSTTR (mean segmental type–token ratio). *See* Chapter 2.

TTR threshold The 0.5 threshold arose from the observation by Templin (1957, p. 115) that in 50 utterances the ratio of different words to the number of words was roughly one to two regardless of age, sex, and social group, and Miller's (1981) calculation of mean TTR from Templin's figures. A TTR of significantly below 0.5 was recommended as a diagnostic of a language deficiency. As there is no stipulation of the number of tokens from which TTR is to be calculated, this advice is spurious (*see* Chapter 2).

Tuldava's T An index of vocabulary diversity:

$$T = \frac{LogLogN}{LogLog\frac{N}{V} + A}$$

where A is a constant whose value depends on the language of a text or, possibly, the genre (Tuldava, 1993). It is not independent of text length (*see* Chapter 2). This index is an extension of SOMERS'S S.

t-unit Also known as minimal terminable unit. The basis of several measures, particularly of second language development, that can be applied to speech or writing and are thought to be sensitive to linguistic complexity. Tonkyn defines the t-unit as consisting 'of a main clause and its associated subordinate clauses; co-ordinated main clauses would not count as one unit' (Tonkyn, 1996, p. 118). *See* Tonkyn for further details and for a range of proficiency measures based on the t-unit. T-units are used as a unit of analysis in the investigation of L1 writing in Chapter 9.

TUR *See* TYPE-UTTERANCE RATIO
TW *See* TNW
type–token ratio *See* TTR
type–type ratio A measure that contains a number of word types in both the numerator and the denominator, that is to say two closed sets. Indices of noun versus verb dominance (e.g. noun types/(noun types + verb types)), early vocabulary composition, and usage of rare words are frequently type–type ratios.
type–utterance ratio (TUR) In this volume, any diversity measure that divides total word types by the number of utterances in the language sample. Examples are Yoder et al.'s (1994) PRORATED NUMBER OF LEXICALLY FREE WORDS and Richards's (1990) 'range of auxiliary forms/100 structured utterances'. As a form of TTR, such measures can be expected to be sensitive to variations in sample size (*see* Chapter 2).

U *See* UBER INDEX.
Uber index A vocabulary measure, U, calculated as: $log^2 N/(log N - log V)$ – see Chapter 2 – and found by Jarvis to provide accurate fits for TTR versus N curves (*See* Jarvis, 2002, and *see* Chapter 3 in this volume). U is the inverse of MAAS'S A^2.
UCLES The University of Cambridge Local Examinations Syndicate, a department of Cambridge University that provides assessment services internationally.

V In equations, the symbol for the number of word types. *See also* N.
verb density A type–type ratio used by Bates et al. (1988), defined as 'total different open-class verbs divided by the total different open-class nouns, verbs and adjectives' (p. 150).
vocabulary richness *See* LEXICAL RICHNESS
vocd A computer program belonging to the CLAN software of the CHILDES project that automatically calculates Malvern and Richards's LEXICAL DIVERSITY measure, D, from transcripts in CHAT format; *vocd* was written by Gerard McKee of the Department of Computer Science at The University of Reading.

W *See* BRUNET'S INDEX
Wells Corpus *See* BRISTOL CORPUS
word length The mean number of orthographic letters of the words in a text (usually written). Longer words are regarded as having more specific and specialised meanings (Biber, 1988). Word length is therefore used as an index of LEXICAL SPECIFICITY. *See* Chapters 8 and 9.
WPM Words per minute, often used as a measure of fluency in studies of both L1 and L2 acquisition. It is one of the measures output by SALT. *See*, for example, Chapter 6.

York Language Aptitude Test A test of foreign language aptitude (Green, 1975a) sometimes used to select school pupils capable of learning a second modern foreign language. It tests the ability to induce grammatical rules from sample phrases and sentences presented in Swedish, and to apply the rules in new linguistic contexts (*see* Green, 1975a, 1975b; Chapter 5).
Yule's characteristic, K Yule studied such considerations as the chance that two noun tokens randomly picked from a text will be of the same type, and derived a constant for a text known as Yule's characteristic K (Yule, 1944).

$$K = 10^4 \frac{\left\{ \sum_{r=1}^{N} v_r r^2 \right\} - N}{N^2}$$

where v_r is the number of types which occur r times in a text of length N. It is a measure of repetition and lower values represent higher diversities (*see* Hess et al., 1986; Tweedie and Baayen, 1998; Jarvis, 2002; Smith and Kelly, 2002). SICHEL'S FORMULATION also predicts that K will indeed be constant (*see* Chapter 3).

Z *See* ORLOV'S Z

Zipf's laws George Zipf made some of the earliest investigations of statistical regularities in language (Crystal, 1987). Of relevance to this volume is the observation that WORD LENGTH is inversely proportional to frequency of usage (*see* Biber, 1988), and his proposal that when the frequencies of words in a text are arranged in rank order (most common first) then frequency × rank = a constant (*see* HARMONIC SERIES HYPOTHESIS and Chapter 3).

References

Afitskaya, N. (2002, Summer). Assessing vocabulary richness: LS* and LS**. *University of the West of England, Faculty of Languages and European Studies Research and Consultancy Bulletin*, **22**, 4–9.
Allen, S. E. (1998). Linguistic change in Inuktitut narratives across ages. Paper presented at the winter meeting of the Society for the Study of the Indigenous Languages of the Americas, New York, January 1998.
Anderson, W. E. (1949). *Aufenthalt in Deutschland*. London: Harrap.
Anglin, J. (1993). Vocabulary development: a morphological analysis. *Monographs of the Society for Research in Child Development*, **58**, Serial No. 238.
Arnaud, P. J. L. (1984). The lexical richness of L2 written productions and the validity of vocabulary tests. In T. Culhane, C. Klein Bradley and D. K. Stevenson (Eds), *Practice and problems in language testing: papers from the International Symposium on Language Testing* (pp. 14–28). Colchester: University of Essex.
Arrhenius, O. (1921). Species and area. *Journal of Ecology*, **9**, 95–9.
Augst, G. (1987). Ist die degressive Struktur des Wortgebrauchs ein Argument für den Rechtschreibgrundwortschatz (RGW)? In K. R. Wagner (Ed.), *Wortschatz-Erwerb* (pp. 115–27). Bern: Peter Lang.
Baayen, R. H. (1996). The effects of lexical specialization on the growth curve of vocabulary. *Computational Linguistics*, **22**, 455–80.
Barnes, S., Gutfreund, M., Satterly, D., and Wells, C. G. (1983). Characteristics of adult speech which predict children's language development. *Journal of Child Language*, **10**, 65–84.
Bassano, D. (2000). Early lexical development of nouns and verbs in French: exploring the interface between lexicon and grammar. *Journal of Child Language*, **27**, 521–59.
Bates, E., Bretherton, I., and Snyder, L. (1988). *From first words to grammar: individual differences and dissociable mechanisms*. Cambridge: Cambridge University Press.
Beals, D. E. (1997). Sources of support for learning words in conversation: evidence from mealtimes. *Journal of Child Language*, **24**, 673–94.
Beals, D. E., and Tabors, P. O. (1995). Arboretum, bureaucratic and carbohydrates: preschoolers' exposure to rare vocabulary at home. *First Language*, **15**, 57–76.
Berman, R. (2000). Developing literacy in different contexts and different languages. Interim final report, September 2000, to The Spencer Foundation, Chicago, Illinois.
Berman, R. A., and Verhoeven, L. (2002). Cross-linguistic perspectives on the development of text-production abilities: speech and writing. *Written Language and Literacy*, **5**, 1–43.
Biber, D. (1988). *Variation across speech and writing*. Cambridge: Cambridge University Press.
Blanken, G., Dittman, J., Haas, J.-C., and Wallesch, C.-W. (1987). Spontaneous speech in senile dementia and aphasia: implications for a neurolinguistic model of language production. *Cognition*, **27**, 247–74.
Bloom, L., Lightbown, P., and Hood, L. (1975). Structure and variation in child language. *Monographs of the Society for Research in Child Development*, **40** (Serial No. 160).
Bornstein, M. H., Painter, K. M., and Park, J. (2002). Everyday language and optimal language in typically developing children. *Journal of Child Language*, **29**, 687–99.

Brainerd, B. (1982a). On the relation between the type–token and species–area problems. *Journal of Applied Probability*, **19**, 785–93.
Brainerd, B. (1982b). The type–token relation in the works of S. Kierkegaard. In R. W. Bailey (Ed.), *Computing in the humanities* (pp. 97–109). Amsterdam: North-Holland.
Breland, H. M., and Jones, R. J. (1984). Perceptions of writing skills. *Written Communication*, **1**, 101–19.
Brimer, M. A., and Dunn, L. (1963). *English Picture Vocabulary Test*. Windsor: NFER.
Broeder, P., Extra, G., and van Hout, R. (1993). Richness and variety in the developing lexicon. In C. Perdue (Ed.), *Adult language acquisition: cross-linguistic perspectives* (Vol. I: Field methods, pp. 145–232). Cambridge: Cambridge University Press.
Broen, P. (1972). The verbal environment of the language-learning child. *ASHA Monograph*, **17**.
Brown, R. (1973). *A first language: the early stages*. London: Allen & Unwin.
Bucks, R. S., Singh, S., Cuerden, J. M., and Wilcock, G. K. (2000). Analysis of spontaneous, conversational speech in dementia of Alzheimer type: evaluation of an objective technique for analysing lexical performance. *Aphasiology*, **14**, 71–91.
Camaioni, L., and Longobardi, E. (2001). Noun versus verb emphasis in Italian mother-to-child speech. *Journal of Child Language*, **28**, 773–85.
Carlson, S., Bridgeman, B., Camp, R., and Waanders, J. (1985). *Relationship of admission test scores to writing performance of native and non-native speakers of English*. Princeton, NJ: Educational Testing Service.
Carpenter, R. H., and Hersh, R. E. (1985). A stylistic index of deteriorating military morale: using form in correspondence for intelligence purposes. *Language and Style*, **18**, 185–91.
Carroll, J. B. (1938). Diversity of vocabulary and the harmonic series law of word-frequency distribution. *The Psychological Record*, **11**, 379–86.
Carroll, J. B. (1964). *Language and thought*. Englewood Cliffs, NJ: Prentice-Hall.
Carroll, J. B., Davies, P., and Richman, B. (1971). *Word frequency book*. Boston, MA: Houghton-Mifflin.
Carroll, J. B., and Sapon, S. M. (1965). *Modern Language Aptitude Test*. New York: The Psychological Corporation.
Carter, R. (1987). *Vocabulary: applied linguistic perspectives*. London: Routledge.
Chafe, W. L. (1982). Integration and involvement in speaking, writing and oral literature. In D. Tannen (Ed.), *Spoken and written language: exploring orality and literacy* (pp. 35–54). Norwood, NJ: Ablex.
Chall, J., and Dale, E. (1995). *Readability revisited and the new Dale-Chall readability formula*. Cambridge, MA: Brookline Books.
Chambers, F., and Richards, B. J. (1992). Criteria for oral assessment. *Language Learning Journal*, **6**, 5–9.
Chambers, F., and Richards, B. J. (1993). Oral assessment: the views of language teachers. *Language Learning Journal*, **7**, 22–6.
Chambers, F., and Richards, B. J. (1995). The 'free conversation' and the assessment of oral proficiency. *Language Learning Journal*, **11**, 6–10.
Chase, C. I. (1968). The impact of some obvious variables on essay test scores. *Journal of Educational Measurement*, **5**, 315–18.
Chen, Y. S., and Leimkuhler, F. F. (1989). A type–token identity in the Simon-Yule model of text. *Journal of the American Society for Information Science*, **40**, 45–53.
Choi, S., and Gopnik, A. (1995). Early acquisition of verbs in Korean: a crosslinguistic study. *Journal of Child Language*, **22**, 497–529.
Chotlos, J. W. (1944). Studies in language behavior: IV. A statistical and comparative analysis of individual written language samples. *Psychological Monographs*, **56**, 75–111.

Colwell, K., Hiscock, C. K., and Memon, A. (2002). Interviewing techniques and the assessment of statement credibility. *Applied Cognitive Psychology*, **16**, 287–300.

Condon, E. V. (1928). Statistics of vocabulary. *Science*, **67**, 300.

Connor, U. (1990). Linguistic/rhetorical measures for international persuasive student writing. *Research in the Teaching of English*, **24**, 67–87.

Conti-Ramsden, G., and Jones, M. (1997). Verb use in specific language impairment. *Journal of Speech, Language and Hearing Research*, **40**, 1298–313.

Cossette, A. (1994). *La richesse lexicale et sa mesure*. Paris: Champion-Slatkine.

Cote, L. R. (2001). Language opportunities during mealtimes in preschool classrooms. In D. K. Dickinson and P. O. Tabors (Eds), *Beginning literacy with language: young children learning at home and at school* (pp. 205–21). Baltimore, MD: Paul H. Brookes Publishing.

Crain-Thoreson, C., Dahlin, M. P., and Powell, T. A. (2001). Parent-child interaction in three conversational contexts: variations in style and strategy. In P. R. Britto and J. Brooks-Gunn (Eds), *The role of family literacy environments in promoting young children's emerging literacy skills* (pp. 23–37). San Francisco, CA: Jossey-Bass.

Croll, P. (1995). Early linguistic attainment, family background and performance in 16+ examinations. *Educational Studies*, **21**, 13–28.

Cronbach, L. J. (1951). Coefficient Alpha and the internal structure of tests. *Psychometrika*, **10**, 3–31.

Cross, T. G. (1977). Mothers' speech adjustments: the contribution of selected child listener variables. In C. E. Snow and C. A. Ferguson (Eds), *Talking to children: language input and acquisition* (pp. 151–88). Cambridge: Cambridge University Press.

Crystal, D. (1982). *Profiling linguistic disability*. London: Edward Arnold.

Crystal, D. (1987). *The Cambridge encyclopedia of language*. Cambridge: Cambridge University Press.

Dale, P., Bates, E., Reznick, S., and Morisset, C. (1989). The validity of a parent report instrument of child language at twenty months. *Journal of Child Language*, **16**, 239–49.

Daller, H., van Hout, R., and Treffers-Daller, J. (2003). Lexical richness in spontaneous speech of bilinguals. *Applied Linguistics*, **24**, 197–222.

Delaney-Black, V., Covington, C., Templin, T., Kershaw, T., Nordstrom-Klee, B., Ager, J., Clark, N., Surendran, A., Martier, S., and Sokol, R. J. (2000). Expressive language development of children exposed to cocaine prenatally: literature review and report of a prospective cohort study. *Journal of Communication Disorders*, **33**, 463–81.

De León, L. (2001). Why Tzotzil (Mayan) children prefer verbs: the role of linguistic and cultural factors over cognitive determinants. In M. Almgren, A. Barreña, M.-J. Ezeizabarrena, I. Idiazabal, and B. MacWhinney (Eds), *Research on child language acquisition. Proceedings of the Eighth Conference of the Association for the Study of Child Language* (pp. 923–7). Sommerville, MA: Cascadilla Press.

Della Corte, M., Benedict, H., and Klein, D. (1983). The relationship of pragmatic dimensions of mothers' speech to the referential-expressive distinction. *Journal of Child Language*, **10**, 35–43.

Dewaele, J.-M., and Pavlenko, A. (2003). Productivity and lexical diversity in native and non-native speech: a study of cross-cultural effects. In V. Cook (Ed.), *Effects of the second language on the first* (pp. 120–41). Clevedon: Multilingual Matters.

Dickinson, D. K. (2001a). Large-group and free-play times: conversational settings supporting language and literacy development. In D. K. Dickinson and P. O. Tabors (Eds), *Beginning literacy with language: young children learning at home and at school* (pp. 223–55). Baltimore, MD: Paul H. Brookes Publishing.

Dickinson, D. K. (2001b). Putting the pieces together: impact of preschool on children's language and literacy development in kindergarten. In D. K. Dickinson and P. O. Tabors (Eds), *Beginning literacy with language: young children learning at home and at school* (pp. 257–87). Baltimore, MD: Paul H. Brookes Publishing.

Dickinson, D. K., and Tabors, P. O. (Eds). (2001). *Beginning literacy with language: young children learning at home and at school*. Baltimore, MD: Paul H. Brookes Publishing.

Duffy, M. E., and Jacobsen, B. S. (2001). Univariate descriptive statistics. In B. H. Munro (Ed.), *Statistical methods for health care research* (4th edn, pp. 29–62). New York: Lippincott.

Dugast, D. (1978). Sur quoi se fonde la notion d'étendue théoretique du vocabulaire? *Le Français Moderne*, **46**, 25–32.

Dugast , D. (1979). *Vocabulaire et stylistique. I Théâtre et dialogue, travaux de linguistique quantitative*. Geneva: Slatkine.

Duncan, S., and Fiske, D. W. (1977). *Face-to-face interaction: research, methods, and theory*. Hillsdale, NJ: Erlbaum.

Dunn, L. M., and Dunn, L. M. (1981). *Peabody Picture Vocabulary Test – Revised (PPVT–R)*. Circle Pines, MN: American Guidance Service.

Durán, P. (2000). Verbal morphology in early Spanish. In R. P. Leow and C. Sanz (Eds), *Spanish applied linguistics at the turn of the millennium* (pp. 36–49). Somerville, MA: Cascadilla Press.

Edwards, S., and Bastiaanse, R. (1998). Diversity in the lexical and syntactic abilities of fluent aphasic speakers. *Aphasiology*, **12**, 99–117.

Ellis Weismer, S., Murray-Branch, J., and Miller, J. F. (1993). Comparison of two methods for promoting productive vocabulary in late talkers. *Journal of Speech and Hearing Research*, **36**, 1037–50.

Ellis Weismer, S., Murray-Branch, J., and Miller, J. F. (1994). A prospective longitudinal study of language development in late talkers. *Journal of Speech and Hearing Research*, **37**, 852–67.

Fairbanks, H. (1944). Studies in language behavior: II. The quantitative differentiation of samples of spoken language. *Psychological Monographs*, **56**, 19–38.

Fenson, L., Dale, P. S., Reznick, J. S., Thal, D., Bates, E., Hartung, J. P., Pethick, S., and Reilly, J. S. (1993). *The MacArthur Communicative Development Inventories: user's guide and technical manual*. San Diego: Singular Publishing Group.

Ferris, D. (1994). Lexical and syntactic features of ESL writing by students at different levels of proficiency. *TESOL Quarterly*, **28**, 414–20.

Fletcher, P. (1985). *A child's learning of English*. Oxford: Blackwell.

Fletcher, P., and Peters, J. (1984). Characterizing language impairment in children: an exploratory study. *Language Testing*, **1**, 33–49.

Foster, P., and Skehan, P. (1996). The influence of planning and task on second language performance. *Studies in Second Language Acquisition*, **18**, 299–323.

Fradis, A., Mihailescu, L., and Jipescu, I. (1992). The distribution of major grammatical classes in the vocabulary of Romanian aphasic patients. *Aphasiology*, **6**, 477–89.

Frase, L., Faletti, J., Ginther, A., and Grant, L. (1999). *Computer analysis of the TOEFL Test of Written English. Research Report No. 64*. Princeton, NJ: Educational Testing Service.

Gass, S. M., and Varonis, E. M. (1985). Variation in native speaker speech modification to non-native speakers. *Studies in Second Language Acquisition*, **7**, 37–57.

Geers, A., Spehar, B., and Sedey, A. (2002). Use of speech by children from total communication programs who wear cochlear implants. *American Journal of Speech-Language Pathology*, **11**, 50–8.

Gentner, D. (1982). Why nouns are learned before verbs: linguistic relativity versus natural partitioning. In S. A. Kuczaj (Ed.), *Language development (Volume 2): language, thought and culture* (pp. 301–34). Hillsdale, NJ: Lawrence Erlbaum Associates.

Gentry, J. R. (1982). An analysis of developmental spelling in Gnys At Wrk. *The Reading Teacher*, **36**, 192–200.

Girolametto, L., Bonifacio, S., Visini, C., Weitzman, E., Zocconi, E., and Pearce, P. S. (2002). Mother-child interactions in Canada and Italy: linguistic responsiveness to late-talking toddlers. *International Journal of Language and Communication Disorders*, **37**, 153–71.

Goldfield, B. (1993). Noun bias in maternal speech to one-year-olds. *Journal of Child Language*, **20**, 85–99.

Good I. J. (1953). The population frequencies of species and the estimation of population parameters. *Biometrika*, **40**, 237–64.

Gopnik, A., and Choi, S. (1995). Names, relational words, and cognitive development in English and Korean speakers: nouns are not always learned before verbs. In M. Tomasello and W. E. Merriman (Eds), *Beyond names for things: young children's acquisition of verbs* (pp. 63–80). Hillsdale, NJ: Erlbaum.

Grant, L. and Ginther, A. (2000). Using computer-tagged linguistic features to describe L2 writing differences. *Journal of Second Language Writing*, **9**, 123–45.

Green, P. S. (1975a). *York Language Aptitude Test*. York: University of York Language Teaching Centre.

Green, P. S. (1975b). *The language laboratory in school: the York Study*. Edinburgh: Oliver and Boyd.

Guiraud, P. (1960). *Problèmes et méthodes de la statistique linguistique*. Dordrecht: D. Reidel.

Gutfreund, M., Harrison, M., and Wells, C. G. (1989). *Bristol Language Development scales*. Windsor: NFER-Nelson.

Halliday, M. A. K. (1985). *Spoken and written language*. Melbourne: Deakin University Press.

Hamilton, A., Plunkett, K., and Schafer, G. (2000). Infant vocabulary development assessed with a British CDI. *Journal of Child Language*, **27**, 689–705.

Hansson, K. (1996). Verb type token ratio in Swedish children with SLI. A reply to Richards and Malvern. *Logopedics Phoniatrics Vocology*, **21**, 112–13.

Härnquist, K., Christianson, U., Ridings, D., and Tingsell, J.-G. (2003). Vocabulary in interviews as related to respondent characteristics. *Computers and the Humanities*, **37**, 179–204.

Hayes, D. P., and Ahrens, M. G. (1988). Vocabulary simplification for children: a special case of 'motherese'. *Journal of Child Language*, **15**, 395–410.

He, A. W., and Young, R. (1998). Language proficiency interviews: a discourse approach. In R. Young and A. W. He (Eds), *Talking and testing: discourse approaches to the assessment of oral proficiency* (pp. 1–24). Amsterdam: John Benjamins.

Heim, A. W., Watts, K. P., and Simmonds, V. (1975). *AH2/AH3 Group Test of General Ability*. Windsor: NFER-Nelson.

Herdan, G. (1960). *Type–token mathematics: a textbook of mathematical linguistics*. The Hague: Mouton.

Hess, C. W., Haug, H. T., and Landry, R. G. (1989). The reliability of type–token ratios for the oral language of school-age children. *Journal of Speech and Hearing Research*, **32**, 536–40.

Hess, C. W., Sefton, K. M., and Landry, R. G. (1986). Sample size and type–token ratios for oral language of preschool children. *Journal of Speech and Hearing Research*, **29**, 129–34.

Hesse, H., and Hesse, B. (1987). Wortschätze der Grundschule. Probleme ihrer Beschreibung. In K. R. Wagner (Ed.), *Wortschatz-Erwerb* (pp. 82–101). Bern: Peter Lang.
Hick, R. F., Joseph, K. L., Conti-Ramsden, G., Serratrice, L., and Faragher, B. (2002). Vocabulary profiles of children with specific language impairment. *Child Language Teaching and Therapy*, **18**, 165–80.
Hickey, T. (1991). Mean length of utterance and the acquisition of Irish. *Journal of Child Language*, **18**, 553–69.
Hoare, R. (2000/2001). Measuring lexical diversity: the TTR and D. *University of the West of England, Faculty of Languages and European Studies Research and Consultancy Bulletin*, **19**, 34–8.
Hoff, E., Baker, M., Isaza, M., Romanoski, S., and Vasquez, J. (2002). Assessing child language using spontaneous speech samples: effects of setting. Paper presented at the Joint Conference of the IXth International Congress for the Study of Child Language and the Symposium on Research in Child Language Disorders, University of Wisconsin-Madison, July 16–21 2002.
Hoff, E., McKay, J., and Noya, M. (2002). Mothers' talk to children: consequences of different methods of measurement. Paper presented at the Joint Conference of the IXth International Congress for the Study of Child Language and the Symposium on Research in Child Language Disorders, University of Wisconsin-Madison, July 16–21 2002.
Hoff, E., and Naigles, L. (2002). How children use input to acquire a lexicon. *Child Development*, **73**, 418–33.
Holmes, D. I. (1994). Authorship attribution. *Computers and the Humanities*, **28**, 87–106.
Holmes, D. I., and Singh, S. (1996). A stylometric analysis of conversational speech of aphasic patients. *Literary and Linguistic Computing*, **11**, 133–40.
Honoré, A. (1979). Some simple measures of richness of vocabulary. *Association of Literary and Linguistic Computing Bulletin*, **11**, 45–60.
Hunt, K. W. (1965). *Grammatical structures written at three grade levels*. NCTE Research Report No. 3. Champaign, IL: NCTE.
Hyltenstam, K. (1988). Lexical characteristics of near-native second-language learners of Swedish. *Journal of Multilingual and Multicultural Development*, **9**, 67–84.
Irwin, O. C. (1946). Infant speech equations for consonant–vowel ratios. *Journal of Speech Disorders*, **11**, 177–80.
Iverson, J. M., Capirci, O., and Caselli, M. C. (1994). From communication to language in two modalities. *Cognitive Development*, **9**, 23–43.
Jarvis, S. (2002). Short texts, best fitting curves, and new measures of lexical diversity. *Language Testing*, **19**, 57–84.
Johnson, M., and Tyler, A. (1998). Re-analyzing the OPI: how much does it look like natural conversation? In R. Young and A. W. He (Eds), *Talking and testing: discourse approaches to the assessment of oral proficiency* (pp. 28–51). Amsterdam: John Benjamins.
Johnson, W. (1944). Studies in language behavior: I. A program of research. *Psychological Monographs*, **56**, 1–15.
Jones, M., and Conti-Ramsden, G. (1997). A comparison of verb use in children with SLI and their younger siblings. *First Language*, **17**, 165–93.
Kauschke, C., and Hofmeister, C. (2002). Early lexical development in German: a study on vocabulary growth and vocabulary composition during the second and third year of life. *Journal of Child Language*, **29**, 735–57.
Kim, M., McGregor, K. K., and Thompson, C. K. (2000). Early lexical development in English- and Korean-speaking children: language-general and language-specific patterns. *Journal of Child Language*, **27**, 225–54.

Klee, T. (1992). Developmental and diagnostic characteristics of quantitative measures of children's language production. *Topics in Language Disorders*, **12**, 28–41.
Köhler, R., and Galle, M. (1993). Dynamic aspects of text characteristics. In L. Hrebicek and G. Altmann (Eds), *Quantitative text analysis* (pp. 46–53). Trier: Wissenschaftlicher Verlag Trier.
Küntay, A. C., and Slobin, D. I. (2001). Discourse behaviour of lexical categories in Turkish child directed speech: nouns vs. verbs. In M. Almgren, A. Barreña, M.-J. Ezeizabarrena, I. Idiazabal and B. MacWhinney (Eds), *Research on child language acquisition. Proceedings of the 8th Conference of the Association for the Study of Child Language* (pp. 928–46). Sommerville, MA: Cascadilla Press.
Laufer, B. (2003). The influence of L2 on L1 collocational knowledge and on L1 lexical diversity in free written expression. In V. Cook (Ed.), *Effects of the second language on the first* (pp. 19–31). Clevedon: Multilingual Matters.
Laufer, B., and Nation, P. (1995). Vocabulary size and use: lexical richness in L2 written production. *Applied Linguistics*, **16**, 307–22.
Layton, T. L., and Savino, M. A. (1990). Acquiring a communication system by sign and speech in a child with Down syndrome: a longitudinal investigation. *Child Language Teaching and Therapy*, **6**, 59–76.
Lazaraton, A. (1992). The structural organization of a language interview: a conversation analytic perspective. *System*, **20**, 373–86.
Lazaraton, A. (1996). Interlocutor support in oral proficiency interviews: the case of CASE. *Language Testing*, **13**, 151–72.
Leech, G., Rayson, P., and Wilson, A. (2001). *Word frequencies in written and spoken English*. Harlow: Longman.
Le Normand, M.-T., and Cohen, H. (1999). The delayed emergence of lexical morphology in preterm children: the case of verbs. *Journal of Neurolinguistics*, **12**, 235–46.
Leonard, L. B. (1996). Characterizing specific language impairment: a crosslinguistic perspective. In M. L. Rice (Ed.), *Towards a genetics of language* (pp. 243–56). Mahwah, NJ: Erlbaum.
Leonard, L. B. (1998). *Children with specific language impairment*. Cambridge, MA: MIT Press.
Leonard, L. B., Miller, C., and Gerber, E. (1999). Grammatical morphology and the lexicon in children with specific language impairment. *Journal of Speech, Language and Hearing Research*, **42**, 678–89.
Lieven, E. V. M. (1978). Conversations between mothers and young children: individual differences and their possible implication for the study of child language learning. In N. Waterson and C. E. Snow (Eds), *The development of communication* (pp. 173–87). Chichester: Wiley.
Linnarud, M. (1983). On lexis: the Swedish learner and the native speaker compared. In K. Sajavaara (Ed.), *Cross language analysis and second language acquisition* (pp. 249–61). Jyväskylä: University of Jyväskylä.
Loban, W. (1976). *Language development: kindergarten through grade twelve*. Urbana, Il: NCTE.
López Ornat, S. (1994). *La adquisición de la lengua Española*. Madrid: Siglo XXI.
Luzzatti, C., Raggi, R., Zonca, G., Pistarini, C., Contardi, A., and Pinna, G.-D. (2001). On the nature of the selective impairment of verb and noun retrieval. *Cortex*, **37**, 724–6.
Maas, H.-D. (1972). Zusammenhang zwischen Wortschatzumfang und Länge eines Textes. *Zeitschrift für Literaturwissenschaft und Linguistik*, **8**, 73–9.

MacWhinney, B. (1994). New Horizons for CHILDES research. In J. L. Sokolov and C. E. Snow (Eds), *Handbook of research in language development using CHILDES* (pp. 408–542). Hillsdale, NJ: Lawrence Erlbaum.
MacWhinney, B. (1995a). Computational analysis of interactions. In P. Fletcher and B. MacWhinney (Eds), *The handbook of child language* (pp. 152–78). Oxford: Blackwell.
MacWhinney, B. (1995b). *The CHILDES project: tools for analyzing talk* (2nd edn). Hillsdale, NJ: Erlbaum.
MacWhinney, B. (2000a). *The CHILDES project: tools for analyzing talk* (3rd edn, Vol. 1: Transcription format and programs). Mahwah, NJ: Erlbaum.
MacWhinney, B. (2000b). *The CHILDES project: tools for analyzing talk* (3rd edn, Vol. 2: The database). Mahwah, NJ: Erlbaum.
MacWhinney, B., and Snow, C. E. (1990). The Child Language Data Exchange System: an update. *Journal of Child Language*, **17**, 457–72.
Malvern D. D. (2000). Mathematical modelling in science and science education. In J. K. Gilbert and C. Boulter (Eds), *Developing models in science education* (pp. 69–90). Dordrecht: Kluwer.
Malvern, D. D., and Richards, B. J. (1997). A new measure of lexical diversity. In A. Ryan and A. Wray (Eds), *Evolving models of language. Papers from the Annual Meeting of the British Association of Applied Linguists held at the University of Wales, Swansea, September 1996* (pp. 58–71). Clevedon: Multilingual Matters.
Malvern, D. D., and Richards, B. J. (2000a). Validation of a new measure of lexical diversity. In M. Beers, B. van den Bogaerde, G. Bol, J. de Jong and C. Rooijmans (Eds), *From sound to sentence: studies on first language acquisition*. Groningen: Centre for Language and Cognition.
Malvern, D. D., and Richards, B. J. (2000b). A new method of measuring lexical diversity in texts and conversations. *Teanga, The Irish Yearbook of Applied Linguistics*, **19**, 1–12. (Special issue on: Integrating theory and practice in LSP and LAP, ed. D. P. O Baoill and M. Ruane).
Malvern, D. D., and Richards, B. J. (2002). Investigating accommodation in language proficiency interviews using a new measure of lexical diversity. *Language Testing*, **19**, 85–104.
Mann, M. B. (1944). Studies in language behavior: III. The quantitative differentiation of samples of written language. *Psychological Monographs*, **56**, 41–74.
Manschreck, T. C., Maher, B. A., and Ader, D. N. (1981). Formal thought disorder, the type–token ratio, and disturbed voluntary movement in schizophrenia. *British Journal of Psychiatry*, **139**, 7–15.
Manschreck, T. C., Maher, B. A., Hoover, T. M., and Ames, D. (1984). The type–token ratio in schizophrenic disorders: clinical and research value. *Psychological Medicine*, **14**, 151–7.
Marcus, G. F., Pinker, S., Ullman, M., Hollander, M., Rosen, T. J., and Xu, F. (1992). Overregularization in language acquisition. *Monographs of the Society for Research in Child Development*, **57**.
Markham, L. R. (1976). Influence of handwriting quality on teacher evaluation of written work. *American Educational Research Journal*, **13**, 277–83.
McCarthy, D. (1954). Language development in children. In L. Carmichael (Ed.), *Manual of child psychology* (2nd edn, pp. 492–630). New York: Wiley.
McEvoy, S., and Dodd, B. (1992). The communication abilities of 2- to 4-year-old twins. *European Journal of Disorders of Communication*, **27**, 73–87.
McKee, G., Malvern, D. D., and Richards, B. J. (2000). Measuring vocabulary diversity using dedicated software. *Literary and Linguistic Computing*, **15**, 323–38.

Meara, P. (1978). Schizophrenic symptoms in foreign language learners. *UEA Papers in Linguistics*, **7**, 22–49.
Meara, P., and Bell, H. (2001). P_Lex: a simple and effective way of describing the lexical characteristics of short L2 texts. *Prospect*, **16**, 5–19.
Meara, P., Lightbown, P. M., and Halter, R. H. (1997). Classrooms as lexical environments. *Language Teaching Research*, **1**, 28–47.
Mehrens, W. A., and Lehmann, I. J. (1978). *Measurement and evaluation in education and psychology* (2nd edn). New York: Holt, Rinehart and Winston.
Ménard, N. (1983). *Mesure de la richesse lexicale*. Geneva: Slatkine.
Mendenhall, T. C. (1987). The characteristic curves of composition. *Science*, **9**, 237–49.
Michéa R. (1969). Répétition et variété dans l'emploi des mots. *Bulletin de la Société de Linguistique de Paris*, 1–24.
Michéa R. (1971). De la relation entre le nombre des mots d'une fréquence déterminée et celui des mots différents employés dans le texte. *Cahiers de Lexicologie*, **18**, 65–78.
Miller, J. F. (1981). *Assessing language production: experimental procedures*. London: Arnold.
Miller, J. F. (1991). Quantifying productive language disorders. In J. F. Miller (Ed.), *Research on child language disorders: a decade of progress* (pp. 211–20). Austin, TX: Pro-Ed.
Miller, J. F. (1996a). Progress in assessing, describing, and defining child language disorder. In K. N. Cole, P. S. Dale and D. J. Thal (Eds), *Assessment of Communication and Language* (pp. 309–24). Baltimore, MD: Paul Brookes Publishing Co.
Miller, J. F. (1996b). The search for the phenotype of disordered language performance. In M. Rice (Ed.), *Towards a genetics of language* (pp. 297–314). Mahwah, NJ: Erlbaum.
Miller, J. F., and Chapman, R. (1993). *SALT: systematic analysis of language transcripts, version 3.0*. Baltimore, MD: University Park Press.
Miller, J. F., Gillon, G., and Johnston, J. (2002). Managing language sample data: new research tools. Paper presented at the Joint Conference of the IXth International Congress for the Study of Child Language and the Symposium on Research in Child Language Disorders, University of Wisconsin-Madison, July 16–21 2002.
Milton, J., and Hales, T. (1997). Applying a lexical profiling system to technical English. In A. Ryan and A. Wray (Eds), *Evolving models of language. Papers from the Annual Meeting of the British Association of Applied Linguists held at the University of Wales, Swansea, September 1996* (pp. 72–83). Clevedon: Multilingual Matters.
Moder, C. L., and Halleck, G. B. (1998). Framing the language proficiency interview as a speech event: native and non-native speakers' questions. In R. Young and A. W. He (Eds), *Talking and testing: discourse approaches to the assessment of oral proficiency* (pp. 117–46). Amsterdam: John Benjamins.
Montes, R. (1987). *Secuencias de clarificación en conversaciones con niños*. (Morphe 3–4): Universidad Autónoma de Puebla.
Montes, R. (1992). *Achieving understanding: repair mechanisms in mother-child conversations*. Unpublished doctoral dissertation, Georgetown University.
Munro B. H. (2001). Regression. In B. H. Munro (Ed.), *Statistical methods for health care research*. New York: Lippincott.
Nation, I. S. P. (1984). *Vocabulary lists: words, affixes and stems*. Wellington, New Zealand: Victoria University of Wellington English Language Institute. Occasional Publication No. 12.
Nation, I. S. P. (1996). *Vocabulary lists*. Wellington, New Zealand: Victoria University of Wellington English Language Institute. Occasional Publication No. 17.

Nelson, K. (1973). Structure and strategy in learning to talk. *Monographs of the Society for Research in Child Development*, **38**.
Nelson, K., Hampson, J., and Kessler Shaw, L. (1993). Nouns in early lexicons: evidence, explanations and implications. *Journal of Child Language*, **20**, 61–84.
Nold, E., and Freedman, S. (1977). An analysis of readers' responses to essays. *Research in the Teaching of English*, **11**, 164–74.
O'Donnell, R. C., Griffin, W. J., and Norris, R. C. (1967). *Syntax of kindergarten and elementary school children: a transformational analysis*. Research Report No. 8. Champaign, Il: NCTE.
Ogura, T. (2002). Caregiver input in Japanese: use of nouns and verbs in book-reading and toy-play contexts. Paper presented at the Joint Conference of the IXth International Congress for the Study of Child Language and the Symposium on Research in Child Language Disorders, University of Wisconsin-Madison, July 16–21 2002.
O'Loughlin, K. (1995). Lexical density in candidate output on direct and semi-direct versions of an oral proficiency test. *Language Testing*, **12**, 217–37.
Onslow, M., Ratner, N. B., and Packman, A. (2001). Changes in linguistic variables during operant, laboratory control of stuttering in children. *Clinical Linguistics and Phonetics*, **15**, 651–62.
Osgood, C. E. (1960). Some effects of motivation on style of encoding. In T. Sebeok (Ed.), *Style in language* (pp. 293–306). Cambridge, MA: MIT Press.
Ouellet, C., Cohen, H., Le Normand, M.-T., and Braun, C. (2000). Asynchronous language acquisition in developmental dysphasia. *Brain and Cognition*, **43**, 352–7.
Owen, A., and Leonard, L. B. (2002). Lexical diversity in the spontaneous speech of children with specific language impairment: application of VOCD. *Journal of Speech, Language and Hearing Research*, **45**, 927–37.
Page, E. B. (1963). Ordered hypotheses for multiple treatments: a significance test for linear ranks. *Journal of the American Statistical Association*, **58**, 216–30.
Page, E. B. (1994). New computer grading of student prose, using modern concepts and software. *Journal of Experimental Education*, **62**, 127–42.
Pan, B. A. (1994). Basic measures of child language. In J. L. Sokolov and C. E. Snow (Eds), *Handbook of research in language development using CHILDES* (pp. 26–49). Hillsdale, NJ: Lawrence Erlbaum.
Pan, B. A., Rowe, M., Spier, E., and Tamis-LeMonda, C. (2002). Parental report and spontaneous speech measures of low-income toddlers' vocabulary at age 2. Paper presented at the Joint Conference of the IXth International Congress for the Study of Child Language and the Symposium on Research in Child Language Disorders, University of Wisconsin-Madison, July 16–21 2002.
Perera, K. (1984). *Children's reading and writing*. Oxford: Blackwell.
Perkins, M. (1994). Repetitiveness in language disorders: a new analytical procedure. *Clinical Linguistics and Phonetics*, **8**, 321–36.
Peters, A. M. (1983). *The units of language acquisition*. Cambridge: Cambridge University Press.
Pimsleur, P. (1966). *Pimsleur language aptitude battery*. New York: Harcourt Brace Jovanowich.
Pine, J. (1992). How referential are 'referential' children? Relationships between maternal-report and observational measures of vocabulary composition and usage. *Journal of Child Language*, **19**, 75–86.
Pine, J. (1994). The language of primary caregivers. In C. Gallaway and B. J. Richards (Eds), *Input and interaction in language acquisition* (pp. 15–37). Cambridge: Cambridge University Press.

Pine, J. M., Lieven, E. V. M., and Rowland, C. (1996). Observational and checklist measures of vocabulary composition: what do they mean? *Journal of Child Language*, **23**, 573–90.

Pinker, S. (1989). *Learnability and cognition: the acquisition of verb-argument structure*. Cambridge, MA: Harvard University Press.

Pinker, S. (1999). *Words and rules: the ingredients of language*. London: Weidenfeld & Nicolson.

Qualifications and Curriculum Authority. (2001). *Marking guidelines for writing*. London: Department of Education and Employment.

Read, J. (2000). *Assessing vocabulary*. Cambridge: Cambridge University Press.

Reid, J. (1986). Using the writer's workbench in composition teaching and testing. In C. W. Stansfield (Ed.), *Technology and language testing* (pp. 167–88). Washington, DC: TESOL.

Reid, J. (1990). Responding to different topic types: a qualitative analysis from a contrastive rhetoric perspective. In B. Kroll (Ed.), *Second language writing: research insights for the classroom* (pp. 191–210). New York: Cambridge University Press.

Reppen, R. (1994). *Variation in elementary student language: a multidimensional perspective*. Unpublished doctoral dissertation, Northern Arizona University, Flagstaff.

Richards, B. J. (1987). Type–token ratios: what do they really tell us? *Journal of Child Language*, **14**, 201–9.

Richards, B. J. (1990). *Language development and individual differences: a study of auxiliary verb learning*. Cambridge: Cambridge University Press.

Richards, B. J., and Chambers, F. (1996). Reliability and validity in the GCSE oral examination. *Language Learning Journal*, **14**, 28–34.

Richards, B. J., and Malvern, D. D. (1996). Swedish verb morphology in language impaired children: interpreting the type–token ratios. *Logopedics Phoniatrics Vocology*, **21**, 109–11.

Richards, B. J., and Malvern, D. D. (1997). *The New Bulmershe Papers. Quantifying lexical diversity in the study of language development*. Reading: The University of Reading.

Richards, B. J., and Malvern, D. D. (1999). Comparing lexical diversity in children with SLI and their siblings. Paper presented at the 1999 Annual Convention of the American Speech-Language-Hearing Association, San Francisco.

Richards, B. J., and Malvern, D. D. (2000). Accommodation in oral interviews between foreign language learners and teachers who are not native speakers. *Studia Linguistica*, **54**, 260–71.

Richards, B. J., and Malvern, D. D. (2004). Investigating the validity of a new measure of lexical diversity for root and inflected forms. In K. Trott, S. Dobbinson and P. Griffiths (Eds), *The child language reader* (pp. 81–9). London: Routledge.

Richards, J. C., Platt, J., and Platt, H. (1992). *Longman dictionary of language teaching and applied linguistics* (2nd edn). Harlow: Longman.

Rollins, P. R. (1994). Language profiles of children with specific language impairment. In J. L. Sokolov and C. E. Snow (Eds), *Handbook of research in language development using CHILDES* (pp. 373–407). Hillsdale, NJ: Lawrence Erlbaum.

Ross, S. (1992). Accommodative questions in oral proficiency interviews. *Language Testing*, **9**, 173–86.

Ross, S., and Berwick, R. (1992). The discourse of accommodation in oral proficiency interviews. *Studies in Second Language Acquisition*, **14**, 159–76.

Sampson, G. (2001). *Empirical linguistics*. London: Continuum.

Sanders, L. M., Adams, J., Tager-Flusberg, H., Shenton, M. E., and Coleman, M. (1995). A comparison of clinical and linguistic indices of deviance in the verbal discourse of schizophrenics. *Applied Psycholinguistics*, **16**, 325–38.

Satterly, D. (1989). *Assessment in schools* (2nd edn). Oxford: Blackwell.
Schegloff, E. A. (1982). Discourse as an interactional achievement: some uses of 'uh huh' and other things that come between sentences. In D. Tannen (Ed.), *Analyzing discourse: text and talk. Georgetown University Round Table on Language and Linguistics, 1981* (pp. 71–93). Washington, DC: Georgetown University Press.
Scholfield, P. (1995). *Quantifying language: a researcher's and teacher's guide to gathering language data and reducing it to figures*. Clevedon: Multilingual Matters.
Scott, C. M., and Windsor, J. (2000). General language performance measures in spoken and written narrative and expository discourse of school-age children with language learning disabilities. *Journal of Speech, Language and Hearing Research*, **43**, 324–39.
Sherblom, J., and Sherblom, A. (1987). TTR: A microcomputer application to language analysis. *Western Journal of Speech Communication*, **51**, 68–77.
Sichel, H. S. (1971). On a family of discrete distributions particularly suited to represent long-tailed frequency data. In N. F. Laubscher (Ed.), *Proceedings of the Third Symposium on Mathematical Statistics*, SACSIR, Pretoria, 51–97.
Sichel, H. S. (1975). On a distribution law for word frequencies, *Journal of the American Statistics Association*, **137**, 25–34.
Sichel, H. S. (1986). Word frequency distributions and type–token characteristics. *Mathematical Scientist*, **11**, 45–72.
Siegel, S., and Castellan, N. J. (1988). *Nonparametric statistics for the behavioral sciences* (2nd edn). New York: Mcgraw Hill.
Silverman, S., and Ratner, N. (2002). Measuring lexical diversity in children who stutter: application of vocd. *Journal of Fluency Disorders*, **27**, 289–304.
Simonton, D. K. (1989). Shakespeare's sonnets: a case of and for single-case historiometry. *Journal of Personality*, **57**, 695–721.
Skehan, P. (1986). Early lexical development and the prediction of foreign language learning success. Paper presented at the CILT/ESRC Conference on Second Language Acquisition, Windsor, Berkshire.
Skehan, P. (1989). *Individual differences in second-language learning*. London: Arnold.
Skehan, P. (1990). The relationship between native and foreign language learning ability: educational and linguistic factors. In H. W. Dechert (Ed.), *Current trends in European second language acquisition research* (pp. 83–106). Clevedon: Multilingual Matters.
Skinner B. F. (1937). The distribution of associated words. *The Psychological Record*, **1**, 71–6.
Smith, J. A., and Kelly, C. (2002). Stylistic constancy and change across literary corpora: using measures of lexical richness to date works. *Computers and the Humanities*, **36**, 411–30.
Snow, C. E. (1989). Imitativeness: a trait or a skill? In G. E. Speidel and K. E. Nelson (Eds), *The many faces of imitation in language learning* (pp. 73–90). New York: Springer-Verlag.
Snow, C. E. (1996). Change in child language and child linguists. In H. Coleman and L. Cameron (Eds), *Change and language* (pp. 75–88). Clevedon: BAAL in association with Multilingual Matters.
Snow, C. E. (2001). Longitudinal study of language and literacy development in low-income children. Inaugural Professorial Lecture of the Language and Literacy Research Centre, University of London Institute of Education, 4 October 2001.
Snow, C. E., Tabors, P. O., and Dickinson, D. K. (2001). Language development in the preschool years. In D. K. Dickinson and P. O. Tabors (Eds), *Beginning literacy with*

language: young children learning at home and at school (pp. 1–25). Baltimore, MD: Paul H. Brookes Publishing.
Somers, H. H. (1966). Statistical methods in literary analysis. In J. Leeds (Ed.), *The computer and literary style* (pp. 128–40). Kent, OH: Kent State University Press.
Spencer, K. (1999). Predicting spelling behaviour in 7 to 11 year-olds. *Reading*, **33**, 72–7.
Spreen, O., and Wachal, R. S. (1973). Psycholinguistic analysis of aphasic language: theoretical formulations and procedures. *Language and Speech*, **16**, 130–46.
Stewart, M., and Grobe, C. (1979). Syntactic maturity, mechanics of writing, and teachers' quality ratings. *Research in the Teaching of English*, **13**, 207–15.
Stewig, J. W. (1994). First graders talk about paintings. *Journal of Educational Research*, **87**, 309–16.
Stickler, K. R. (1987). *Guide to analysis of language transcripts*. Eau Claire, WI: Thinking Publications.
Stokes, S. F., and Fletcher, P. (2000). Lexical diversity and productivity in Cantonese-speaking children with specific language impairment. *International Journal of Language and Communication Disorders*, **35**, 527–41.
Strömqvist, S., Johansson, V., Kriz, S., Ragnarsdóttir, H., Aisenman, R., and Ravid, D. (2002). Toward a crosslinguistic comparison of lexical quanta in speech and writing. *Written Language and Literacy*, **5**, 45–67.
Tabors, P. O., Beals, D. E., and Weizman, Z. O. (2001). 'You know what oxygen is?': Learning new words at home. In D. K. Dickinson and P. O. Tabors (Eds), *Beginning literacy with language: young children learning at home and at school* (pp. 93–110). Baltimore, MD: Paul H. Brookes Publishing.
Tabors, P. O., Roach, K. A., and Snow, C. E. (2001). Home language and literacy environment: final results. In D. K. Dickinson and P. O. Tabors (Eds), *Beginning literacy with language: young children learning at home and at school* (pp. 111–38). Baltimore, MD: Paul H. Brookes Publishing.
Tabors, P. O., Snow, C. E., and Dickinson, D. K. (2001). Homes and schools together: supporting language and literacy development. In D. K. Dickinson and P. O. Tabors (Eds), *Beginning literacy with language: young children learning at home and at school* (pp. 313–34). Baltimore, MD: Paul H. Brookes Publishing.
Tardif, T. (2001). When all things are not equal: contextualizing the noun bias in Mandarin and English. In M. Almgren, A. Barreña, M.-J. Ezeizabarrena, I. Idiazabal, and B. MacWhinney (Eds), *Research on child language acquisition. Proceedings of the Eighth Conference of the Association for the Study of Child Language* (pp. 970–80). Sommerville, MA: Cascadilla Press.
Tardif, T., Gelman, S., and Xu, F. (1999). Putting the 'noun bias' in context: a comparison of English and Mandarin. *Child Development*, **70**, 620–35.
Tardif, T., Shatz, M., and Naigles, L. (1997). Caregiver speech and children's use of nouns versus verbs: a comparison of English, Italian, and Mandarin. *Journal of Child Language*, **24**, 535–65.
Templin, M. (1957). *Certain language skills in children*. Minneapolis: University of Minneapolis Press.
Thakerar, J. N., Giles, H., and Cheshire, J. (1982). Psychological and linguistic parameters of speech accommodation theory. In C. Fraser and K. R. Sherer (Eds), *Advances in the social psychology of language* (pp. 205–55). Cambridge: Cambridge University Press.
Theakston, A. L., Lieven, E. V. M., Pine, J. M., and Rowland, C. F. (2001). The role of performance limitations in the acquisition of verb-argument structure: an alternative account. *Journal of Child Language*, **28**, 127–52.

Thomson, G. H., and Thompson, J. R. (1915). Outlines of a method for the quantitative analysis of writing vocabularies. *British Journal of Psychology*, **8**, 52–69.

Thordardottir, E. T., and Ellis Weismer, S. (1998). Mean length of utterance and other language sample measures in early Icelandic. *First Language*, **18**, 1–32.

Thordardottir, E. T., and Ellis Weismer, S. (2001). High frequency verbs and verb diversity in the spontaneous speech of school-age children with specific language impairment. *International Journal of Language and Communication Disorders*, **36**, 221–44.

Tonkyn, A. (1996). The oral language development of instructed second language learners: the quest for a progress-sensitive proficiency measure. In H. Coleman and L. Cameron (Eds), *Change and language* (pp. 116–30). Clevedon: BAAL in association with Multilingual Matters.

Tuldava, J. (1993). The statistical structure of a text and its readability. In L. Hřebíček and G. Altmann (Eds), *Quantitative text analysis* (pp. 215–27). Trier: Wissenschaftlicher Verlag Trier.

Tweedie, F. J., and Baayen, R. H. (1998). How variable may a constant be? Measures of lexical richness in perspective. *Computers and the Humanities*, **32**, 323–52.

Ukrainetz, T. A., and Blomquist, C. (2002). The criterion validity of four vocabulary tests compared with a language sample. *Child Language Teaching and Therapy*, **18**, 59–78.

Ure, J. (1971). Lexical density and register differentiation. In G. E. Perren and J. L. M. Trim (Eds), *Applications of linguistics: selected papers of the Second International Congress of Applied Linguistics, Cambridge 1969* (pp. 443–52). Cambridge: Cambridge University Press.

Van Kleeck, A., and Carpenter, R. L. (1980). The effects of children's language comprehension level on adults' child-directed talk. *Journal of Speech and Hearing Research*, **23**, 546–66.

Van Lier, L. (1989). Reeling, writhing, drawling, stretching and fainting in coils: oral proficiency interviews as conversation. *TESOL Quarterly*, **23**, 489–508.

Vermeer, A. (2000). Coming to grips with lexical richness in spontaneous speech data. *Language Testing*, **17**, 65–83.

Wachal, R. S., and Spreen, O. (1973). Some measures of lexical diversity in aphasic and normal language performance. *Language and Speech*, **16**, 169–81.

Wagner, K. R., Altmann, G., and Köhler, R. (1987). Zum Gesamtwortschatz der Kinder. In K. R. Wagner (Ed.), *Wortschatz-Erwerb* (pp. 128–42). Bern: Peter Lang.

Walker, V. G., Roberts, P. M., and Hedrick, D. L. (1988). Linguistic analyses of the discourse narratives of young and aged women. *Folia Phoniatrica*, **40**, 58–64.

Watkins, R. V., Kelly, D. J., Harbers, H. M., and Hollis, W. (1995). Measuring children's lexical diversity: differentiating typical and impaired language learners. *Journal of Speech and Hearing Research*, **38**, 1349–55.

Watkins, R. V., Rice, M. L., and Moltz, C. C. (1993). Verb use by language-impaired and normally developing children. *First Language*, **13**, 133–43.

Weigle, S. C. (2002). *Assessing writing*. Cambridge: Cambridge University Press.

Weitzman, M. (1971). How useful is the logarithmic type–token ratio? *Journal of Linguistics*, **7**, 237–43.

Weizman, Z. O., and Snow, C. E. (2001). Lexical input as related to children's vocabulary acquisition: effects of sophisticated exposure and support for meaning. *Developmental Psychology*, **37**, 265–79.

Wells, C. G. (1975). *Coding manual for the description of child speech* (2nd edn). Bristol: University of Bristol Press.

Wells, C. G. (1978). What makes for successful language development? In R. Campbell and P. Smith (Eds), *Recent advances in the psychology of language* (Vol. 4A). New York: Plenum.
Wells, C. G. (1979). Learning and using the auxiliary verb in English. In V. Lee (Ed.), *Language development*. London: Croom Helm.
Wells, C. G. (1985). *Language development in the pre-school years*. Cambridge: Cambridge University Press.
Wesche, M. B. (1994). Input and interaction in second language acquisition. In C. Gallaway and B. J. Richards (Eds), *Input and interaction in language acquisition* (pp. 219–49). Cambridge: Cambridge University Press.
Wimmer, G., and Altmann, G. (1999). Review article: on vocabulary richness. *Journal of Quantitative Linguistics*, **6**, 1–9.
Wright, H. H., Silverman, S. W., and Newhoff, M. (2003). Measures of lexical diversity in aphasia. *Aphasiology*, **17**, 443–52.
Yamada-Yamamoto, A., and Richards, B. J. (Eds). (1998). *Japanese children abroad*. Clevedon: Multilingual Matters.
Yoder, P. J., Davies, B., and Bishop, K. (1994). Adult interaction style effects on the language sampling and transcription process with children who have developmental disabilities. *American Journal on Mental Retardation*, **99**, 270–82.
Young, R., and Milanovic, M. (1992). Discourse variation in oral proficiency interviews. *Studies in Second Language Acquisition*, **14**, 403–24.
Yule, G. U. (1944). *The statistical study of literary vocabulary*. Cambridge: Cambridge University Press.
Zagona, K. (2002). *The syntax of Spanish*. Cambridge: Cambridge University Press.
Zipf, G. K. (1932). *Selected studies of the principle of relative frequency in language*. Cambridge, MA: Harvard University Press.
Zipf, G. K. (1935). *Psycho-biology of languages*. Cambridge, MA: MIT Press.
Zipf, G. K. (1937). Observations of the possible effect of mental age upon the frequency-distribution of words from the viewpoint of dynamic philology. *Journal of Psychology*, **4**, 239–44.
Zipf, G. K. (1949). *Human behavior and the principle of least effort*. Reading, MA: Addison Wesley.

Appendices

I
Key to the CHAT Transcripts in Appendices II–IV

Selected CHAT codes in order of occurrence

(See MacWhinney, 2000a for full details)

-	boundary of an inflection
#	pause
#2	two-second pause
%alt	tier for alternative transcription
%com	tier for comments by transcriber
%err	error coding tier
%mor	morphosyntax tier
%par	tier for paralinguistics
&s	phonological fragment 's'
@e	English words
[*]	error
[/]	retracing without correction
[//]	retracing with correction
[+ bch]	back channel
[>] [<]	overlapping speech
+···	the utterance trails off
<aft>	occurs after the utterance
3S	third person singular
adv	adverb
co	communicator
det	determiner
det:poss	possessive determiner
n	noun
n:prop	proper noun
neg	negative marker
PERF	past participle
POSS	possessive
prep	preposition
PRES	present
pro	pronoun
pro:dem	demonstrative pronoun
PROG	progressive
v	verb
v:aux	auxiliary verb
wh:pro	wh-question pronoun
xxx	unintelligible speech

II
Extract from a Transcript in the Bristol Corpus Following Editing

Jonathan at 42 months

@Begin
@Coding: Childes 1.1
@Participants: JON Jonathan Target_Child, MOT Mother, FAT Father, PAU Paul Child, UNK Unidentified
@Birth of JON: 20-APR-1972
@Age of JON: 3;5.24
@Date: 14-OCT-1975
@Time Start: 10:07
@Location: Verandah
@Activities: Other non+play
@Situation: J is watching dustmen
@Situation: M is in the kitchen
*MOT: Alright #2?
*CHI: Yes mummy [: mum] [=! vocative] #2.
*MOT: What are you doing #2?
*CHI: Oh #1.
*CHI: I (a)maux watch-ing the dust #1 man #2.
*CHI: Put-ing that up there.
*MOT: Oh #40.
%par: <aft> intermittently whispering
@Time Start: 10:37
@Location: Living room
@Activities: Talk as the main activity
@Situation: J is pretending to choose a recipe for dinner by looking at cookery cards
*CHI: <We (wi)ll have that.> [>]
*MOT: <xxx.> [<]
*CHI: Shall we have that for dinner #1?
*MOT: What #1?
*CHI: That for dinner?
*MOT: Yes #1.
*CHI: That for dinner?
*MOT: Yes #3.
*CHI: That for dinner?
*MOT: Yes #1.
*MOT: Going to have tummy ache aren't you?
%alt: tooth
*CHI: Why?
*MOT: Having all these things for dinner #1.

*CHI: Can we have that for dinner #2?
%com: Points to a card
*CHI: How about all these for dinner?
*CHI: One two #1 three #2 four #2 five #1 six #1 seven #1.
*MOT: Eight.
*CHI: No #1.
*CHI: Eight #1.
*MOT: Nine.
*CHI: Nine #3.
*CHI: Fifteen.
*MOT: Ten.
*CHI: No that one (i)s fifty.
*MOT: Oh.
*CHI: Ten #1.
*CHI: Eleven #1.
*CHI: Thirteen.
*MOT: Twelve #2.
*CHI: Thirteen.
*MOT: Twelve comes before thirteen #2.
*CHI: Well that was thirteen though #3.
*CHI: That was.
*CHI: That was thirteen #2.
*CHI: xxx #1 xxx #2.
*CHI: xxx #3.
*CHI: xxx #1.
*MOT: One paperback.
%com: M is tidying books
*CHI: No <paperback.> [>]
*MOT: <Two> [<] #1.
*MOT: Three #1.
*MOT: Four.
*MOT: Five #2.
*MOT: Six seven eight.
*CHI: Mum [=! vocative] can we have all #1 those thing-es I (a)maux go-ing to have for dinner #2?
*MOT: Yes alright.
*CHI: All those thing-es?
*MOT: Mm?
*CHI: When we have a +···
....

....

@End

III
A French Transcript from the Reading Corpus

The example selected is the student who had a median score for the oral test and the score closest to the mean for the whole sample for the aggregated marks for listening, speaking, reading and writing.

@Begin
@Filename: W07.cha
@Tape location: candidate 7, side A, tape 1
@Participants: TEA teacher, STU student
@ID: 7.1=TEA
@ID: 7.2=STU
@Sex of STU: male
@Sex of TEA: male
@GCSE examination grade: C
@Oral mark: 4
@Date: 2-May-1990
@Coder: Francine Chambers, Brian Richards
@Warning: the errors on the error tier are anglicised pronunciations, and the standard French spelling has been retained here and on the main speaker tier
*TEA: euh pour commencer parle moi un peu de ton collège James.
*STU: euh <le collège> [//] euh #3 euh <je> [//] j' arrive au collège à huit heures <dans> [>] matin.
*TEA: <oui> [<]. [+ bch]
*STU: euh le collège commencer à neuf heures moins trois.
*TEA: oui. [+ bch]
*STU: <à> [/] # à neuf heures # cinq <> [>] euh le cours commencer.
*TEA: <oui>. [+ bch]
*TEA: oui. [+ bch]
*STU: euh dans le jour # il y a euh huit cours.
*STU: euh je étudie français euh la physique le éducation physique le secrétaire.
*TEA: oui. [+ bch]
*STU: euh #2 l' anglais et maths.
*TEA: oui. [+ bch]
*TEA: # d' accord.
*TEA: et quelle matière préfères tu?
*STU: euh je préfère le éducation physique.
*TEA: pourquoi?
*STU: c' est intéressant et c' est drôle.
*TEA: oui d' accord.
*TEA: et qu' est ce que tu vas faire l' année prochaine au mois de septembre?
*TEA: tu vas retourner au collège ou <tu vas travailler> [>]?

*STU: <aah oui> [<] euh je retourner au collège for@e deux [*] ans.
%err: deux /du/ = deux /d3/ ;
*TEA: pour deux ans oui.
*TEA: et quelle matière vas tu <&s> [//] euh étudier?
*STU: euh je étudier euh les maths et la physique et <le information technique> [//] l' information technologie.
*TEA: aah euh oui euh je vois ce que vous voulez dire oui informatique.
*TEA: d' accord.
*TEA: et euh tu as un ordinateur à la maison?
*STU: aah oui # euh il y a le Atari eight@e hundred@e.
*TEA: oui. [+ bch]
*STU: oui <c' est> [/] c' est en panne.
*TEA: en <panne xxx> [>]?
*STU: <aah oui> [<].
*TEA: aah bon.
*TEA: #2 et d' habitude tu travailles souvent avec l' ordinateur?
*STU: euh # non #2 euh pardon monsieur.
*TEA: tu <&tra> [//] #2 tu joues tu travailles souvent avec euh ton ordinateur?
*STU: aah euh de temps de temps.
*TEA: de temps en temps xxx oui.
*TEA: et où est l' ordinateur?
*TEA: #3 [% no response] euh dans le salon?
*STU: euh <dans> [/] dans ma chambre.
*TEA: aah bon tu as de la chance.
*TEA: # ok.
*TEA: et euh qu' est ce que tu vas faire pendant les grandes vacances en été?
*STU: euh dans ma grande vacance de je visiter #3 euh l' Espagne.
*TEA: aah bon l' Espagne.
*TEA: qu' est ce que tu vas faire en Espagne?
*STU: # je # nager.
*TEA: oui. [+ bch]
*STU: et je visiter le monument <historiques xxx> [>].
*TEA: <oui> [<]. [+ bch]
*TEA: aah bon oui.
*STU: euh <j' ai acheté> [//] euh j' achète des xxx sportifs.
*TEA: oui. [+ bch]
*STU: t+shirt et + ···
*TEA: d' accord oui.
*TEA: bon et euh pourquoi veux tu aller en Espagne?
*STU: euh &s # <c' est drôle et> [/-] no@e les discothèques xxx très discothèques.
*STU: euh #3 xxx #4 le soleil.
*TEA: le soleil oui xxx le soleil et les discothèques bon.
*TEA: d' accord très bien.
*TEA: ok James merci et au revoir.
*STU: au revoir monsieur.
@End

IV
Extract from the Manchester Corpus Illustrating the %mor Tier

Anne at 1;10.7

....
....
*MOT: what-'is baby do-ing ?
%mor: wh:pro|what n-cl|v:aux|be&3S n|baby v|do-PROG ?
*CHI: Anne .
%mor: n:prop|Anne .
*MOT: is that Anne ?
%mor: v|be&3S pro:dem|that n:prop|Anne ?
*MOT: is it ?
%mor: v|be&3S pro|it ?
*CHI: what-'is that ?
%mor: wh:pro|what n-cl|v|be&3S pro:dem|that ?
*CHI: what-'is that ?
%mor: wh:pro|what n-cl|v|be&3S pro:dem|that ?
*MOT: who-'is that ?
%mor: wh:pro|who n-cl|v|be&3S pro:dem|that ?
*MOT: who do you think it is ?
%mor: wh:pro|who v:aux|do pro|you v|think pro|it v:aux|be&3S ?
*CHI: baby [/] baby Mummy .
%mor: n|baby n|baby n:prop|Mummy .
*MOT: baby-'s Mummy ?
%mor: n|baby- n-cl|POSS n:prop|Mummy ?
*CHI: car .
%mor: n|car .
%act: gets toy car out
*MOT: put them on the table, look .
%mor: v|put pro|them prep|on det|the n|table co|look .
*MOT: then they will-'nt get lost, will they ?
%mor: adv|then pro|they v:aux|will v-cl|neg|not v|get v|lose&PAST v:aux|will pro|they ?
*MOT: what-'re you gonna [: going+to] do ?
%mor: wh:pro|what n-cl|v:aux|be&PRES pro|you v|going+to v|do ?
*CHI: hair .
%mor: n|hair .
*MOT: hair ?

```
%mor:   n|hair ?
*MOT:   have her hair brushed ?
%mor:   v:aux|have det:poss|her n|hair v|brush-PERF ?
*CHI:   xxx .
%mor:   .
..........
..........
```

V
Documentation for *vocd*

The *vocd* program was written in C by Gerard McKee of the Department of Computer Science at The University of Reading.

The documentation supplied here applies to the UNIX version of the software for which the use of inverted commas in the command line is obligatory in certain contexts. While these are not necessary in the Windows and Macintosh versions of *vocd*, their inclusion will not affect the running of the program.

Using *vocd*

Vocd can be used to investigate lexical diversity in samples of speech or writing provided that they are transcribed accurately in CHAT format. Three things should be noted:

1 *vocd* is less tolerant of small deviations from the conventions laid down in the CHILDES manual (MacWhinney, 2000a) than are the other CLAN programs;
2 since all of the options in *vocd*'s command lines are case sensitive, the case of all elements should be modelled on the examples given below; and
3 unlike other CLAN programs, *vocd* looks for 'exclude files' (see below) in the working directory.

Sample size

By default, the software plots the TTR versus token curve from 35 tokens to 50 tokens (see Chapter 3 of this volume). *vocd* therefore requires a minimum of 50 tokens to operate. It must be stressed, however, that even if the software will output a value of D from a sample of 50 tokens, it does not guarantee that values obtained from such small samples will be reliable. The matter of minimum sample size needs further investigation. It should also be noted that random sampling without replacement causes the software to run noticeably more slowly when samples approach this minimum level.

Preparation of files

We recommend the procedures outlined in Part 2 of the CHILDES manual (MacWhinney, 2000a, pp. 109–10) for preparing files. These entail running files through the CHILDES *check* program to ensure correct CHAT syntax. Using the +g3 switch with *check* will also help to track down some typographical errors within words. The *freq* program can then be used to create a complete wordlist that should be scanned for further errors. The output from *freq* also allows the researcher to see exactly what *freq* (and therefore *vocd*) will treat as a word and as a *different* word. From this information an 'exclude file' of non-words can be compiled (e.g. hesitations, laughter, etc.). These can then be filtered out of the analysis (see the use of the '-s' switch below). As noted above, exclude files need to be held in the current working directory, rather than the 'lib' directory as with other CLAN programs.

Exclude files contain only ASCII characters and list the words to be omitted one per line with a carriage return after each word. In addition, one can create an 'include' file consisting of a list of only those words one wishes to be included in the analysis. This would be useful, for example, if a lexical diversity value for just closed-class items were required.

The minimum command line

The minimum requirements for a *vocd* command line are:

vocd filename.cha

where: **vocd** executes the program;

filename.cha is a transcript in CHAT format.

This command would only be valid in cases where there is one single main speaker tier (this might be the case if you used *vocd* to analyse a monologue or a sample of writing). In practice, it is usual to designate the speaker tier:

vocd +t"*CHI" filename.cha

where:

+t"*CHI" selects only the child speaker tier for analysis.

The output from *vocd*

Output consists of:

- A sequential list of utterances by the selected speaker that contains *only those tokens that have been retained for analysis*.
- Total types, tokens, and TTR for these items.
- Tables showing the data which produce the empirical curve: number of tokens for each point on the curve, average TTR, and the standard deviation for each point and, in addition, the value of D obtained from the equation for each point. Three such tables appear, one for each time the program takes random samples and carries out the curve-fitting.
- At the foot of each table is the average of the Ds obtained from the equation and their standard deviation, as well as the value for D that provided the best fit, and the residuals.

- Finally, a Results Summary repeats the command line and file name, and the type and token information for the lexical items retained for analysis, and gives the three optimum values of D and their average.

A sample print-out of *vocd*'s standard output is contained in Appendix VI.

Text-handling options

+c   includes capitalized words only:

vocd +t"*CHI" +c filename.cha

Only those words with an initial capital letter are retained for analysis.

+d   outputs a list of the utterances processed and number of types, tokens, and TTR but does not calculate D:

vocd +t"*CHI" +d filename.cha

+d4   outputs number of types, tokens and TTR only:

vocd +t"*CHI" +d4 filename.cha

+DS   split-half reliability function.
The +DS switch allows separate analysis of odd- and even-numbered words in the transcript. The results of this can then be fed into a split-half reliability analysis. This switch can have one of two values: +DS0 (for even-numbered words) or +DS1 (for odd-numbered words):

vocd +t"*CHI" +DS0 filename.cha

This command would return a D value for even-numbered words only.

+f   directs output to files.
By default, *vocd* directs output to the screen. The +f switch sends output to a file. A three-letter combination can be chosen to follow +f. This will serve as the file extension name. The command:

vocd +t"*CHI" +fchi filename.cha

would output the file 'filename.chi'.
Up to 256 files can be processed in a batch using wildcards (e.g. *.cha) and the +f switch causes a separate output file to be produced for each input file. In a directory containing 10 CHAT files, the command:

vocd +t"*CHI" +fchi *.cha

would output ten results files, each with the extension .chi.

If the separate results from each input file are required as a *single* output file, the redirect symbol (>) can be used followed by the name of the output file:

vocd +t"*CHI" *.cha > filename

+g calls up the limiting relative diversity (LRD) sub-routine (see Chapter 8 in this volume) to compare the relative diversity of two different word classes coded on the %mor tier.

This procedure operates in three stages and extracts the words to be included from the %mor tier where the word classes are coded. First, the speaker, the %mor tier, and the file name are specified in the usual way, plus the +g switch to invoke the subroutine:

vocd +t"*CHI" +t"%mor" -t"*" +g filename

Second, the user is prompted twice to specify the word classes to be compared. The following would compare verb and noun diversity and limit the analysis to word stems:

+s"v|*" +s"*-%%"

+s"n|*" +s"*-%%"

The first word class entered will be the numerator and the second will be the denominator.

+k treats upper and lower case words as different word types.

By default, vocd would treat 'may' (modal verb) and 'May' (the month) as the same word type. The +k switch allows them to be counted as different types:

vocd +t"*CHI" +k filename.cha

-m segments words into their component morphemes so that an overall morpheme diversity measure will be returned.

This feature relates particularly to analyses of polysynthetic and agglutinative languages where, because of complex morphological structure, the definition of a 'word' may be problematic. In these cases morpheme diversity may be more meaningful than word diversity.

CHAT uses the following morpheme boundary markers:

\# for a prefix;
− for a suffix;
~ for clitics and contractions;
& for fused forms ('went' transcribed as 'go&ed'); and
+ for compounds and rote forms ('all+right').

To allow users the greatest flexibility, *vocd* will segment words according to any of these five boundary markers or any combination of them. This is achieved by placing the boundary markers relevant for the analysis in inverted commas after the -m switch. Thus:

vocd +t"*CHI" –m"-#~&+" filename.cha

would provide all possible word segmentations.

vocd always lists utterance by utterance the items that have been entered into the curve-fitting so it is possible to check easily that these correspond with the grammatical units required.

+r1,+r2,+r3   treatment of non-completed words.

Words frequently occur in a shortened form: 'till' for 'until' or 'cos' for 'because'. Sometimes a speaker will alternate between the full and shortened form. This might distort analyses if *vocd* treated them as different word types. However, in CHAT it is possible to transcribe non-completed words using brackets so that consistency of spelling is achieved: (un)til, (be)cause (see MacWhinney, 2000a, pp. 43–4).

The +r1, +r2 and +r3 switches cause the bracketed material to be processed as follows:

+r1: (be)cause is processed as because (this is the default);
+r2: (be)cause is processed as (be)cause;
+r3: (be)cause is processed as cause.

For example:

vocd +t"*CHI" +r3 filename

+r4   removes prosodic symbols contained within words.
For example:

vocd +t"*CHI" +r4 filename.cha

would cause the removal of the symbols for stressed syllables and syllable lengthening in rhi/noceros and bana:nas (see MacWhinney, 2000a).

+r5   prevents text replacement indicated by [: text].
In the utterance:

'*CHI: it goed [: went] in there.'

the child's 'goed' is followed by the adult form in square brackets. By default, preceding text is replaced by the text in square brackets, so the form processed by *vocd* would be 'went'. This coding allows alternative realisations of a word (e.g. 'yes', 'yeah', 'yep') to be treated as the same word type.

This facility can be overridden using the +r5 switch so that 'goed' would be returned rather than 'went':

vocd +t"*CHI" +r5 filename.cha

+r6   excludes retracing.
By default, retraced material indicated by [/] and [//] in the transcript is included in the analysis. In the utterance:

'*CHI: <I can't> [//] I can see [/] see you.',

vocd would by default process all seven words. To exclude the retraced material and limit the analysis to the remaining four words, the +r6 switch is added:

vocd +t"*CHI" +r6 filename.cha

+s/−s   includes or excludes single words, a list of words or whole utterances marked with postcodes. Thus:

vocd +t"*CHI" −s"uhoh" filename.cha

excludes the single word 'uhoh';

vocd +t"*CHI" −s@exclude filename.cha

excludes a word list held in a text file with the name 'exclude';

vocd +t"*CHI" −s"[+text]" filename.cha

excludes all utterances that are followed by a certain postcode, for example back channels [+ bch] or imitations [+ I].

In some cases, the researcher might wish to restrict the analysis to a list of words (e.g. closed-class items) held in an 'include' file. Thus:

vocd +t"*CHI" +s@include filename.cha

includes only those words listed in a text file with the name 'include'.

To confine the analysis to one word class, for example to obtain a measure of verb diversity, the relevant +s switch (e.g. +s"v*") can be made to apply to the %mor tier for the specified speaker:

vocd +t"*CHI" +t"%mor" −t"*" +s"v*" filename

In this case all verbs would be included, but there can be further limiting as follows:

> +s"v:aux*" would include auxiliaries only;
> +s"v|*" includes all verbs except auxiliaries;
> a combination of +s"v|*" and −s"v|be*" would include all verbs except copulas and auxiliaries.

+s"*−%%"   strips off regular inflections and returns the word stem.

234 *Appendix V*

+s"*&%%" returns root forms.

By default, *vocd* treats morphemicised inflected words (go, go-es, go-ing, go&ed) as different word types.

+s"*-%%"(or +s"*&%%") causes *vocd* to ignore the hyphen (or the ampersand) and the elements that follow it, and treat inflected words or irregular forms as tokens of a single word type:

vocd +t"*CHI" +s"*-%%" filename.cha
vocd +t"*CHI" +s"*&%%" filename.cha

If required, +s and –s switches may be included in the same command line.

+t specifies which tier of the transcript is to be analysed.

vocd +t"*CHI" filename.cha

includes material from the child main tier only.

vocd +t"*MOT" filename.cha

includes material from the mother's main tier only.

An analysis of material on the %mor tier would require the following:

vocd +t"*CHI" +t" % mor" –t"*" filename

where –t"*" prevents material from the main tier from being included.

Combining options in the command line

In the analysis of French foreign language oral interviews reported in Chapter 6 of this volume the following command line was used:

vocd +t"*TEA" –s@ttrexclu +r6 –s"[+ bch]" w01.cha

where:

vocd executed the program;
+t"*TEA" limited analysis to the teacher's speaker tier;
–s@ttrexclu filtered out a list of items held in an exclude file called 'ttrexclu';
+r6 removed retraced material;
–s"[+ bch]" filtered out the content of utterances coded as 'back channels'; and
w01.cha was the filename for the first interview.

VI

Example of Standard Output from *vocd* Using a Transcript from the New England Corpus

Command line:

vocd +t"*CHI" +r6 −s@exclude +s"* − %%" d096132.cha

Output:
reading exclude file <exclude>

UTTERANCES: (vocd<d096132.cha>)
where are the toy
yeah
yeah
book
book
book
book
book
two
where the two booko@
i want two booko@
okay
baby
bug
duck
there
yeah
what
what
yeah
comb
comb
that
comb
brush
brush
soap
yeah
purple
that yellow
no purple

purple
milk there
no
yeah
me
yeah
yeah
there
purple
yeah
get more book
puppet show
puppet
puppet
mommy
no more cookie
no
hello
hello
yeah
hello
no
yeah
yeah
that box
yeah
mommy color
mommy color too
three color
here mommy
purple

235

that purple
yeah
here mommy
help me
help
help
help me
yeah
eye
the nose
all done
house
house
the house

me
down
go down
out
there
car
car
car
car
nope
want to put it away mommy
i want it away
yeah
no

tokens	samples	ttr	st.dev	D
35	100	0.6951	0.053	27.739
36	100	0.6925	0.053	28.072
37	100	0.6905	0.052	28.507
38	100	0.6887	0.058	28.946
39	100	0.6790	0.056	28.003
40	100	0.6703	0.061	27.247
41	100	0.6566	0.051	25.735
42	100	0.6605	0.054	26.981
43	100	0.6567	0.050	27.016
44	100	0.6466	0.050	26.026
45	100	0.6531	0.050	27.667
46	100	0.6461	0.052	27.128
47	100	0.6336	0.048	25.751
48	100	0.6225	0.051	24.636
49	100	0.6214	0.044	24.992
50	100	0.6248	0.049	26.011

D: average = 26.903; std dev. = 1.221
D_optimum <26.85; min least sq val = 0.001>

tokens	samples	ttr	st.dev	D
35	100	0.6937	0.058	27.496
36	100	0.6897	0.061	27.598
37	100	0.6876	0.062	27.993
38	100	0.6705	0.055	25.928
39	100	0.6833	0.060	28.754
40	100	0.6672	0.059	26.760
41	100	0.6671	0.061	27.400
42	100	0.6633	0.052	27.446
43	100	0.6612	0.049	27.737
44	100	0.6541	0.048	27.211
45	100	0.6504	0.058	27.232
46	100	0.6450	0.046	26.954
47	100	0.6381	0.047	26.437
48	100	0.6388	0.054	27.106

tokens	samples	ttr	st.dev	
49	100	0.6198	0.042	24.754
50	100	0.6290	0.047	26.660

D: average = 27.092; std dev. = 0.874
D_optimum <27.06; min least sq val = 0.000>

tokens	samples	ttr	st.dev	D
35	100	0.6966	0.055	27.984
36	100	0.6786	0.059	25.792
37	100	0.6832	0.059	27.264
38	100	0.6897	0.059	29.133
39	100	0.6764	0.059	27.571
40	100	0.6700	0.051	27.206
41	100	0.6732	0.055	28.424
42	100	0.6607	0.059	27.020
43	100	0.6588	0.050	27.355
44	100	0.6593	0.044	28.071
45	100	0.6544	0.046	27.888
46	100	0.6504	0.048	27.836
47	100	0.6387	0.051	26.537
48	100	0.6323	0.047	26.094
49	100	0.6271	0.049	25.844
50	100	0.6262	0.045	26.226

D: average = 27.265; std dev. = 0.937
D_optimum <27.24; min least sq val = 0.001>

VOCD RESULTS SUMMARY
= = = = = = = = = = = = :
Command line: vocd +t*CHI +r6 −s@exclude +s*−%% d096132.cha
File name: d096132.cha
Types,Tokens,TTR: <52,129, 0.403101>
D_optimum values: <26.85,27.06,27.24>
D_optimum average: 27.05

VII
Output from the Limiting Relative Diversity (LRD) Option in *vocd* Using a File from Anne (anne03a.cha) in the Manchester Corpus

The analysis below provides an index of the relative diversity of verbs and nouns. Main command line and responses to the two prompts:

vocd +t"*CHI" +t"%mor" –t"*" anne03a.cha +g

Enter NUMERATOR **+s/–s directives** > +s"v|*" +s"*-%%"

Enter DENOMINATOR **+s/–s directives** > +s"n|*" +s"*-%%"

Output:
compute TYPE_TYPE_D for each file

UTTERANCES: (vocd<anne03a.cha>)
v|fit	v|fit
v|thank	v|pop
v|fit	v|look
v|thank	v|leave
v|move	v|think
v|move	v|go
v|drive	v|go
v|drive	v|go
v|drive	v|give
v|drive	v|sleep
v|do	v|tidy
v|go	v|lie
v|go	v|fit
v|want v|go	v|fit
v|go	v|sleep
v|go	v|sleep
v|hurt	v|go&perf
v|let v|go	v|cry
v|go	v|cry
v|land	v|cry
v|let v|do	v|sleep
v|work	v|brush

LRD Output from vocd – Manchester Corpus

v|brush
v|slip
v|sleep
v|do
v|chase
v|get
v|get
v|sleep
v|sleep
v|sleep
v|tuck
v|tuck
v|tuck
v|tuck
v|brush
v|brush
v|brush
v|sleep

v|sleep
v|be
v|fit
v|fit
v|err
v|fit
v|look
v|fit
v|finish
v|show
v|show
v|look
v|put
v|show
v|show
v|be&pres
v|drink
v|look

tokens	samples	ttr	st.dev	D
35	100	0.5629	0.058	12.683
36	100	0.5494	0.051	12.061
37	100	0.5592	0.050	13.123
38	100	0.5550	0.053	13.152
39	100	0.5456	0.047	12.778
40	100	0.5420	0.053	12.828
41	100	0.5290	0.048	12.182
42	100	0.5257	0.045	12.237
43	100	0.5144	0.048	11.717
44	100	0.5141	0.046	11.966
45	100	0.5224	0.041	12.860
46	100	0.5067	0.038	11.973
47	100	0.5053	0.044	12.130
48	100	0.5033	0.042	12.242
49	100	0.4955	0.038	11.924
50	100	0.4890	0.039	11.699

D: average = 12.347; std dev. = 0.468
D_optimum <12.34; min least sq val = 0.001>

tokens	samples	ttr	st.dev	D
35	100	0.5686	0.056	13.113
36	100	0.5628	0.052	13.039
37	100	0.5454	0.050	12.106
38	100	0.5503	0.054	12.792
39	100	0.5482	0.046	12.971
40	100	0.5388	0.055	12.585
41	100	0.5317	0.049	12.376
42	100	0.5314	0.048	12.657
43	100	0.5240	0.048	12.399

240 Appendix VII

44	100	0.5191	0.044	12.327
45	100	0.5211	0.042	12.759
46	100	0.5130	0.049	12.432
47	100	0.5051	0.042	12.115
48	100	0.5023	0.041	12.166
49	100	0.4992	0.037	12.190
50	100	0.4922	0.040	11.927

D: average = 12.497; std dev. = 0.351
D_optimum < 12.50; min least sq val = 0.000 >

tokens	samples	ttr	st.dev	D
35	100	0.5657	0.056	12.896
36	100	0.5647	0.059	13.188
37	100	0.5538	0.056	12.715
38	100	0.5421	0.046	12.194
39	100	0.5408	0.054	12.417
40	100	0.5310	0.049	12.024
41	100	0.5371	0.056	12.773
42	100	0.5240	0.047	12.117
43	100	0.5200	0.051	12.112
44	100	0.5207	0.042	12.444
45	100	0.5131	0.040	12.167
46	100	0.5030	0.044	11.712
47	100	0.5062	0.041	12.192
48	100	0.5019	0.033	12.136
49	100	0.4908	0.038	11.591
50	100	0.4912	0.039	11.855

D: average = 12.283; std dev. = 0.420
D_optimum <12.28; min least sq val = 0.001>

VOCD RESULTS SUMMARY
= = = = = = = = = = = =
Command line: vocd +t*CHI +t%mor −t* anne03a.cha +g
File name: anne03a.cha
Types,Tokens,TTR: <33,83,0.397590>
D_optimum values: <12.34, 12.50, 12.28>
D_optimum average: 12.37

UTTERANCES: (vocd<anne03a.cha>)

n|fit	n|bit
n|fit	n|bit
n|bit	n|car
n|bit	n|car
n|morning	n|bit
n|boy	n|bit
n|piece	n|car
n|bit	n|lorry
n|bit	n|lorry
n|bit	n|lorry

n|helicopter
n|fit
n|helicopter
n|fit
n|house
n|house
n|house
n|house
n|house
n|toy
n|wash
n|wash
n|wash
n|wash
n|wash
n|monkey
n|monkey
n|monkey
n|monkey
n|cat n|mouth
n|water
n|water
n|baby
n|night
n|baby
n|baby
n|rabbit
n|teddy
n|teddy
n|box
n|teddy
n|bit
n|bit
n|bit
n|baby

n|baby
n|boy
n|baby
n|baby
n|baby
n|baby
n|teddy
n|cuddle+cuddle
n|doll
n|baby
n|baby
n|teddy
n|eye
n|hair
n|hair
n|ear
n|ear
n|hair
n|teddy
n|teddy
n|tomato
n|tomato
n|cream
n|crisp
n|jelly
n|sausage
n|knife
n|fork
n|drink
n|milk
n|drink
n|milk
n|strawberry
n|strawberry
n|garden

tokens	samples	ttr	st.dev	D
35	100	0.5909	0.053	14.932
36	100	0.5842	0.056	14.772
37	100	0.5846	0.055	15.220
38	100	0.5800	0.056	15.218
39	100	0.5777	0.047	15.410
40	100	0.5658	0.051	14.741
41	100	0.5605	0.048	14.653
42	100	0.5564	0.049	14.658
43	100	0.5465	0.048	14.160
44	100	0.5455	0.045	14.400
45	100	0.5331	0.047	13.696
46	100	0.5309	0.040	13.817

47	100	0.5315	0.053	14.169
48	100	0.5296	0.044	14.309
49	100	0.5165	0.042	13.520
50	100	0.5124	0.041	13.462

D: average = 14.446; std dev. = 0.592
D_optimum <14.44; min least sq val = 0.001>

tokens	samples	ttr	st.dev	D
35	100	0.6009	0.063	15.829
36	100	0.5972	0.058	15.940
37	100	0.5816	0.054	14.958
38	100	0.5782	0.051	15.056
39	100	0.5708	0.051	14.800
40	100	0.5620	0.052	14.422
41	100	0.5593	0.053	14.549
42	100	0.5493	0.049	14.058
43	100	0.5470	0.049	14.199
44	100	0.5368	0.047	13.688
45	100	0.5458	0.034	14.755
46	100	0.5402	0.043	14.599
47	100	0.5283	0.038	13.905
48	100	0.5344	0.042	14.719
49	100	0.5202	0.040	13.818
50	100	0.5126	0.045	13.478

D: average = 14.548; std dev. = 0.678
D_optimum <14.54; min least sq val = 0.001>

tokens	samples	ttr	st.dev	D
35	100	0.5886	0.053	14.735
36	100	0.5864	0.065	14.964
37	100	0.5814	0.052	14.935
38	100	0.5771	0.047	14.963
39	100	0.5674	0.052	14.515
40	100	0.5678	0.046	14.915
41	100	0.5534	0.051	14.059
42	100	0.5514	0.049	14.235
43	100	0.5449	0.044	14.026
44	100	0.5459	0.049	14.438
45	100	0.5387	0.042	14.152
46	100	0.5322	0.048	13.924
47	100	0.5245	0.041	13.593
48	100	0.5225	0.040	13.722
49	100	0.5320	0.040	14.820
50	100	0.5136	0.038	13.558

D: average = 14.347; std dev. = 0.490
D_optimum <14.34; min least sq val = 0.001>

VOCD RESULTS SUMMARY
============:
Command line: vocd +t*CHI +t%mor -t* anne03a.cha +g
File name: anne03a.cha
Types,Tokens,TTR: <36,91,0.395604>
D_optimum values: <14.44, 14.54, 14.34>
D_optimum average: 14.44

VOCD: LIMITING-TYPE–TYPE-RATIO RESULTS SUMMARY
=============================
Command line: vocd +t*CHI +t%mor -t* anne03a.cha +g
Numerator: +sv|* +s*-%%
Denominator: +sn|* +s*-%%
File name: anne03a.cha
Numerator D_optimum: 12.37
Denominator D_optimum: 14.44
SQRT(Num.)/SQRT(Den.):   0.93

Index

accommodation 95–109, 187
Adams, J. 14
Ader, D. N. 14, 25, 97
adjective density 135, 187
adjective-noun ratio 122, 136
advanced Guiraud 128, 133, 187
advanced TTR 128, 133, 187
Afitskaya, N. 64, 126, 132
Ager, J. 11, 179
AH2 79, 89, 187
Ahrens, M. G. 124, 126, 129
Aisenman, R. 6, 116, 152, 173, 181, 183
Allen, S.E. 180
Altmann, G. 3, 5, 28, 52, 180, 192
Alzheimer's disease 13, 14, 126, 188, 189, 191
Ames, D. 14
Anderson, W. E. 127
Anglin, J. 119, 158
aphasia *see* language impairment and delay
aptitude *see* foreign language aptitude
Arnaud, P. J. L. 3, 4, 27, 127
Arrhenius, O. 40
Augst, G. 135, 136
authorial style 5, 7, 39–40, 122, 125, 134
averaging 143, 144, 145, 146, 187, 189

Baayen, R.H. 28, 29, 39–40, 44, 45–6, 51, 53, 55, 65, 72, 187, 202
back channels 101, 181, 187
Baker, M. 10
Barnes, S. 26
Bassano, D. 139, 140
Bastiaanse, R. 14
Bates, E. 22, 64, 70, 84, 90, 135, 136, 187, 188, 194, 196, 197, 201
Beals, D. E. 130, 132, 134
Bell, H. 65, 68, 123, 124, 125, 126, 132, 133, 159, 160, 162, 189, 191, 197
Benedict, H. 135
Berman, R. 9, 116, 152, 156, 176, 181, 182, 183

Berwick, R. 96, 109
Biber, D. 124, 125, 158, 160, 172, 193, 201, 202
bilingualism research 8, 127–8
bilogarithmic TTR *see* Herdan's index
binomial probability 32–6, 38, 43, 55, 187, 199
Bishop, K. 10, 24, 26, 140, 197, 201
BLADES *see* Bristol Language Development Scales
Blanken, G. 13, 189
Blomquist, C. 5, 9
Bloom, L. 135
Bonifacio, S. 10, 183
Bornstein, M. H. 10
Brainerd, B. 40, 41, 44, 199
Braun, C. 11, 179
Breland, H. M. 156
Bretherton, I. 22, 135, 136, 187, 188, 196, 201
Bridgeman, B. 156
Brimer, M. A. 79, 189
Bristol Corpus 76–94, 110, 111–13, 114, 181–2, 185, 187
  language measures from 78–80, 195
  and language sampling 77
  and population sample 76, 77
  sample transcript from 222–3
Bristol Language Development Scales (BLADES) 78–9, 86–7, 91, 92, 112, 113, 187–8
Broeder, P. 6, 22, 27, 134
Broen, P. 23
Brown, R. 17, 78, 91, 156, 195
Brunet's index 188
Bucks, R. S. 13, 126, 188, 189, 191

Camaioni, L. 139, 140, 141
Camp, R. 156
Cantonese 117, 141, 197
Capirci, O. 26
Carlson, S. 156
Carpenter, R. H. 7, 97
Carpenter, R. L. 10

Carroll, J. B. 26, 37, 79, 126, 189, 190, 195, 198
Carroll's lexical diversity measure (CTTR) 26–7, 29, 30, 189
Carter, R. 192
Caselli, M. C. 26
Castellan, N. J. 82, 85
CDI *see* MacArthur Communicative Development Inventories
Chafe, W. L. 6
Chall, J. 126, 130
Chambers, F. 99, 101, 197
Chapman, R. 198
Chase, C. I. 155
CHAT 56, 63, 77, 80, 99, 142, 161, 188, 228, 232
 key to transcripts 221
 sample transcripts 222–7
check 188, 228
Chen, Y. S. 23
Cheshire, J. 96, 187
CHILDES 56, 188
 database 63, 64, 77, 114, 142, 188, 196
 see also CHAT; CLAN
child language *see* D, early child language; early lexical style; vocabulary composition
Chipere, N. 186
Choi, S. 138, 140
Chotlos, J. W. 24, 25, 37, 51, 69, 151, 198, 200
Christianson, U. 8, 27
CLAN 56, 64, 78, 80, 99, 100–1, 142, 161, 162, 188, 189, 190, 195, 196, 198, 200, 201, 228–9
Clark, N. 11, 179
closed-class style 135, 136, 188
cochlear implants 13, 17, 180
Cohen, H. 11, 12, 179
Coleman, M. 14
Colwell, K. 7, 180
Communicative Development Inventories (CDI) *see* MacArthur Communicative Development Inventories
Condon, E. V. 36, 191
Connor, U. 156
Contardi, A. 14
contiguity rating (CR) 188–9

Conti-Ramsden, G. 12, 121, 141
corrected TTR (CTTR) *see* Carroll's lexical diversity measure
Cossette, A. 52
Cote, L. R. 130, 131
Covington, C. 11, 179
CR *see* contiguity rating
Crain-Thoreson, C. 5, 10, 129, 131, 180
Croll, P. 87, 88, 92, 185
Cronbach, L. J. 87, 198
Cross, T. G. 96
cross-linguistic comparisons *see* lexical diversity
Crystal, D. 5, 37, 80, 202
CTTR *see* Carroll's lexical diversity measure
Cuerden, J. M. 13, 126, 188, 189, 191
cumulative plot 142, 143, 146, 187, 189

D
 and academic writing 181–2
 developmental trends in 82, 85–6
 and early child language 63–94, 110–11, 112, 115–16, 181–2
 and English as a second language 181–2
 equation for 47, 50
 and first language writing 160, 162, 169–71, 172, 173, 175–6, 182–3
 and goodness of fit 50–1
 indicative values for 70, 82, 85, 181–3
 and learners and teachers of French as a foreign language 95–109, 181–2
 reliability of 68–9, 87–9, 185, 197–8, 228, 230
 for Spanish 115
 validity of 70–1, 73, 86–7, 89, 90, 102–3, 180–1
 see also lexical diversity, a mathematical model for; *vocd*; sample size, sensitivity of measures to
Dahlin, M. P. 5, 10, 129, 131, 180
Dale, E. 126, 130
Dale, P. S. 64, 70, 84, 90, 136, 194, 196
Daller, H. 3, 8, 128, 133, 183, 187
DAT *see* Alzheimer's disease
Davies, B. 10, 24, 26, 140, 197, 201
Davies, P. 126
Delaney-Black, V. 11, 179

De León, L. 139
Della Corte, M. 135
Dewaele, J.-M. 5, 8, 15, 64, 183, 190
diary data 136–8, 139
Dickinson, D. K. 127, 129, 130, 131, 132, 189, 192, 197
Dittman, J. 13, 189
Dodd, B. 21
Duffy, M. E. 88
Dugast, D. 28, 198
Dugast's U *see* Uber index
Duncan, S. 187
Dunn, L. M. 79, 130, 189
Dunn, L. M. 130
Durán, P. 113

early lexical style 134–8
echolalia 5, 189
Edwards, S. 14
Ellis Weismer, S. 9, 12, 13, 18, 141, 142, 190, 199
English Picture Vocabulary Test (EPVT) 79, 87, 91–2, 189
errors 3, 4, 192, 196
exclude files 70, 73, 80, 81, 101, 189, 228, 229, 233
Extra, G. 6, 22, 27, 134
extrinsic measures 125, 126–31, 189–90
see also intrinsic measures

Fairbanks, H. 14, 25, 97, 200
Faletti, J. 156, 157
family background *see* social class
Faragher, B. 141
Fenson, L. 70, 90, 136, 194
Ferris, D. 156
Fiske, D. W. 187
Fletcher, P. 12, 20, 22, 24, 117, 123, 141, 197
foreigner talk 96
foreign language 95–109, 132, 191
 oral proficiency interviews 95–109
 teachers of 95–109
foreign language aptitude 79–80, 89, 92–3
 see also AH2; Modern Language Aptitude Test; Pimsleur Language Aptitude Battery; York Language Aptitude Test
forensic linguistics 7, 180
Foster, P. 181

Fradis, A. 5
Frase, L. 156, 157
Freedman, S. 156
French 95–109, 224–5
freq 56, 64, 80, 190, 196, 200, 228–9

Galle, M. 122, 136
GAP verbs 12, 13, 141, 190, 194
Gass, S. M. 96
GCSE *see* General Certificate of Secondary Education
Geers, A. 13, 17, 180
Gelman, S. 139, 140, 149
gender 8, 71, 73, 87, 92
General Certificate of Secondary Education (GCSE) 98, 99, 190
 French oral scores 100, 102, 105–8
Gentner, D. 11, 121, 138, 139, 196
Gentry, J. R. 157
Gerber, E. 12
Giles, H. 96, 187
Gillon, G. 9, 198
Ginther, A. 156, 157
Girolametto, L. 10, 183
Goldfield, B. 139, 140, 200
Good I. J. 42
Gopnik, A. 138, 140
Grant, L. 156, 157
granularity 5, 8, 15, 190
Green, P. S. 79, 201
Griffin, W.J. 156
Grobe, C. 156
Guiraud, P. 26, 128
Guiraud's index (RTTR) 26–7, 28, 29, 30, 50, 51, 128, 134, 180, 187, 198
Gutfreund, M. 26, 78, 187

H *see* Herdan's index
Haas, J.-C. 13, 189
Hales, T. 42, 129, 133
Halleck, G. B. 95, 96
Halliday, M. A. K. 135, 192
halo effects 103–4, 154–5, 157, 173
Halter, R. H. 129, 133
Hamilton, A. 90
Hampson, J. 139
handwriting 154–5
Hansson, K. 141
hapax dislegomena 38, 39, 41, 44, 45, 125, 132, 190, 195

hapax legomena 38, 39, 41, 44, 45, 125–6, 132, 134, 190
Harbers, H. M. 5
harmonic series hypothesis 36–7, 42, 190
Härnquist, K. 8, 27
Harrison, M. 78, 187
Hartung, J. P. 70, 90, 136, 194
Haug, H. T. 27, 65, 69
Hayes, D. P. 124, 126, 129
He, A. W. 95
hearing impairment *see* cochlear implants
Hedrick, D. L. 5
Heim, A. W. 79, 187
Herdan, G. 27, 190
Herdan's index 27, 28, 29, 30, 40, 50, 51, 190, 193, 198
Hersh, R. E. 7, 97
Hess, C. W. 27, 29, 65, 68–9, 198, 202
Hesse, B. 5, 126
Hesse, H. 5, 126
Hick, R. F. 141
Hickey, T. 195
Hiscock, C. K. 7, 180
historical documents 7, 97
Hoare, R. 64, 181
Hoff, E. 10–11
Hofmeister, C. 139, 140
Hollander, M. 40–1, 194
Hollis, W. 5
Holmes, D. I. 13, 126, 157, 188, 191
Home-School Study of Language and Literacy Development 129–31, 189, 197
Honoré, A. 39, 126, 191
Honoré's statistic 39, 126, 190
Hood, L. 135
Hoover, T. M. 14
Hunt, K. W. 156
Hyltenstam, K. 123, 126, 127

inflectional diversity (ID) 110–17, 191
  developmental trends in 111–12
  and productivity 117
inflectional morphology, development of 81, 83–4, 110, 113
inflections per utterance 111, 113, 117, 191

input and interaction 10–11, 96, 129–31, 139, 179–80, 183
intrinsic measures 125–6, 191
  see also extrinsic measures
inverse Gaussian distribution 42–3, 191
inverse Gaussian-Poisson formulation 43–4, 57, 191, 198
Irwin, O. C. 26, 122
Isaza, M. 10
Iverson, J. M. 26

Jacobsen, B. S. 88
Jarvis, S. 6, 9, 47, 50–1, 53, 55, 181, 192, 201, 202
Jipescu, I. 5
Johansson, V. 6, 116, 152, 173, 181, 183
Johnson, M. 96
Johnson, W. 20, 25, 97, 196, 200
Johnston, J. 9, 198
Jones, M. 12, 121
Jones, R. J. 156
Joseph, K. L. 141

k *see* Rubet's k
K *see* Yule's characteristic K
Kauschke, C. 139, 140
Kelly, C. 5, 7, 125, 134, 202
Kelly, D. J. 5
Kershaw, T. 11, 179
Kessler Shaw, L. 139
Key Stage (KS) 153, 191
Kim, M. 138, 140
Klee, T. 16, 17, 196
Klein, D. 135
Köhler, R. 5, 122, 136
Kriz, S. 6, 116, 152, 173, 181, 183
Küntay, A. C. 139, 140

lambda 133, 160, 167–8, 170–1, 172, 173, 174, 175–6, 197
  see also P_Lex
Landry, R. G. 27, 29, 65, 69, 198, 202
language assessment 8–10, 95–109
language dominance 8
language environment *see* input and interaction; rare words
language impairment and delay 5, 10, 11–14, 179, 183, 188, 193, 199
  aphasia 13–14, 25, 74, 97, 126, 181, 188, 191

SLI   12–13, 16, 65, 74, 121, 123, 141–2, 181, 190, 196, 197, 198–9
stuttering   12, 13, 74, 91–2, 180, 181
Laufer, B.   5, 8, 128, 132, 133, 159, 160, 180, 192, 193
Layton, T. L.   22, 26
Lazaraton, A.   95, 96
LDV   192
Leech, G.   126
Lehmann, I. J.   69, 87
Leimkuhler, F. F.   23
lemmatisation   192
Le Normand, M.-T.   11, 12, 179
Leonard, L. B.   12, 13, 65, 74, 75, 181, 198
lexical density   3–4, 135, 158, 172, 192
lexical diversity
  and cross-linguistic comparisons   116, 183–4
  definition of   59, 192
  interpretation of   5–6
  a mathematical model for   47–55, 57–9
  and rare words   123–4, 160, 174
  and research topics   6–14
  and spelling   160
  and word length   124, 158
  see also D, and first language writing
lexical frequency profile (LFP)   128–9, 132, 133, 160, 193, 197
lexical individuality *see* lexical originality
lexical originality   127, 192
lexical richness, definition of   3–4, 192
lexical sophistication (LS)   3, 123, 192, 193
  see also rare words
lexical specificity   124, 158, 193, 201
lexical variability quotient (LVQ)   193
lexical variation (LV)   3, 4, 192, 193
LFP *see* lexical frequency profile
Lieven, E.V.M.   21, 137, 138, 142, 193–4
Lightbown, P.M.   129, 133, 135
limiting relative diversity   147–50, 151, 193, 231
  output from   238–43
Linaza Corpus   114
linearisation   27–8, 30, 193
Linnarud, M.   127, 192, 193
Loban, W.   156
LogTTR *see* Herdan's index

Longobardi, E.   139, 140, 141
López Ornat, S.   114
LRD *see* limiting relative diversity
Luzzatti, C.   14
LV *see* lexical variation
LVQ *see* lexical variability quotient

M *see* Michéa's M
Maas, H.-D.   28, 193
Maas's a^2 28, 193, 201
MacArthur Communicative Development Inventories (MCDI)   9, 70–1, 73, 90, 91, 99, 136, 137, 139, 194
MacWhinney, B.   20, 56, 63, 64, 77, 80, 114, 142, 185, 188, 194, 195, 196, 197, 221, 228, 232
Maher, B. A.   14, 25, 97
Malvern D. D.   25, 48, 50, 59, 67, 69, 70, 72, 95, 97, 98, 110, 111, 136, 140, 141, 179, 181, 185, 186, 189, 191, 193
Manchester Corpus   142–7, 149–51, 193–4, 238–43
  sample transcript   226–7
Mann, M. B.   14, 25, 97, 200
Manschreck, T. C.   14, 25, 97
Marcus, G. F.   40–1, 194
Markham, L. R.   155
mark-recapture   40, 42, 194
Martier, S.   11, 179
McCarthy, D.   5, 26
MCDI *see* MacArthur Communicative Development Inventories
McEvoy, S.   21
McGregor, K. K.   138, 140
McKay, J.   10
McKee, G.   56, 67, 69, 72, 189, 201, 228
mean length of turn (MLT)   100, 101, 102, 105, 106, 187, 195
mean length of utterance (MLU)   65, 71, 73, 78, 79, 86, 87, 90–1, 92, 100, 102, 105, 106, 111, 113, 117, 185, 195
mean polysemy   122–3, 194
mean segmental type–token ratio (MSTTR)   24–5, 53, 95, 97–8, 100, 102–3, 105, 106, 108, 134, 196, 198, 199, 200
mean word frequency (MWF)   28, 195, 200

Meara, P. 14, 65, 68, 97, 123, 124, 125, 126, 129, 132, 133, 159, 160, 162, 183, 186, 189, 191, 197
Mehrens, W. A. 69, 87
Memon, A. 7, 180
Ménard, N. 3, 27, 28, 38, 64, 122–3, 124, 127, 132, 134, 136, 192, 194, 195, 196, 199
Ménard's rarity measure 127, 195
Mendenhall, T. C. 157
Michéa R. 38, 44, 195
Michéa's M 39, 44, 51, 195
Mihailescu, L. 5
Milanovic, M. 95, 96
Miller, C. 12
Miller, J. F. 9, 12, 13, 16, 17, 20–1, 23, 49, 196, 198, 200
Milton, J. 42, 129, 133
minimal terminable unit *see* t-unit
MLAT *see* Modern Language Aptitude Test
MLT *see* mean length of turn
MLU *see* mean length of utterance
MLUS *see* mean length of utterance
Moder, C. L. 95, 96
Modern Language Aptitude Test (MLAT) 79, 89, 195
Moltz, C. C. 12, 141
monosemic rate 122–3, 195
Montes, R. 114
Morisset, C. 64, 84, 196
morpheme diversity measure 231
morphemicisation 63–4, 69–70, 71, 73, 81, 194, 195
MSTTR *see* mean segmental type–token ratio
Murray-Branch, J. 13
MWF *see* mean word frequency

Naigles, L. 10, 139, 140
narrative writing *see* writing
Nation, I. S. P. 128, 132, 133, 159, 160, 162, 193
National Curriculum 153, 154, 156–7
native speakers 96–7
natural partitions hypothesis 11, 138, 196
NDW *see* number of different words
Nelson, K. 135, 139

New England Corpus 63–75, 84, 90, 91, 110, 111, 185, 186, 196, 235
Newhoff, M. 13, 74, 181
Nold, E. 156
Nordstrom-Klee, B. 11, 179
Norris, R. C. 156
'noun bias' research 11, 121, 138–41, 196
  measures used in 140
noun density 135, 196
noun–pronoun ratio 135
noun TTR 140
noun–verb ratio 122, 136, 140, 142–50, 151, 201
Noya, M. 11
Noyou, C. 8, 190
number of different words (NDW) 16–19, 22, 23, 24, 25, 29, 74, 100, 102–3, 179, 180, 185, 196
  related measures 25–6

O'Donnell, R. C. 156
Ogura, T. 139, 140
oligosemic rate 122–3, 196
O'Loughlin, K. 135
Onslow, M. 13, 180
open-class style 135, 136, 196
oral proficiency interviews *see* foreign language
Orlov's Z 39, 51, 196
Osgood, C. E. 7
Ouellet, C. 11, 179
Owen, A. 13, 65, 74, 75, 181

Packman, A. 13, 180
Page, E. B. 153, 155, 156, 173
Page, E. B. 85
Painter, K. M. 10
Pan, B. A. 9, 20
Park, J. 10
Pavlenko, A. 5, 8, 15, 64, 183, 190
Pearce, P. S. 10, 183
Perera, K. 172
Perkins, M. 6, 188–9, 193, 197, 199, 200
perseveration 5, 14, 197
Peters, A. M. 135
Peters, J. 12
Pethick, S. 70, 90, 136, 194
Pimsleur, P. 80, 197
Pimsleur Language Aptitude Battery (PLAB) 80, 89, 92–3, 197

Pine, J. M. 96, 136, 137, 138, 142, 193–4
Pinker, S. 13, 40–1, 112, 126, 190, 194
Pinna, G.-D. 14
Pistarini, C. 14
PLAB *see* Pimsleur Language Aptitude Battery
Platt, H. 192
Platt, J. 192
P_Lex 133, 134, 160, 162, 174, 186, 197
  see also lambda
Plunkett, K. 90
Poisson distribution 33–5, 43, 197
Powell, T. A. 5, 10, 129, 131, 180
proportional diversity 123, 197
prorated number of lexically free words 24, 26, 140, 197

Qualifications and Curriculum Authority (QCA) 154

Raggi, R. 14
Ragnarsdóttir, H. 6, 116, 152, 173, 181, 183
rare words 3, 5, 123–34, 180, 192, 193, 195, 197, 201
  density of 130–1, 192, 197
  exposure to 129–31, 189
  and writing 158–60, 162, 167–8
  see also lambda; lexical diversity, and rare words; lexical sophistication; P_Lex
Ratner, N. B. 12, 13, 74, 91, 180, 181
Ravid, D. 6, 116, 152, 173, 181, 183
Rayson, P. 126
Read, J. 3, 123, 127, 135, 158, 192, 193, 196
Reading Corpus 98–100, 197
  sample transcript 224–5
referential style 135, 197
Reid, J. 156, 157
Reilly, J. S. 70, 90, 136, 194
reliability *see* D, reliability of
repetition 5, 14, 188, 193, 196, 198, 199, 200
  see also echolalia; perseveration; retracing; topic bias
Reppen, R. 157
retracing 63, 64, 69, 70, 71, 73, 80, 101, 114, 181, 198
Reznick, J. S. 64, 70, 84, 90, 136, 194, 196

Rice, M. L. 12, 141
Richards, B. J. 22, 25, 26, 27, 50, 65, 67, 69, 70, 72, 95, 97, 98, 99, 101, 110, 111, 135, 136, 140, 141, 179, 180, 181, 185, 186, 191, 193, 197, 201
Richards, J. C. 192
Richman, B. 126
Ridings, D. 8, 27
Roach, K. A. 131
Roberts, P. M. 5
Rollins, P. R. 17
Romanoski, S. 10
root TTR (RTTR) *see* Guiraud's index
Rosen, T. J. 40–1, 194
Ross, S. 96, 109
Rowe, M. 9
Rowland, C. F. 137, 138, 193–4
RTTR *see* Guiraud's index
Rubet's k 28, 198

SALT 196, 198, 200, 201
sample size, sensitivity of measures to 16–18, 22–4, 27, 28–9, 64–8, 71–5, 122, 123, 131–4, 136, 142–7, 151, 179, 180
sampling 10
  random 18–19, 52–4, 56–7, 66–8, 71–3
  sequential 66–7, 72
Sampson, G. 156
Sanders, L. M. 14
Sapon, S. M. 79, 195
Satterly, D. 26, 88
Savino, M. A. 22, 26
Schafer, G. 90
Schegloff, E. A. 101, 187
schizophrenia 14, 25, 97
Scholfield, P. 69, 122, 200
Scott, C.M. 11
second language research 8, 127–9, 181–2
Sedey, A. 13, 17, 180
Sefton, K. M. 27, 29, 65, 69, 198, 202
Serra/Sole Corpus 114
Serratrice, L. 141
SES *see* social class
Shatz, M. 139, 140
Shenton, M. E. 14
Sherblom, A. 5

Sherblom, J. 5
Sichel, H. S. 38, 41–6, 50, 51, 55, 56, 57, 124, 125, 132, 190, 191, 195, 198, 202
Sichel's S *see* Michéa's M
Siegel, S. 82, 85
Silverman, S. W. 12, 13, 74, 91, 181
Simmonds, V. 79, 187
Simonton, D. K. 5
Singh, S. 13, 126, 188, 189, 191
Skehan, P. 79, 80, 93, 181
Skinner B. F. 36
SLI *see* language impairment and delay
Slobin, D. I. 139, 140
Smith, J. A. 5, 7, 125, 134, 202
Snow, C. E. 17, 64, 84, 110, 124, 129, 130, 131, 132, 188, 189, 196, 197
Snyder, L. 22, 135, 136, 187, 188, 196, 201
social class 8, 11, 71, 73, 77, 87, 92
Sokol, R. J. 11, 179
Somers, H. H. 199
Somers's S 28, 199, 200
Spanish 113–16
species–area problem 40, 199
specific language impairment *see* language impairment and delay
Spehar, B. 13, 17, 180
spelling 156–7, 162, 164–5, 170–1, 172, 173–4, 175
  coding of 161
Spencer, K. 157, 174
Spier, E. 9
Spreen, O. 5, 25, 97
stem type–token ratio (STTR) 199
stem variability quotient (SVQ) 199
Stewart, M. 156
Stewig, J. W. 5
Stickler, K. R. 20, 21, 23
Stokes, S. F. 12, 117, 123, 141, 197
Strömqvist, S. 6, 116, 152, 172, 181, 183
STTR *see* stem type–token ratio
stuttering *see* language impairment and delay
Surendran, A. 11, 179
SVQ *see* stem variability quotient

T *see* Tuldava's T
Tabors, P. O. 127, 129, 130, 131, 132, 134, 189, 197
Tager-Flusberg, H. 14
Tamis-LeMonda, C. 9
Tardif, T. 139, 140, 149
Templin, M. 20–2, 24, 49, 65, 200
Templin, T. 11, 179
text length 156, 164, 170–1, 172, 173
  calculation of 161
Thakerar, J. N. 96, 187
Thal, D. 70, 90, 136, 194
Theakston, A. L. 142, 194
theoretical vocabulary 38, 54, 134, 199
Thompson, C. K. 138, 140
Thompson, J. R. 5, 6, 31–6, 38, 40, 41, 42, 43, 51–2, 53, 57
Thomson, G. H. 5, 6, 31–6, 38, 40, 41, 42, 43, 51–2, 53, 57
Thordardottir, E. T. 9, 12, 18, 141, 142, 190, 199
threshold *see* TTR theshold
Tingsell, J.-G. 8, 27
TNW *see* total number of words
token–type ratio *see* mean word frequency
Tonkyn, A. 200
topic bias 5, 200
total active vocabulary *see* vocabulary size
total number of words (TNW) 100, 102–3, 105, 106, 198, 200
  see also text length
transcripts, preparation of 80, 99, 114, 228–9
  see also CHAT
Treffers-Daller, J. 3, 8, 127, 128, 133, 183, 187
TTR *see* type–token ratio
TTR threshold 20–2, 200
Tuldava, J. 5, 27–8, 30, 200
Tuldava's T 28, 200
t-unit length 155–6, 162–3, 170–1, 172, 173, 175–6, 200
  calculation of 161
TUR *see* type–utterance ratio
TW *see* total number of words
Tweedie, F. J. 28, 29, 39–40, 44, 45–6, 51, 53, 55, 65, 187, 202

Tyler, A. 96
type–token ratio (TTR) 14, 19–24, 26, 29–30, 31, 66, 74, 83, 100, 102, 124, 147–8, 179, 180, 183, 185, 193, 195, 198, 200
  transformations of 26–9, 31
  see also TTR threshold
type–type ratio 121–51, 201
  see also limiting relative diversity
type–utterance ratio (TUR) 24, 26, 197, 201

Uber index (U) 28, 29, 50, 51, 180, 193, 201
Ukrainetz, T. A. 5, 9
Ullman, M. 40–1, 194
University of Cambridge Local Examinations Syndicate (UCLES) 154, 201
Ure, J. 3, 135, 192
urn model 31–6

Van Hout, R. 3, 6, 8, 22, 27, 127, 128, 133, 134, 183, 187
Van Kleeck, A. 10
Van Lier, L. 95
Varonis, E. M. 96
Vasquez, J. 10
verb–adjective ratio 122, 136
verb density 135, 201
verb–noun ratio 140, 142–50, 151
verb TTR 140, 151
Verhoeven, L. 9, 116, 152, 156, 176, 181, 182, 183
Vermeer, A. 3, 9, 27, 29, 123
Vila Corpus 114
Visini, C. 10, 183
vocabulary checklists see MacArthur Communicative Development Inventories
vocabulary composition 134–8, 201
vocabulary lists see word lists
vocabulary richness see lexical richness
vocabulary size 5, 29, 31, 32, 40, 41, 53
vocd 55–7, 63–4, 65–6, 69, 80, 81, 134, 148–9, 162, 190, 193, 198, 201
  command lines for analyses 70, 81, 101, 149
  documentation for 228–34
  flowchart for 58
  sample output from 235–43
  see also D; lexical diversity, a mathematical model for; limiting relative diversity

W see Brunet's index
Waanders, J. 156
Wachal, R. S. 5, 25, 97
Wagner, K. R. 5
Walker, V. G. 5
Wallesch, C.-W. 13, 189
Watkins, R. V. 5, 12, 141
Watts, K. P. 79, 187
Weigle, S. C. 153
Weitzman, E. 10, 183
Weitzman, M. 27
Weizman, Z. O. 124, 130, 131, 132
Wells, C. G. 17, 25–6, 76, 78, 79, 81, 91, 92, 110, 112, 187, 188, 195
Wells Corpus see Bristol Corpus
Wesche, M. B. 96
Wilcock, G. K. 13, 126, 188, 189, 191
Wilson, A. 126
Wimmer, G. 3, 28, 52, 180, 192
Windsor, J. 11
word length 124, 157–8, 165–7, 170–1, 172, 173, 174, 175–6, 193, 201, 202
  calculation of 161
word lists 42, 126–7, 128, 133, 162, 193
WPM (words per minute) 100, 102, 105, 106, 201
Wright, H. H. 13, 74, 181
writing 152–76, 181–3
  measures of 155–62:
    inter-correlations 170, 174; regression analysis 170–1, 172–3, 175–6

Xu, F. 40–1, 139, 140, 149, 194

Yamada-Yamamoto, A. 181
Yoder, P. J. 10, 24, 26, 140, 197, 201
York Language Aptitude Test 79, 89, 201
Young, R. 95, 96

Yule, G. U. 38, 44, 201
Yule's characteristic K 38, 39, 44, 45, 51, 134, 180, 198, 201–2

Z *see* Orlov's Z
Zagona, K. 113

Zipf, G. K. 36, 37, 41, 42, 51, 124, 157, 190
Zipf's laws 36–7, 39, 124, 157, 158, 174, 196, 202
Zocconi, E. 10, 183
Zonca, G 14